Poke a Stick at It

Poke a Stick at It

Unexpected True Stories

Connie Cronley

University of Oklahoma Press : Norman

Dedicated to the librarians of Oklahoma
and to
Angie Debo, who loved them

Library of Congress Cataloging-in-Publication Data

Names: Cronley, Connie, author.
Title: Poke a stick at it : unexpected true stories / Connie Cronley.
Description: Norman : University of Oklahoma Press, 2016.
Identifiers: LCCN 2016000700 | ISBN 978-0-8061-5395-7 (pbk. : alk. paper)
Classification: LCC PS3603.R6646 A6 2016 | DDC 814/.6—dc23
LC record available at http://lccn.loc.gov/2016000700

The paper in this book meets the guidelines for permanence and durability of
the Committee on Production Guidelines for Book Longevity of the Council on
Library Resources, Inc. ∞

1 2 3 4 5 6 7 8 9 10

Contents

Poke a Stick at It

Introduction

One hot Oklahoma summer, I set out on a literary crime spree. I was scheduled on a book tour to public libraries in the central part of the state. The title of my talk was "Gasp. Gulp. Giggle. Sigh. My Love Affair with the English Language." I stole part of that title from the actress Joan Fontaine. It was the first of many shameless thefts. I also stole jokes and punch lines and bits of poetry, but I confessed readily. What I learned in college, I told my audiences, is that to steal from one is plagiarism. But to steal from many is called academic research.

I told lots of cheesy jokes like that, and they always got laughs. The audiences wanted to laugh. "We need more humor these days," they told me.

They liked the story of Mrs. Brown in my neighborhood sending me off on the book tour with wisdom about the power of books. "If you don't want anyone to sit beside you on a plane," she said, "hold two books prominently displayed. One should be the Holy Bible and the other an Amway catalog. People will pass you right by."

When authors go on book tours, they usually go to New York, Los Angeles, Chicago, Paris. Where my book tour took me was more off the beaten path—Tecumseh, Shawnee, McCloud, Newcastle, Noble, and Purcell, Oklahoma. In larger cities, such as Norman, the audience was at least thirty people. In smaller Blanchard, set in the middle of open fields, the library was an old Methodist church and I had a crowd of three. Two were librarians who worked there. The other was a woman who had hurt her back falling off a ladder and couldn't go to work that day.

Day after day I drove along Highways 9 and 77, lined with great wheels of hay just harvested, cornfields so thick I couldn't see through them, expanses of green prairie and yellow wildflowers—black-eyed Susans or coreopsis, I think—fireworks stands, American flags flapping in the wind, small towns with water towers, and wide blue skies with fluffy white clouds like the drop biscuits my grandmother made from scratch. My car radio picked up stations with music from the 1940s, '50s, and '60s—Frank Sinatra, Dean Martin, Doris Day, and Duke Ellington, the last playing, oh so appropriately for me on this occasion, "Don't Get Around Much Anymore."

Librarians are wonderful hosts. When I arrived at their libraries, they had posters up announcing my visit, plates of donuts and cookies laid out, a podium for me, and an ambitious number of seats arranged for the audience.

Whatever the size of the audience, we had a good time discussing books and authors. I told them stories about Angie Debo, Pearl Buck, Truman Capote, Emily Dickinson, and other writers they knew. I quoted from famous books, and I paraphrased beloved authors. I told them colorful Spanish, Chinese, and African proverbs. We exchanged titles of books we liked—*The Pat Conroy Cookbook: Recipes and Stories of My Life,* Ivan Doig's *The Whistling Season,* and *Being Dead Is No Excuse: The Southern Ladies' Guide to the Perfect Funeral* by Gayden Metcalfe and Charlotte Hays.

Debo, who wrote thirteen books and hundreds of articles, told me that for every one Oklahoman who reads a book, two Oklahomans write one. Sure enough, each sparse audience always included someone who had come only to ask how to get his or her book published. Mostly, though, the people I met on my book tour, primarily women, were readers. I learned from talking with them that the books we read are like a second language. What we read and how we talk with one another about books is a way of exploring what's in our hearts. We are a storytelling people, and talking about books is a way of telling our own stories.

Some of their stories made me laugh so hard I got a stitch in my side. Other times, people told me stories that broke my heart—illness, death, disappointment, loss. One woman told me about an incident in her life that was so sad, after the audience had left and the library had locked the doors, I sat in my car and sobbed into my steering wheel.

How did she find the strength to go on? I wondered. Neither that woman nor anybody else told me their stories with self-pity or pathos. Even the most tragic stories were told just as Oklahomans talk—plain and simple as steak and eggs but with a little humor for spice, like peach pie on the side.

Emily Dickinson wrote that "the Soul has bandaged moments." I met many bandaged souls. I met hearts that had been patched together with baling wire and bubble gum. No wonder the Oklahoma women particularly liked the Chinese adage about two tears floating down a river. One tear said, "I'm the tear of a woman who lost her lover." The second tear said, "And I'm the tear of the woman who found him."

When I discovered that my essay books are classified as memoir, I puffed up like a blowfish. "Memoir" sounds so artful, doesn't it? This pride collapsed when I read a critic's disdain of memoirs in general, calling the genre "the Barbie doll of biography."

Memoirs come in many flavors: gruesome childhoods, even more gruesome illnesses, debilitating grief, colorful addictions, humiliating downfalls, glorious triumphs, and bizarre life experiments (often titled *A Year of . . .*).

I try to avoid these, but it's like giving up white wine. I keep looking for a wagon to fall off. Confessional memoirs appeal to my voyeuristic tendencies, but these are occasionally lapses. Most of all, I like memoirs by people with a healthy self-identity who can laugh at themselves. Come to think of it, those are the kind of people I like.

I recommend Debbie Bull's *Blue Jelly,* which she claims was inspired by being dumped by her boyfriend. She was so depressed, she says, she knew she had hit rock bottom when she identified with a country-and-western song's lyrics, "I'm so miserable without you, it's almost like I've got you back again." I like people who don't take themselves too seriously.

My all-time favorites are James Thurber's wild-eyed adventures of everyday occurrences, such as "The Day the Dam Broke" and "The Night the Bed Fell." These stories make me laugh until my stomach aches. I identify with Thurber's teetering-on-the-edge-of-hysteria disasters. My tombstone might read "How Did I Get into This Mess?"

If I have a tombstone. I once mused to my ex-husband that when I die I'd like to be cremated and have my ashes spread on the Oklahoma prairies. "When you die," he said, "I'll have you cremated and your ashes thrown on the kitchen floor where nobody will notice them."

I think I write with typical southwestern humor, which is different from southern humor or western humor or tall-tale humor. We don't take ourselves too seriously in the Southwest, and we can find humor in almost anything. My Uncle Hal, one of the funniest people I ever knew, told a story about how a local farmer named Cornfield Brown got his name. One night, Brown walked to town, got drunk, and passed out in his cornfield on the way home. His wife got into their Model T to go look for him, took a shortcut through the cornfield, drove over him, and broke his leg. She thought she had hit something, so she backed up to see what it was and broke his other leg. That's a very funny story in the small town I come from. It might even be true.

One reviewer of my book of memoir-essays mentioned my guts as a writer and my being an adventurer at heart. Guts? Adventurer? That surprised me.

Maybe southwestern humor, self-deprecating and candid, comes across as guts. Or maybe it is my training as a journalist that makes me admire a writing style that is simple, clear, and direct. I explain that style by quoting the prize-winning newspaper story about a deadly tornado in Udall, Kansas. The lead on that story was "This quiet town died in its sleep last night." Simple, clear, and direct.

A young reporter tried to emulate that style when he was sent to Kentucky to cover a mine cave-in. The story he wired to his paper began "God sat on a mountain top and surveyed the disaster that lay at His feet below." The editor wired back, "Forget mine cave in. Get interview with God. Pictures if possible."

I don't think of myself as adventurous. I go through change like a cartoon cat clawing at the doorframe. Still, once I'm on the other side—fired, or divorced, upright, and walking around again—I'm OK with it. Often, I even like it. I recognize that I'm not good at change; I'm trying to change that.

Perhaps more than adventurous, I'm curious. Maybe that comes from journalism or maybe from growing up bored in a small town in the 1950s, when we kids had to entertain ourselves. Without an imagination, all we could do in the hot, windless Augusts was hang in a tire swing and wait for school to start.

Maybe it's genetic. My parents were lively people who eagerly took up new hobbies or adventures—square dancing, making a bathtub full of tamales, creating art from paint-by-number kits. On family vacations, they liked to stop and talk to the natives. During a trip through Louisiana, my mother learned how to make a roux, we went crawdad fishing with two young boys, and on a picnic we met a local man who proselytized for several hours about the virtues of goat's milk. When we toured a plantation house, my father—alert to learning opportunities—shrewdly told the tour director, "I notice that whenever we go into a room, you reach behind a piece of furniture near the door. Why do you do that?" She looked at him in silence for a long moment and replied, "I'm turning on the light." That, too, is a funny story where I come from.

"You never know till you ask" is a sound piece of advice. Or until you read about it and study it. This book is a collection of true stories and adventures that sprang from my enthusiastic curiosity about people and things I bump into. I will tell you all I know about same-sex insects, reptiles, and animals; vampire literature; accordions; air-dried laundry; ex-husbands; women's lib among young women today; Gregg shorthand; appropriate business attire; Emily Post etiquette; some Oklahoma history; spiders; stars; and more. It's a big world, and there's a lot to know.

"Enthusiastic curiosity" might be a phrase too exalted for a blue-collar worker's daughter like me. Where I come from, what we say when we come upon something new, strange, and baffling is "Let's poke a stick at it and see what happens."

Everyday Life—What Fun!

I know a woman who sees the world as a glass, not half empty but completely empty. And cracked.

Not me.

I see life as a writer does, which means everything is material for a story. A spray-on suntan goes south the day before a gala event? So what if I'm the color of a kumquat? It's all material.

"Do your work sincerely, but don't take yourself seriously," a favorite professor told me. Or, as Bob Marley sang, "lively up yourself." Same thing.

My Ex-husband

Nobody makes me laugh like my ex-husband. Nobody is more exasperating, tells bigger whoppers, or keeps life real like my ex-husband. Here are three examples.

A Really Scary Neighborhood Story

This is a true story. Not even the names have been changed. My hairdresser, George, who is a good friend, lives in the country but has a salon in my neighborhood. The other morning, he came into town early and wanted to spend a couple of hours at my house before opening his shop. He brought his little dog, Cammie, about the size of a fuzzy house shoe.

My ex-husband Jay, who is a good friend, lives in the neighborhood but has no tools or lawn equipment of his own. Why should he, he reasons, when I have plenty?

The hairdresser and I had coffee, and I set off for work. "Wait," said George the hairdresser. "Let me see that skirt. I love the fabric." Before I could get out the door, he gave my hair a disapproving look and rearranged my bangs. I felt like a first-grader on the way to school.

No sooner was I out of sight when George the hairdresser decided to be helpful and run the dishwasher just as Jay the ex-husband showed up to borrow my lawn mower. Jay called me immediately. "Why didn't you tell me your hairdresser was there?" he asked.

"Scared me to death. You'd better call him, and I mean right now. He said the whole house is flooded. And who is that other guy in the house with him?"

I called. "What's going on?"

George blurted out the whole horrible story. When he turned on the dishwasher, the washing machine overflowed into the garden room. He had mopped up the mess and was going to pull out the washing machine to find the problem.

"No, no," I said. "Don't do that. I'll call a plumber. And who else is there? Jay saw a second guy."

"Oh, my God," said George. "I heard him talking to someone outside, but I don't know who it is. I won't go to the salon. I'll stay here

Bingo and me *(author's collection)*

and guard your house. And by the way, your dog tried to kill me. I tried to put him outside, and he nearly took my arm off."

I forgot to tell you that I have a dog named Bingo. The size of a pony. Hates everyone but me.

I instructed George to (a) leave my dog alone, (b) leave my washing machine alone, (c) leave my house alone, and (d) go to the salon.

I went home to wait for the plumber. Just as I arrived, Jay showed up to return the lawn mower, and when he opened the garage door, George's little fuzzy dog ran out.

"Oh, my God," Jay said. "Nearly scared me to death. What dog is that?" I chased down the little fuzzy dog, tearing my new black tights in the chase, and put her back in the garage.

"What guy were you talking to in the driveway?" I asked Jay. "You scared George."

Turns out, he wasn't talking to a person; he was talking to Louie, my orange cat. I forgot to tell you I have a cat.

Turns out, he didn't see a second guy in the house. What he saw was George's reflection in the windows.

So, to summarize: my dog scared the hairdresser, the hairdresser's dog scared the ex-husband, and the hairdresser and the ex-husband scared each other.

All was explained and all was well. I settled in to wait for the plumber. And then—both men reverted to their natural selves.

George called and said in a rather chilly voice, "You know, you have a hair appointment this afternoon."

"Let's forget the hair appointment," I said, "I'm waiting for the plumber."

"Hasn't the plumber come yet?" he asked.

Then Jay called and said in a rather scolding voice, "Hasn't the plumber come yet? You should have called someone else. By the way, something's wrong with your lawn mower. It's not cutting right."

Both men called repeatedly to ask about the plumber. "Isn't the plumber there yet?"

On his last call, George said, "By the way, I can't reschedule your appointment until next week. And I'm allergic to cats."

David the plumber arrived. He had his own tools. He had no dog. He had no cat. Nothing scared him. He fixed the problem in twenty minutes. I wish David the plumber (instead of other people I won't mention) lived and worked in the neighborhood.

Dog Bite

This is a little story about a dog bite. And the ensuing reactions of friends and family.

One lazy Saturday evening, my dog, Bingo, and I were sharing an order of barbecue ribs. I would eat my part, then hold the bone in my fist so he could chomp off the soft end with his back teeth.

Eat, eat. Chomp. Eat, eat. Chomp. It was a pleasant routine. And then.

Oh, how many dark chapters of our lives begin with those two words—"and then." And then, I got distracted by something I was reading in the Cherokee newspaper, held the bone out absentmindedly, got my finger in his mouth, and chomp!

I thought he had bitten off the end of my finger. You talk about something hurting. You talk about carrying on!

I called my ex-husband and told him what had happened. I said, "Jay, I need for you take me to urgent care."

He said, "Oh, just put some antibiotic on it."

I said, "I need for you to take me to urgent care."

He said, "What do you think they can do that you can't do yourself? It's not like one of your cat bites. A dog's mouth is cleaner. It's not going to get infected."

I said, "I need to go to urgent care."

He wanted to know where urgent care was. He wanted to know how late it was open. I told him I had checked all of that and we needed to go now.

He said, "I'm watching golf. Can't you call around and find one that's closer?"

Eventually he did drive me to urgent care, where the doctor looked at my finger and said, "Boy, he really nailed you, didn't he?"

Now, if there's anything we do not want, it is for our doctors to be excited about our illnesses or injuries. We want them nonchalant. Bored, almost. We want them to say, "Oh, it's not as bad as you think."

What this doctor said was, "Wow, how big is this dog?"

After injections and X-rays and stitches, I was sent home with a fistful of prescriptions. I told my ex-husband that we needed to stop at a pharmacy to get them filled.

He said, "Oh, brother, how long is this going to take? I need to get home. Golf's on."

The next day I began telling friends and family about the dog bite.

Anna, a pianist, said, "Which hand? Which finger? Did you call in a hand specialist?"

Joe, a writer, said, "Are you going to lose your nail? Can you type? You're a writer; you have to have use of your hands."

Another friend said, "Did they give you good pain meds? Because if they didn't, I have a cabinet full I can share."

Michele said, "How gruesome. I would be more sympathetic if you hadn't told me last week to stop being such a southern belle and complaining about all of my aches and pains."

David, a retired architect, saw my first finger, bandaged, in a metal cage and held pointing heavenward. He asked what happened, and when I told him, he said, "What! You fed your dog *rib bones?* You could have killed him! Never do that."

My sister said, "Did the dog get to finish his bone?"

A little boy named Deon looked closely at the black stitches through the fingernail and said, "Gross. Can I show my little brother?"

I have learned, yet again, that I am not cut out for multitasking. I cannot feed the dog treats while reading a newspaper any more than I can trim my own bangs while drinking chardonnay. I've tried both actions with grim results.

P.S. I don't know what happened to the rib bone the dog and I were eating. I lost interest in it. But I can report that both the dog and I are alive and well.

Makin' Whoopee

This is a story about how music can inspire creativity.

The other evening I was listening to a Frank Sinatra album. One with the song "Makin' Whoopee." You know, the song that begins

> Another bride,
> Another June,
> Another sunny honeymoon.

I started thinking about June and weddings, and that's when creativity struck.

What I thought I would do was swing by my neighborhood Gold and Silver Exchange store and sell some of my old wedding rings. From some of my old marriages. So I did.

I felt a bit out of place. Like I think I would feel in a blood bank among people selling plasma. I had to wait my turn, and the longer I waited, the more out of place I felt. I was overdressed, for one thing, wearing my work clothes, including heels, sitting primly with my pocketbook on my lap. The owner of the Gold and Silver Exchange was padding around barefoot. The other customers were two women wearing overalls and tattoos—not that I'm stereotyping by tattoos. It's just that I don't have any tattoos. Or overalls. Plus, I had shoes.

To clear things up, I didn't have all that many wedding rings to sell. One was stolen years ago. But I did have the other one, which I don't think I'll ever use again, and I had some odds and ends of jewelry and a couple of old gold dental crowns. I don't think I'll be needing those, either.

Lest you get the wrong idea, there was no rancor involved in selling the wedding ring. Neither was there any sentimentality. I've had lots of fun with marriages but not much luck.

My first husband, John Chick, was a popular TV star of the local kids' show *Mr. Zing and Tuffy*. I was nobody. So this was the newspaper headline announcing our marriage: "Mr. Zing Weds."

On the other hand, my second husband got short shrift recently when he was identified in a local publication this way: "Connie Cronley, former wife of a local newspaper columnist, . . ." As they say, what goes around.

Ah, the lengths media sometimes go to avoid mentioning the competition. I worked at KTUL-TV a hundred years ago; that's where I met the famous Mr. Zing. At that time, local newspapers were so loath to mention television stations by name—unless they paid for an ad—that weatherman Don Woods joked not even a miracle would persuade them to do it. He said, "I can see the headline now: 'Virgin Mary Appears—at a Local TV Station.'"

So I called Jay, the ex-husband and newspaper columnist, and told him my idea about selling the old wedding ring. He thought it was funny, like something Lucy and Ethel would do. He had no grounds for complaint anyway; he'd lost his ring at a car wash a week after the wedding.

Well, the price of gold being what it is, I came away with a little windfall. I called Jay immediately to brag about it.

First, a long silence. Then he said, "You know what? I've got an old gold ID bracelet around here somewhere. You can go sell it for me."

"Me go sell it?" I said. "What'll *you* be doing?"

He said, "Oh, I'll be getting ready to go to the race track."

> So don't forget folks,
> That's what you get folks,
> For makin' whoopee.

Postscript

Here's what happened to some of the people above.

George the hairdresser finagled his way into moving into my garage apartment for a year. What began as a jolly arrangement—he would do my hair for free, mow the lawn, and help with gardening improvements—ended on a grimmer note. He was disappointed that I wouldn't let him put my library in boxes and store them in the attic so he would have more space. He spent most weekends sleeping off late nights of dancing, while I tiptoed quietly to keep from disturbing him. He was allergic to Virginia creeper and couldn't go near the garden. He was saddened that the garage quarters had no cable connection and he couldn't watch *So You Think You Can Dance* unless he watched it in my house, while I sat outside in the garden waiting for it to end. He was accident-prone and spent much time recuperating from misadventures: a camping trip ended with an asthma attack; he cut his hand helping a friend build a dock at the lake, after which the cut got infected; he tripped over a curb and broke his big toe.

On the positive side, George is happy and upbeat. He has lots of friends who help him. One of them fixed my garden watering system; another one laid a lovely flagstone path. After George moved out, he drove his motorbike into a tree and dislocated his shoulder.

Jay the ex-husband hired a lawn service to mow his lawn.

I now have my garden, my garage apartment, and my lawn tools to myself.

Gang Funeral

On a recent Saturday afternoon that was brilliant with sunshine, I went to the funeral of a young man killed in a drive-by gang shooting. I had met the handsome young man. He struck me as polite and reserved. I know his hardworking and honorable family. I went to the funeral to pay my respects to them.

A line of law enforcement officers stood at the chapel door. Police cars were parked across the street. The chapel was full to standing room, about four hundred people. I was one of five white faces there. Some of the young men looked at one another suspiciously; some looked back with eyes like blades. Most of the gathering wore black or gray. A few of the young men wore red pants or shirts as a defiant display of gang colors—the Bloods.

This funeral began like those at my Episcopal church: a minister led the processional, reciting, "I am the resurrection and the life . . . ," followed by a white casket and the family. From there on, everything was different to me.

Throughout the service, a pianist noodled on a keyboard to provide background music. People walked in and out—women taking small children to the bathroom and teen girls changing seats. The congregation was casual, but there was nothing relaxed about the rest of the funeral.

An aunt of the deceased delivered a fiery testimonial. She raised an arm above her head and shouted that this violence has got to stop. This street killing of our young men and women must end. She said she had already heard rumors of revenge. "Don't do it," she told the young mourners. "Take your guns to the church and leave them there."

Sitting beside me was a young black man in sunglasses. Sometimes he was angry and cursed a speaker: "Who the f___ does he think he is?" Sometimes he held his head in his hands and wept quietly. He told me he was a friend of the dead gang member.

The preacher's sermon shook the walls. "We must make a change in the way fathers raise their children," he said. "This death must be a detour for the young men present. All of you who pledge to make a change, stand up."

All through the chapel, men began to stand. Some older men, some younger. Beside me, the young man in sunglasses stood up.

Then the preacher said, "Those of you standing, take the hands of the people sitting to your left and your right." The young man took my hand.

"Now," the preacher said, "look at those people and ask, 'Will you help me make this change?'" The young man answered yes, and I answered that I would support him.

At the front of the chapel, a young man wearing a red and white sports shirt paced about during the service, clearly agitated and upset. When the casket was opened for viewing, he was the first one there. Everybody sat back and gave him time and space. Time and again he leaned over the casket—talking? praying?—then strode away. Then back to the casket, leaning close again. Finally he left the chapel, walking outside quickly, followed by several law enforcement officers.

"Why did they escort him out?" I whispered to the young man in sunglasses.

"That's his brother," he answered. "He's in the penitentiary. They let him out to come to the funeral."

My heart broke. Again.

When I walked out of the chapel, I stepped into a mob of thirty or forty young men from the funeral, young men about to explode with anger. They pushed and shoved and shouted at one another. I saw one take a swig from a bottle of Jack Daniel's.

Adult men waded into the mob, separating the boys, trying to calm them. A member of the family told me, "You better go on and go. These kids are acting stupid." A woman said to me, "Some of them have guns." Just before I drove away, the last thing I saw was my young man in sunglasses. He was in the middle of a roiling crowd of youths. He was butting his chest against another young man. Defiant. Challenging. Threatening. No longer was he weeping and pledging to change. At this moment, he was aggressive with young male rage.

Why do young people in Tulsa join gangs? Why do young people riot in London streets and massacre in Paris neighborhoods?

We know the answers. I'm not sure we know what to do about it. I don't. So we bury our young people and mourn.

Lost Boys

I can't speak for the other animals, but we humans are a storytelling species. That's how we pass along our legends, history, and religious tenets—we wrap the information in a compelling story.

Our primitive ancestors used to squat on their haunches around a fire as they told their stories, sometimes scratching illustrations on cave walls. We are so sophisticated we hardly ever squat on our haunches, but we still tell our stories. We tell them in many forms—songs, poems, narratives.

A clever, new story form is to tell our life story in only six words. This began as a readers' contest in *SMITH* online magazine. Now a compilation of these teensy biographies has come out in a book titled *Not Quite What I Was Planning.* That's the title of one of the six-word memoirs.

Here are some examples from the book:

Born in California. Then nothing happened."

"After Harvard, had baby with crackhead."

"Former child star, seeks love, employment."

"Love New York. Hate Self. Equally."

"Professional canoe guide. Lost only once."

"You wouldn't know, looking at me."

"Catholic school backfired. Sin is in."

"The psychic said I'd be richer."

One popular theme of our culture's storytelling is that of lost boys. Think of J. M. Barrie's play *Peter Pan* and the cute lost boys of Neverland who never grow up. They have names like Nips, Tootles, and Cubby. Think of the movie *Lost Boys* with its "Wait 'til mom finds out" teen vampires.

Then there are America's real-life lost boys, young men who spend more time playing games than growing up. In American pop psychology, the "Peter Pan principle" defines a type of immature young man who is lots of fun but makes a dreadful long-term boyfriend or husband.

Half a world away in Africa, a more grim definition is the Lost Boys of Sudan. First in the 1980s and again recently, tens of thousands of boys and some girls have been orphaned and displaced by ethnic war. Some were conscripted to be child soldiers or enslaved; others traveled a thousand miles by foot for years to find safe refugee camps. Recently, I found a camp of lost boys in Tulsa. Not really a camp, but the drop-in shelter at Youth Services of Tulsa. This is a safe haven for homeless young men and women ages eighteen to twenty-four. Some have aged out of foster care, some couch surf among friends' homes, others live on the street or under downtown bridges. I went there to teach a creative writing class to about a dozen young men and two young women.

A couple were zoned out and didn't participate, but I was impressed by how attentive the rest were, how polite and eager. I wanted the classwork to be fun, so we did a couple of word games and short writing assignments. One assignment was to write their life—in only six words. They jumped right in. Here are some of the mini self-portraits the homeless young Tulsans wrote. Spoiler alert: Guard your heart.

"Bags of linen, but no Laundromat."

"I live, but really I'm dead."

"I am mean, but really scared."

"I can't talk. Call me please."

"Fall in love, hope it lasts."

"I'm not racist, I hate everyone."

"Graduate from school of hard knocks."

"Born and lived in complete sorrow."

"State to state, peddling my life."

I warned you. In only six words, their lives can pierce our hearts. I hope these lost boys and girls in Tulsa get found. I hope they get to live the lovely line that Barrie wrote in *Peter Pan:* "All the world is made of faith and trust and pixie dust."

The Cherokee Word for Water
and Creek Fry Bread as Big as Your Face

"Life beats down and crushes the soul," said the great acting coach Stella Adler. "Art reminds you that you have a soul."

I thought of that after seeing the made-in-Oklahoma movie *The Cherokee Word for Water*. This is the story of the late Wilma Mankiller, principal chief of the Cherokee Nation, and Charlie Soap, her husband. As young activists, they organized and inspired a small, poor community to voluntarily dig and install eighteen miles of waterline. This brought running water to the town of Bell, Oklahoma. Of course, they didn't do it alone. The Cherokee Nation and other donors and supporters were behind them, but these two people were the activists.

This is a feel-good movie that made me want to applaud. It had gentle humor and gentle sadness. The movie felt personal to me because it was filmed in a landscape I know: eastern Oklahoma. I saw the resilient spirit of the Cherokee Nation. I saw quiet, courageous people coming together as a community. I saw all of this and thought: I forgot how much I love turquoise jewelry!

Face it, I told myself, you're never going to dig a waterline in the rocky soil of eastern Oklahoma or anywhere else. You're part magpie and attracted to shiny objects, so enjoy who you are.

Recently I was assigned to a booth at the Episcopal diocese's state convention. My job was to hand out literature about the soup kitchen where I work. I showed up on time, a soldier about to do her duty, when what should I see but an Indian jewelry booth right next door. No wonder I believe in miracles.

They didn't take credit cards or checks. "I've got to find an ATM booth." I said.

"Ask the bishop," said Mr. Whitebird, the elderly artisan in the jewelry booth. "He knows where it is because he's already been here buying moccasins."

It was Whitebird who told me lots about turquoise. It is a mineral related to copper. The bluer it is, the more copper. The greener, the more iron. I once bought a cheap turquoise ring so blue I suspect it is really a melted Clorox bottle.

When I did some research, I discovered that the blue-green gem got the name turquoise in the sixteenth century when Turks took it to Europe from mines in Iran. In ancient Persia, palaces were domed with turquoise because blue symbolized heaven on earth. Aristotle, Pliny, and Marco Polo referred to turquoise.

In history, people wore turquoise as a talisman against death or evil. Turquoise is still thought to bring the wearer good luck, good fortune, wisdom, happiness, and connection to the spirit world. One legend says that throwing a piece of turquoise in a river will bring rain. I know for a fact that wearing turquoise brings scrutiny and comparison from Indians who are also wearing turquoise. My cousin Carole Greenfeather Moore, half Shawnee, looks at my humble turquoise choices with laser analysis for fear I'll embarrass the family.

Ancient Egyptians mined turquoise in the Sinai Peninsula, so it is logical that turquoise was found in the dry geography of the southwestern United States, especially Arizona and New Mexico. Albuquerque has a turquoise museum. According to one Native American legend, here's how turquoise was formed: When the rains came, ancient peoples danced and wept for joy. Their teardrops mingled with raindrops and seeped into Mother Earth, where it became turquoise, sometimes called skystone, pieces of the sky fallen to earth for our pleasure.

Ah, turquoise, the gem worn by Aztec kings, Jewish high priests, and me.

The Cherokee word for thanks is *wado*. It is more than a cursory, "Hey, thanks a bunch." *Wado* means a big, great, genuine, heartfelt thank you.

I say *wado* for the wonderful little film *The Cherokee Word for Water*. *Wado* for leaders who can bring people together as a community. And *wado* for turquoise.

....

The title of this tale is "A Native American Magi." It's about Oklahoma filmmaker Sterlin Harjo, who is a Seminole/Creek from Holdenville.

He has directed three feature films (*Four Sheets to the Wind, Barking Water,* and *Meeko*), a feature documentary (*This May Be the Last Time*), and a short film. They premiered at either the prestigious Sundance Film Festival or the Toronto International Film Festival. He is thirty-five years old.

The mystery at the heart of his documentary is the disappearance of his grandfather's body after a car accident in the 1960s. The whole community searched for his body while singing traditional songs of faith.

Then the film segues into the story of those Creek hymns, which are disappearing with the elders, and the origin of the Native songs from Scottish missionaries. The missionaries planted the same song form—called line singing—among the Appalachians in Kentucky, where it became country and bluegrass music, and with black slaves in Alabama, where the song form became spirituals and gospels. The film traces the title song, "This May Be the Last Time," from the Trail of Tears to popular versions by the Staple Singers and the Rolling Stones. By the end of the film, all of the Natives in the movie audience seemed to be singing along, so maybe the traditional songs aren't disappearing.

Before I knew about Harjo's feature films, I saw a short news film he and his film partner Matt Leach had done for Tulsa's This Land Press. The video features Jimmy Washington, a full-blood Cherokee. I happen to know Washington. He had come to Tulsa from Tahlequah to find work, but life didn't turn out that way. He became alcoholic and homeless. He was often beaten, and his stuff was stolen, even some of his clothes. You can see the video on This Land Press's website.

One cold winter day, long after the video was made, Harjo saw Washington on the street without a coat. Harjo stopped his car and put his own coat on Jimmy Washington; it was his Sundance Film Festival jacket.

How many of us would love to have a Sundance jacket? And Sterlin gave it away—to what many people would call a homeless drunk. I don't think Sterlin knows that I know the story of his jacket. He is quiet and modest, and it was a spontaneous act of kindness.

It reminds me of O. Henry's famous Christmas short story "The Gift of the Magi," in which a poor young wife sells her beautiful long hair to buy her beloved husband a watch chain, while he has sold his treasured watch to buy her combs for her hair. O. Henry tells us it's a story of sacrificing treasures to show our love for someone else. We know the biblical story of the three kings, but O. Henry says the real magi are people like the poor husband and wife in his story—and, I would add, Sterlin Harjo.

I hope he doesn't read this. He would be so embarrassed.

....

My mother was the best cook in Nowata County. Sadly, the cooking gene passed me by.

When I called my mother to tell her I was going to work for a soup kitchen, she didn't reply. A heavy silence lay on the phone. "But I'm not doing the cooking," I said quickly.

"Oh, thank God," she said.

Although I am not a good cook, I have spent many hours in kitchens—trying, watching, cleaning, talking with friends and family around a kitchen table. The kitchen is the heart of a home; it's where the best communication takes place.

Recently, I spent some special time at the soup kitchen watching Indian women make fry bread for eight hundred people. Native American Days at the Iron Gate soup kitchen were organized by Cherrah Giles, an official with the Muscogee (Creek) Nation. She marshaled an army of Native American volunteers to provide the food, cook, and serve authentic dishes, then clean the kitchen.

Fry bread was an important part of those meals. The cooks were of the Creek, Cherokee, Osage, Ponca, and other tribes. They were of several generations, many were related, and all were friends. It was a happy kitchen, full of laughter with flour flying, dough rising into mountains, and lots of prayer.

"We always pray before we cook," Giles told me. "And we pray while we cook. That's what goes into fry bread—love and prayer."

That's what brings us together as a people, she said. Caring about one another and feeding one another.

"And praying is what keeps them from killing one another," she said, glancing at her mother and aunt at the stoves.

"We are fry bread divas," her mother proclaimed.

Each cook had her own recipe and style. Some used self-rising flour, a little dried buttermilk, and warm water. Some used only warm water and Red Corn Native Foods Mix, produced by the Red Corn family business in Pawhuska. I saw no measuring going on. The real artistry was the mixing, rolling, patting, and cutting. After being lightly kneaded, the dough was turned out onto a floured counter. Some rolled it out with a rolling pin the size of a child's baseball bat. Some patted it out.

Then they cut the thick dough like big biscuits. One cook used a tin can as a cutter. For fry bread the size of your face, another used a small saucepan. Some cooks, I understand, cut the dough with a butcher knife or pizza cutter. Still others don't roll out their dough at all; they pat and stretch individual balls into large patties. Some cooked it immediately; some let the dough rise overnight at room temperature.

Just before the dough was dropped into hot oil, it was stretched slightly and the center of each patty was poked with a finger or a knife. That makes the bread crisper; the indentation better holds honey or the juice of beans and meat for an Indian taco. Others, as befitting a chef's prerogative, did not indent their bread at all.

Making fry bread is both a skill and a fine art. That's why there's a movie titled *More Than Frybread,* a pseudo-documentary about an Arizona fry bread contest, and a funny play titled *The Fry Bread Queen.* That's why a National Indian Taco Championship was held in Pawhuska a couple of years ago. That's why it's an honor to have Oklahoma Red Corn Native Foods fry bread mix available in the gift shop at the National Museum of the American Indian. That's why South Dakota named fry bread the official state bread.

And yet, fry bread has a dark and painful history. During the years 1864–68, the U.S. government forcibly evicted the Navajos from their homeland in Arizona to New Mexico. The three-hundred-mile journey, at gunpoint, became known as the Long Walk. The Navajos subsisted on government-issued flour, sugar, salt, and lard, which they transformed into fry bread. It is not a healthy food. Because a piece of fry bread contains seven hundred calories, much of which comes from carbohydrates (plus twenty-seven grams of fat), nutritionists say it has contributed to diabetes among traditional people.

Now fry bread is a festive dish associated with fairs, powwows, and special occasions. Making it, in large quantities, is part of the celebration. What an adventure I had in the kitchen with Indian fry bread divas. What an honor, welcomed into a parallel culture that is so close, yet separate. What a universal experience, a tribe of women cooking traditional foods.

Although fry bread is not a traditional dish, the cooks made it anyway because it is so popular. Hominy was also on the menu, as was "fried meat." I was so enjoying this Creek cooking experience, I asked the woman tending the big kettle of oil and deep frying chunks of pork, "What's the name of that? What's it called?"

"Fried meat," she said.

"What's the name of it in Creek?" I asked.

She consulted the other cooks, murmuring in Creek. They came to an agreement, and she came back to me with an answer.

"Fried meat," she said.

Mvto is the Creek word for thank you.

A Dab of Humility

Lives there a human with ego so humble she doesn't beam at the idea of having her portrait painted?

Not in my house. When I was asked if I would sit for a local art project, I fairly swooned with delight. This is a project by local artists depicting Tulsans of various occupations. Surely I would join a celebrated galaxy of famous portraits: John Singer Sargent's *Madame X,* Jan Vermeer's *Girl with a Pearl Earring,* Gustav Klimt's glittering *Adele Bloch-Baur,* and perhaps Andy Warhol's *Marilyn* with emerald green eye shadow and scarlet lipstick.

I bought a white blouse ruffled at the neck especially for the occasion. A hint of Emily Dickinson, I thought, timeless and poetic. Plus, the tiniest suggestion of strength and royalty from Elizabethan ruff collars. And the ruffles just might hide surplus chins.

Some fifteen painters with easels and drawing boards were set up waiting for me. "Oh, ruffles," one of them said. "What fun."

I took my place, a chair on a small platform, and the timekeeper called out, "Twenty minutes—begin." They would paint, and I would sit motionless, for about four hours with breaks every twenty minutes. I fixed my eyes on a distant tree bough and pasted on an expression intended to be both charming and intelligent. Instantly I had to sneeze. My ear itched. I had a slight cramp in my back.

"You're turning to the right," one painter barked.

"A little more to the left," another said. "All we're getting is a profile."

During the break, as they talked amiably with me, they revealed some hard truths: "It's hard to paint teenagers," one said. "They're pretty but don't have any character in their faces. We're so happy *you're* here."

"You see *a lot* when you look at a person for four hours."

I began to get an uneasy feeling. The painters began to grumble about the ruffles. "Too much white," somebody murmured.

At the next break, I asked timidly if I could peek at their works in progress. It was a sobering experience. In an array of media—oil, pastels, pencils, charcoal—I was depicted as a cross between *Whistler's Mother* and George Washington, with a vague resemblance to the Pillsbury Doughboy and a profile to rival Alfred Hitchcock. In their portraits, the white, ruffled blouse ballooned around me as if I were parachuting slowly to earth. Somebody, weary of too much white and blonde, had painted the blouse—and my face—green.

Sargent said famously that "a portrait is a likeness with a little something wrong with the mouth." Picasso turned portraits into geometry and animal parts. Were my painters, chattering quietly like a flock of merry birds, venturing where no artist had dared to go before?

In the spring of 1985, I did the publicity for what the legendary Angie Debo called her "public hanging." It was the unveiling of her portrait by Charles Banks Wilson in the state capitol—the first portrait of a woman to be hung there. Wilson told me he discarded his early sketches of the famed historian. "She looked like an old woman whose highlight of her life was picking green beans in a garden."

The final portrait depicts her as I often saw her, wearing a Mexican jacket given to her by historian friends and sitting in her favorite, vintage, mauve armchair. Behind her, Wilson painted a shelf of her books. They stand like the rugged landscape she wrote about. Her expression in semiprofile is proud, strong, and determined. She doesn't look directly at the viewer, she looks off into a past she examined fearlessly or into a future she saw hopefully. One of those hopes was that ambitious, smart, hardworking young women would have equal opportunities, far more than she had had at their age. This was the Debo that I knew. "I won't be writing any more books," she told me, "but you will be writing them and I will be reading them."

In the middle of the afternoon of my portrait adventure, I limped off the platform, stiff from sitting motionless, and the artists went off to work on my portrait for several months. Then the drawings and paintings went on display in the Tulsa Historical Society's gallery. How interesting it was to see a dozen or so images all similar, yet so different. I visited the exhibit several times, slack-jawed at the various faces the artists saw of me when I see only one face in the mirror.

I understood this better when I read about the unveiling in 1964 of Jamie Wyeth's portrait of the famous children's cardiologist Helen Brooke Tausig. When the painting was revealed, her friends gasped. One burst into tears. They said the portrait looked evil and witchy. They hid it away in a closet. Today, the painting is considered a masterpiece. Where others saw her as kindly and beloved, Wyeth said he painted the forcefulness and intensity he saw in the woman. He painted the personality that drove her to greatness. That's what artists do, isn't it?—see and interpret.

After Debo's funeral service, Anne Morgan and I collected Wilson to drive with us to the cemetery for the interment. Rather, we tried

Sitting for my portrait *(author's collection)*

to collect him. He was the epitome of a Western hero, tall and thin with his flowing white hair and dramatic moustache, charming all the women. He kissed so many hands, we fell far behind the funeral procession and got lost. On that flat prairie outside of Marshall, Oklahoma, we couldn't find the cemetery. I still have never seen her gravesite.

Wilson is dead too, now. The famous portrait painter of Native Americans and historical figures did more than paint faces and murals; he told stories in paint. Oklahoma's most famous artist was buried in Miami, Oklahoma. He was ninety-four when he died. Debo died at age ninety-eight.

My own portraits, all of my faces at the time, are packed away in artists' storage. Now it's just me and my everyday face facing the world. Here's the lesson I learned. For beauty, tour the renovated Tulsa Historical Society and Museum and the gardens with the Five Moons statues of Oklahoma's Indian ballerinas. For humility, have your portrait painted. For a legacy, write or paint or dance fearlessly and with truth.

What You Ought to Do Is . . .

Here's a tip: If you want lots of advice, invite your sister to visit.

Some sisters invite themselves. As in, "I'll be flying from Minneapolis back to Tucson and thought I'd stop over for a few days."

My sister doesn't visit often—more frequently than the biblical seven-year plagues but about as ferociously. She cannot stay with me, because she is allergic to cats and afraid of my dog, so there are respites when she goes back to her lodging. The rest of the visit is boot camp.

"No wonder you're tired and run down," she declared. "You're not eating right. You're not eating regularly and you're not eating enough." So we went out to eat a lot, at least three solid meals a day. Sometimes more. And we started early.

"You're not up yet?" She was calling the first morning. "I slept in, until almost seven thirty. Let's go have breakfast."

And boy, did we—big, field-hand breakfasts at Brookside by Day and Wild Fork. Breakfasts with piles of fried potatoes, sausage, eggs, and a side of gravy.

Beverage was another topic she addressed. "You drink too much coffee. No wonder you don't sleep well. I have all of my coffee in the morning, then only iced tea the rest of the day. And plenty of water."

She looked closely at me. "That's another thing. You don't drink enough water. You're probably dehydrated." We bought a case of bottled water to take with us in the car.

Since she doesn't drink alcohol, there was no cocktail hour. No wine with dinner. No nightcap. Instead, we sat in the garden, drank water, watched fireflies, and had deep conversations.

"We don't have fireflies in Tucson."

"Do you have mosquitoes?"

I forget the answer.

Then we went out for ice cream.

Holding her breath against the danger of cat dander, she made a couple of sprints through my house to do her laundry. With barely any criticism in her voice, she looked around the laundry room and asked, "Do you have a broom?" Then she tidied up a bit during the dry cycle. Despite the brevity of her in-house time, she spent the rest of the visit fastidiously picking (imaginary) cat hair off her clothes.

Outside, she looked around the yard and asked, "Don't you have a blower?" It was so hot, she left that chore to me to handle later, content that she had brought the oversight to my attention.

Since we couldn't spend much time in my house and since even we could eat only so many meals a day, we were on the road a great deal.

"You're not going to watch the bicycle race? You haven't planned on seeing the exhibit at Philbrook? You've never been to the Hard Rock gift shop? That's another thing. You're in a rut. All you do is work. Remember what happened the last time you overworked and overstressed yourself?"

I drove us at least four hundred miles around Tulsa. We went to movies and museums and galleries. We had spa days. We walked around the hopping downtown, drove by the big Gathering Place Park construction, and cruised through neighborhoods commenting on the houses. We drank lots of water. We went to bed early because we had another full day ahead of us.

I tried to limit the number of times I asked her when her flight left.

Like curious chimpanzees, we examined one another's jewelry and clothes. We exchanged silent looks that said, "What in the world have you done to your hair?" We talked about books, eviscerated old boyfriends, debated the best way to cook potatoes, and remembered our father's regular disasters with backyard barbecues.

We tiptoed around sensitive topics, like the time—and surely it was just once and that was thirty years ago—that I referred to her son and daughter as "the sacred grandchildren." Not that I was bitter, but nobody drove cross-country in a pilgrimage to spend holidays with my cats.

"And another thing," she volunteered out of the blue. "You ought to get a memory foam mattress cover. That might help you sleep better."

My sister had dropped in like much like Mary Poppins to sort out my life.

Then she flew away. I'm feeling much better.

Look at Me, Look at Me

1. Laurence Olivier said when he made a stage entrance he imagined himself carrying a pink umbrella. He thought that helped call the audience's attention to him. That's because actors want people to look at them when they're on stage.

2. When television was becoming popular, white shirts created an on-screen glare, so men were asked to wear pastel dress shirts on camera. Soon, lots of men were wearing pastel dress shirts so that other people might think that they, too, were appearing on television.

3. I like the joke about a redneck's last words: "Hey, watch this!"

4. I hate Facebook.

What do these four things have in common? Some vague theory I'm developing about our desperate need for attention. Celebrity culture is not new. It's as old as women in ancient Rome collecting the perspiration of famous gladiators or of primitive people eating the flesh of fierce warriors.

We are far beyond being a celebrity culture. What we're after now is individual celebrity. Not just fifteen minutes of fame but daily, constant, chattering, clamoring for attention like a two-year-old child.

When I caved in to peer pressure and signed up on Facebook, one of the first messages was from a person reporting to everybody, "I just ate a peanut butter sandwich and am going to bed." This stop-the-press report cooled me forever on Facebook. Or perhaps it implanted the fear that I, too, would succumb to such innocuous posts.

Brooding over this craving to be in the public eye led me to thinking about eye contact in general and its complexities—the different connotations, implications, and plain old misunderstandings. There's even a polysyllabic word for the study of eye contact in nonverbal communication: oculesics.

Supposedly, when my cat looks at me and blinks slowly it means that she loves me. But if I blink slowly at another human, it means that I'm either disinterested, sleepy, or drugged. Whereas if I blink excessively it could mean that I'm flirting, stressed, or lying. Or, I suppose, all of the above.

Not making eye contact could mean lying, too, or guilt. I think of this when I'm trying to explain something to somebody and look away to gather my thoughts. "Uh-oh," I remind myself and snap back to eye contact so sincere I'm bug-eyed. This is equally disconcerting to the other person, who often jumps back startled. No wonder I find myself frequently misunderstood.

Good eye contact is hard to master. Looking too long at someone—akin to staring—can be rude, creepy, or threatening, as in, "What are *you* looking at?"

Unless we smile when we look at the other person, which can be interpreted as either friendly or invitational. Unless we're in France, where smiling at someone we don't know suggests to the reserved French that we are simpletons.

Eye contact in other cultures can mean entirely other things. In an Argentine tango club, a woman stares at a man to convey "Ask me to dance. And I mean only dance." Whereas in Japan, a woman who does not make eye contact can be considered polite and proper. Same thing for some traditional American Indians and for a couple of ex-cons I know.

My day job is at a soup kitchen, where I learned that homeless people say one of the most painful things about being homeless is becoming invisible. People don't look at them. Maybe the people think recognition of their condition will embarrass the homeless. Maybe they're afraid they will be asked for money. Strangers look away or even cross the street to avoid the homeless.

When I learned that the homeless felt unseen, I started taking photographs of the people who eat at the soup kitchen, always with their permission. We put the pictures on the bulletin board. We print the photos in newsletters and brochures. We include them in our online e-news. It's our way of saying, "We *see* you. You're a person."

Sometimes the homeless ask for a copy of the photo to send to a relative for a holiday, to a fiancé in prison, or to friends far away. I usually take close-up portraits, but a man called L.A. asked me to take a full-length shot. "I want to send it to my mother in California," he said. "I was just diagnosed HIV positive, and I want her to see me while I'm healthy."

Sometimes they want the photo for themselves, for the same reason we all want pictures of ourselves. It's not look-at-me ego. A photograph reminds us: I'm here.

Tell Me, Who Am I?

Here's my take on an old joke.

"Knock knock."

"Who's there?"

"You tell me."

Some people play games on the computer for relaxation. To me, the computer is a tool. Playing computer games would be like playing with the vacuum cleaner. That changed when I discovered Play-Buzz and other quizzes that ask something like, "If you were a rock and roll band, what band would you be?" A short series of questions follow, then your parallel identity is revealed.

Here is who I am:

If I were a classic cartoon character, I'd be Bugs Bunny.

If I were a storm in nature, I'd be an ice storm.

If a jewel, I'd be a sapphire.

If a famous novel, I'd be *Pride and Prejudice.*

If an animal, a cat.

If a vegetable, a carrot.

If a crook, I'd be an art thief.

The charm of these personality quizzes is that they combine a little bit of self-recognition with a hint of flattery. And yet, there's an aftertaste of doubt. An ice storm sounds silent and menacing. Is that how people see me? Is that how I behave?

Maybe I can't get past being identified with smarty-pants, fast-talking Bugs Bunny. Would I rather be Elmer Fudd? Maybe fearless little Henry Hawk?

Is there a purpose to self-identity quizzes? A slightly distasteful hint of narcissism and self- absorption hovers over the whole thing, another brick in the Me Me Me era. Fred Astaire said the only time he looked at himself in the mirror was in the morning when he shaved. Lauren Bacall said, "Looking at yourself in the mirror isn't exactly a study of life." That was another era. In some ways, a better era.

On the other hand, self-awareness can be healthy. I know people who don't have a clear self-identity; they keep changing their personality, trying to find one that fits. Some act a role so believably that others believe that's who they are. Cary Grant was so famous both on- and offscreen for his suave, debonair persona that he once said, "Everybody wants to be Cary Grant. Even me. I want to be Cary Grant, too."

(Note to self: Once in a while, refer to some hero figure besides actors.)

It must be scary and exhausting to live hiding behind a made-up self, much like the fearful little Wizard of Oz behind his curtain and smoke.

(Another note to self: Referring to a fictional character isn't much of an improvement.)

I know people who seem to pick a single persona and stick with it: entertainer, authority, cynic, et cetera. That's fun for a while, but then I want different levels of conversation. I want to talk to an authentic person and wade into the deep end of a conversation.

Brené Brown is an author and researcher who says—among a lot of other stuff—that authenticity involves letting go of what we think we should be and embracing who we are.

The concept of an individual self hasn't always been around. Saint Augustine, about A.D. 400, was the first Western writer to define the concept of a personal identity. He thought the reason for knowing our self was to grow beyond that individual self toward a higher identity, or God.

In our more secular world, self-improvement is more likely to be for personal gain. Executive coaches offer advice for businesspeople who want to develop their presence. Here are some tips from a *Wall Street Journal* article: Ask for honest feedback from your boss or colleagues. Solicit constructive criticism from your spouse, family, and friends. Ask a few trusted people what they like and dislike about you.

(Note to others: This is not going to happen with me. Ever.)

I've been dabbling with silly "who am I" quizzes for amusement, headed down that slippery slope toward self-absorption. I need to get back on track. I need to remember the higher purpose of understanding my personal self. I need to take a serious look at myself in the mirror and ask, "What's up, Doc?"

Committee Work

This is a little rumination on the question "Why do I put myself through this agony?" It's about committees. Or councils or boards or any small group of people that gathers together to run something and to drive one another crazy.

A sign I like says, "For God so loved the world, he didn't send a committee." Can I have an amen to that?

I came away from a particularly frustrating committee meeting recently with this query stuck on repeat: Why am I doing this? Why am I doing this? Why am I doing this? I can't flatter myself that it's because I'm invaluable to the organization. The organization is like the snow in the lovely little poem by e. e. cummings: "The snow doesn't give a soft, white damn whom it touches."

The organization I'm volunteering with doesn't need me. It doesn't give a soft, white damn about me. It just wants the work done. I remember a woman in South Africa talking to me about her city's fumbling administration. "I don't care what party is in office," she said. "I just want running water to my house."

Good point. Excellent point.

So if I'm not vital to whatever committee, board, or council that is agitating me, obviously I am offering my time and services for my own reasons. Such as ego.

An economist I admire once asked, "Why would you want to know only people like yourself?" At the time, I *did* want to know only people who think as I do. I've changed. A little. Now I see that it's good for us to get outside our comfort zone. I think it's also good for us to try to work as a chorus, not just sing our solos.

The English actress Glenda Jackson said she didn't want to live like a movie star. She said she liked to do her own shopping and join the ordinary people on the streets because she liked the friction of daily life. She said roughing up the nerves a bit made her a better actress. She left acting to become a member of Parliament, which, I presume, keeps her nerves roughed up admirably.

I taught journalism at a university, trying to communicate that the goal of good, print journalism style is to write with directness, simplicity, and clarity. I also held some administrative positions, and it was in these roles that I was called into the dean's office.

"Connie," he said, "you are a very direct person. You say what you think very clearly and directly." I was squirming in my seat over this high praise. Then he lowered the boom: "If you want to succeed in academia, you've got to get over that."

I have come to learn that I am not cut out for diplomacy. However I try, I am not diplomatic. I am not subtle. I am not gushy. I excuse myself by saying I have enough trouble communicating when I'm trying to be clear. Any embellishment only muddies things. Therefore I know that I am not an ideal committee member. And yet . . .

Over the years as different committees have pounded me down to the ground, I've recognized some stereotypes as bad as or worse than I:

> The guy who doesn't have power at his workplace, so by God he's going to have it here.

> The woman so passive-aggressive you could slice salami with her fixed little smile.

> The person who never quite understands the organization's mission or financial statement or bylaws.

> The one with a blank stare thinking about dinner plans or a plumbing problem or tee-off time.

> The one trying to placate both sides and annoying everybody.

The one who wants to win, the one who missed the last meeting and wants an update, the one with a hidden agenda, the one whose cell phone rings, the one whose hearing aid is on the fritz, and the one who keeps saying, "We need to run this organization like a business" (meaning, like his own business). The one who never speaks, the one who never listens, the one who never votes yea or nay but always abstains. The one who wants her name and photograph in the newspaper. Sometimes there's even the one who really does have the organization's best interest at heart and knows how to move in that direction.

In short, committees are like microcosms of the world, full of people who irritate one another while trying to do the most good for the most people.

There's a reason we use the verb "serve" when we talk about committees, boards, trusts, and councils. We serve on them in the sense of public service. Or sometimes like serving a jail sentence.

And yet, as wise and mellow as I have become, I know deep down that every committee I've served on would have operated so much better if everybody had just done it my way. That makes me much like H. G. Wells, who considered for his epitaph, "I was right. You damned fools."

Maybe It's Me

The whole world ought to be more like a hardware store.

I love hardware stores. Small ones, neighborhood ones, big box ones—I love them all.

And here's why. The salesmen—and they're usually men—are so positive and helpful. No matter what do-it-myself project I go in with, no matter how tentative I am or how inexperienced, the hardware salesmen are full of positive support.

"Sure you can do that. Of course you can. Easiest thing in the world."

Not only do they have helpful directions and inside advice, they have the tools and supplies needed for the job. Not only do they have the stuff, they're happy to sell it to me. What's more, they have personal testimonials to go with it.

"I got one just like this for my wife. It's lightweight, and I thought she could handle it easier. Turns out, I liked it so much I kept it for myself. Got another one just like it for her."

I strut out of hardware stores puffed like a toad with my new-found self-confidence.

When my do-it-myself project takes an ugly turn, I can go back to the hardware store the next day without fear of disapproval. I can go back for more encouragement and more helpful tips. Plus, they've got stuff to sell me to fix what I messed up the first time. Or second time.

More people ought to be like hardware salesmen. Just think how productive we would all be if more parents, business colleagues, teachers, and dog trainers were former hardware salesmen. We'd never hear "Shame on you" or "Bad dog." We'd never have to look at someone wearing a "What were you thinking?" expression on her face. We'd never hear cursing from the office next door.

Same for drivers. There would be no more angry honking, yelling, or rude gestures. People would smile at us and say, "Hey. I can get stuff to fix this little scratch you put on my fender." They would wait patiently behind us while we tried, yet again, to parallel park. They'd give us the "thumbs up" sign as we took another crack at it. They might even assure us that we can repair the smashed taillight ourselves.

It's not just the tools, materials, and equipment that give hardware salesmen their mojo, it's their attaboy attitude. Imagine going into an office supply story and saying in a small, quiet voice, "Do you have something to help me write a novel?"

"Have I got it?" the salesclerk would exclaim. "Heck, yeah, I've got it. But why is a person like you thinking of only one novel? Think trilogy. Now, for that, you're going to need a heavy-duty printer, so let me show you this one.

"Of course, for a big job like a trilogy, which will require hours of typing, you'll need an ergonomic keyboard. Lucky you. Got one left.

"Woman bought one just like it last Wednesday, and by Saturday she had written a book of poetry. A whole book. But wait, what kind of desk chair do you have? You can't slump when you're on a creative streak."

It's not that I want everybody to be like *The Music Man*'s Professor Harold Hill with his "think method," but when I dive into unchartered waters—and that includes all of my home improvement projects—I need lots of help.

Come to think of it, people offer me advice all the time, and most of it is unsolicited. My friends have voluntarily advised me on everything from makeup application and hairstyles to appliance purchases and garden maintenance. Advice isn't as welcome when I don't ask for it.

Maybe it's me. Maybe I look like a person who needs lots of handholding as I trip through life as merry as a breeze. At the soup kitchen one morning a homeless man told me, "Mama, those shoes you have on don't go with that outfit. In fact, nothing you have on today goes together." I went to a mirror, and he was right. I'm getting fashion critiques from the homeless. And they're bad.

Maybe it is me.

The Work Crew and Me

Is there anything you want to know about plumbing? Or Roto-Rooting?
Or sump pumps? Or the city's sewer lines? Or surface water under
the house?

Because if there is, I'm your woman.

This is not an expertise I sought out. No, like most of the other
unpleasant lessons in life, it found me. And it found me after some of
Oklahoma's gully-washing rains.

Water backed up in the bathtub, the toilet wouldn't work, even
a hardwood floor buckled. The plumbing and water problems were
so complicated, for some time I thought I was going to have to quit
my day job, stop writing, resign from the book club, and deal with
plumbing issues full time. I thought I would set up a little card table
in the front yard and check in the workmen who arrived in waves.

Every cloud has a silver lining, though, right? And so did this one.
My dog Bingo could not have been happier. These were his kind of
guys—many of them big, strapping lads who patted him, scratched
him roughly, and admired him for the fine, overfed specimen that
he is.

The dog said to me, "Now, this is more like it. Real guys. I'm
cooped up in this house day after day with you and those cats
talking about Emily Dickinson and listening to classical music. Let's
get outside and roll on our backs in the sunshine."

And I have to admit, we did meet some interesting folks during
this home repair saga. Some of them were chatty lots, and we had
interesting conversations. We learned about the kidney infection that
turned into a bladder infection. "Yep," one said, "flat on my back for
three weeks."

We met the oldest plumber in Tulsa who has the permit to
prove it. He's a man called Strawberry, because he used to ride a
strawberry roan horse and now has a dog he loves so much he has
insured it for $10,000.

We met guys who start a lot of sentences with "Well, here's your
problem, right here." Unfortunately, this optimistic statement was
often followed with the more depressing sentence "Nope, that ain't
her after all."

We met a big plumber, too large for the crawl space, who had an innovative solution to finding the source of the water leak. "What I'll do is," he said, "I'll cut some holes in the floor and stick my head down to see what I can see." We vetoed that idea.

We met a smaller plumber who relied on his intuition. "I've just got this hunch," he said, "that the problem is out in the garage quarters. We bust up that cement floor, we find our problem." We had a hunch this wasn't a very scientific approach, so we vetoed this idea, too.

We had unexpected conversations about music. A particularly nice young man volunteered this information: "I'm getting a little sick of Ernest Tubb."

"Really?" I said.

"I always liked Ernest Tubb," he said, "until I got a tape stuck in the tape deck of my truck. That's all I've been able to listen to. After about three months of Ernest Tubb, I'm getting a little tired of him."

I pondered this on two levels:

1. The idea of listening to "Walking the Floor over You" and "Yellow Rose of Texas" for three months, and
2. The tiniest concern that a guy who can't get a tape out of his tape deck could fix my stuff.

I met, at least by phone, a sympathetic young woman at a plumbing company. I sounded like a caller on public radio's *Car Talk* as I described the symptoms of my plumbing problems—the burble sound, the whoosh-whoosh noise, the color of the water that backed up in the tub, the flow of water that poured out of the crawl space. She responded to everything I said with "Oh, no!"

At first this took me aback. Maybe things were worse than I thought. "Does that sound really bad to you?" I asked her.

"Oh, no," she said. "I'm just thinking how I would feel if I were you."

How I'm feeling now is better. Most of the problems seem to be solved. Water is flowing properly. The cats have crept out from under the bed where they hid to avoid the foot traffic. And the dog is back to being lethargic and bored.

Not a bad way to be. I'm looking forward to it myself.

The Ancient Mariner

This is a story about how four young women—Andrea, Erin, Becky, and Ashley—taught me an ancient language.

Turns out, I'm the one that speaks it. I didn't know this until I discovered a generational language gap akin to the Grand Canyon between me and my young colleagues. This all started with Gregg shorthand. I was sitting between Andrea and Erin at a meeting, happily taking notes in shorthand. After the meeting, one of them said, "What were you drawing?"

"Not drawing," says I. "Shorthand notes." And I demonstrated. They exploded with laughter. "Oh, you're making that up," one said. "You're just drawing squiggles and making up meanings."

"Wait," said the other one. "I think I've heard of shorthand. But I've never known anyone to actually *do* it."

There I was—the Ancient Mariner and her shorthand pad. All the time I spent in high school learning to take 120 words a minute only to have it fall on me in derision.

These young women, whizzes at the Internet, could discover in a keystroke that in 1888 John Robert Gregg invented a system of pen stenography—cursive strokes and sharp angles of phonetic spelling—called Gregg shorthand. It gained popularity in the United States in the early twentieth century. Sadly, in the past twenty years or so it has fallen out of fashion. Does any high school still offer shorthand and typing classes?

If I wanted to refresh my skills, I could order the 1949 *Simplified* book or, even more nostalgic, the 1903 edition. Although as a purist, I might prefer the 1988 *Centennial* version. Would I have the patience to do the repetitive drills, page after page?

I have reverent admiration for the patience of Mrs. Brant, the high school teacher who graded our shorthand books: pages of the stairstep symbols for "is," "for," and "have." We used to do our shorthand homework during meetings of Rainbow girls. Rainbow—that's another custom of yore the young women wouldn't know.

About the same time, in yoga class, my young teacher, Ashley, had us do a routine that involved balancing large inflated balls with our legs. "That was fun," I told her. "Made me feel like Esther Williams."

"Who?" she asked.

It's as if they said they had once heard of button shoes and whalebone corsets and lazy Susans and Tweed perfume and Nehru jackets and poodle skirts and I had them. Maybe I could also put my hair into a French twist, get a mustard-seed necklace, wear a charm bracelet, and do the dirty bop. I could talk in a swoon about Johnnie Ray, Sal Mineo, and Tab Hunter.

I thought I found a book that might help us communicate over our generational gap: *Merriam-Webster's Dictionary of Allusions.* Maybe this book could help us translate our common English language. But here's what I found in the book—entries like grassy knoll, Rosebud, *Silent Spring, Peyton Place,* yellow journalism. Do you think my young friends know what these mean?

The dictionary is meant to explain the colorful terms of the English language, but what it showed me is how quickly language can age. Do we all know that a Mickey Finn is gangster slang from the 1800s? Or that the origin of the term "hat trick" comes from a play in cricket? I can't imagine explaining to my young colleagues that "double whammy" is a term introduced by a character named Evil Eye Fleegle in *Li'l Abner,* which was a comic strip drawn by Al Capp in the 1950s. I don't think they've heard of the 1950s.

But these young women have their own language. I was driving to lunch with Becky, who suddenly said to me, "Look! A choo-choo!" Do I need to explain that she is the mother of a toddler? They have their own language.

I know some toddler language. I can say "choo-choo" and "bye-bye," and I can write those words in shorthand, too.

Hooked on Hookah

So, the other evening when I was at the hookah lounge . . .
What? You don't think I'm hip enough to go to a hookah lounge?
I worried about that myself. For starters, I didn't know what a
hookah lounge is. I see them popping up—usually around colleges—
but they sound illegal. Like an opium den. But surely not, what
with hookah painted in big letters outside. I am neither advocating
hookah smoking nor denouncing it. I'm reporting. To be colloquial,
"I'm not saying, I'm just saying."

First, I did some research. I learned that the smoke is inhaled
through the long tube of a hookah pipe and passes through a water
bowl to cool and purify it. In Southeast Asia the hookah pipe is
called a *shisha*. Other places it is called a hubble-bubble.

Hookah cafes are popular social places in the Arab world. The
first recorded mention of hookah was in Persia in the 1500s. The
Brits discovered the pleasures of hookah during the British Raj
colonial era in India in the late 1800s. The United States discovered
hookah in the 1960s and 1970s and now again. Here in Tulsa, an
average pipe costs about $15 or $20 and lasts about forty minutes,
but in larger cities and more upscale lounges, the price can go up to
$150. Usually no alcohol or food is served in a hookah den, only soft
drinks, tea, and coffee.

Armed with this information, I strolled into my neighborhood
hookah lounge. I was a bit disappointed with the décor. I had hoped
the place would be dripping with bright color, stacks of Persian rugs,
and piles of satin pillows with tassels. I imagined I would sit cross-
legged on a cushion, puff from an ornate water pipe, and exhale colored smoke rings, much like the caterpillar in *Alice in Wonderland*.

Wrong. It wasn't like that. Except for the water pipes. The hookah
lounge itself was chockablock with low, mismatched tables, sofas,
and chairs. It was comfortable but ordinary and looked like many of
my college apartments.

I arrived at the hookah lounge right after work, and the place was
practically empty except for two very young men sitting in a corner. I
said to the waitress, "It's my first time here. Where do I sit and what
do I do?" She guided me to ordering a mango-flavored tobacco.

One of the young men came over and said, "If you're alone, would you like to join us?" I've watched enough true-crime TV shows to have second thoughts—"When last seen, the missing woman was accompanied by two young men . . ." My fearful hesitation lasted only a split second. I jumped right into their party, and soon we were joined by the mother of one of the young men. She is a nurse who often works thirty-six-hour shifts. She and her son meet regularly at the hookah lounge to spend time together. They said it's quieter than dinner out and costs about the same.

The three of them showed me the ropes—how to smoke and savor the flavored tobacco; how to lean back, relax, and talk quietly; how to enjoy a cup of hot chai with the hookah. They told me that the place is completely different at night, crammed with people and sometimes having belly dancers and Middle Eastern music for entertainment.

What I liked best was the gentle smell of the tobacco. It clung to my clothes and to my hair. I drove home thinking how nice and welcoming the three people had been and how vaguely relaxed I felt, as if I'd shed a heavy coat. I drove home singing to the tune of the Oscar Mayer commercial, "I'm hooked on hookah and hookah's hooked on me." People smiled and waved at me.

When I got home, everything changed. An icy message on my answering machine was the veterinarian's office saying they were closing for the day and I had forgotten to pick up my cat. She would have to spend the night there.

Forgot my cat! Oh egregious, slattern pet owner am I. Guilt kicked the mellow hookah right out of me. Now I'm going to have to go back to the hookah lounge and begin my research all over. First, I'll retrieve my cat from the vet's. Next time I'll tape a note to myself on the dashboard: Collect your pets before going home. Roll up the car windows when you sing.

Scaredy Cat?

I've stumbled into an idea that could make a lot of money. The only hitch is, I can't figure out how to translate the idea into profit. Here's my thought sequence in the labyrinth of popular culture.

1. Mysteries and detective books are popular because we like suspense, but we like everything to be tidied up in the ending. That's how we would like life to be—tidied up and with good triumphing over evil.
2. We like thrillers because they are titillating. We like to experience fear, but at a distance. This is much like a child's running up to touch a scary—maybe haunted!—house.
3. What are the two most popular creatures in thrillers? Vampires and zombies. People make a fortune writing in these genres. I've known two writers who made fortunes writing detective books. I know a woman who has made several fortunes writing about vampires.

So here is how I blundered into my guaranteed moneymaking idea.

1. I remember my elderly neighbor Mrs. Brown's experiences with a young neighbor she sees every day on her walk. "I always say hello," Mrs. Brown told me, "but she never answers. I think she's afraid that if she speaks to me, I'll ask her to drive me to the doctor."
2. I remember another neighbor, a pleasant young man who was an airplane mechanic. Occasionally we chatted over the fence. One Saturday morning as I headed out on an errand I told him I was involved in a home improvement project. I was going to replace the toilet lid.

"That ought to be easy," he said and waved me on my way.

Well, it wasn't easy. Later that day he stepped out onto his front porch while I was in the flower garden.

"How did your home improvement project go?" he called.

"Terrible," I said. "I can't get the screw to work."

He leapt back inside and yelled through a tiny crack, "I think that it turns to the left. Try that." And he slammed the door.

"What was that about?" I thought. Then I got it. He was afraid I would ask him to come do the repair for me.

And that is how I came to my brilliant idea. I have discovered the next popular horror creature—seniors! Senior citizens and old people, anyone over sixty. We are the scariest beings on earth. Especially old women.

Younger people see us coming, and they run the other way. They're afraid we're going to ask them to do something for us—lift something, move something, fix something, go get something for us, take us somewhere, listen to us. Oh, the list of possible torments goes on and on.

We don't have to prowl the neighborhoods by night on our walkers or stalk the shopping malls with our canes. We don't even have to *have* walkers or canes: just the look of maturity will do it. Especially if we are women of a certain age.

I love that phrase—a woman of a certain age. It is fraught with innuendo in literature. Sometimes (in English literature) it means spinsterhood; sometimes (in French) it is charged with sexual implications.

Not now and not in America. It just means older women who are most likely to be needy. Or dangerous. They used to burn us at stakes or drown us, especially if we have cats. The scariest of all is an older women wearing a robe or patio dress midday and tottering down the driveway; one look, and neighbors, workmen, and passersby scatter like birds.

Unless she's an older woman who has a lot of money and power. That woman is not scary; she is courted, especially by gigolos, ambitious young people, and nonprofit organizations.

Why is it that older men aren't so scary?

....

Isn't it fun to discover that you're right and everybody else is wrong? I have arrived at this epiphany in a circuitous route with three parts:

1. I believe that 99 percent of the reading audience is women, and however diverse our lives, we all speak one common language: books. Women communicate some of our most personal feelings and experiences by discussing what we have read and what it means to us.

2. I see that new books, like movies and TV shows, come in waves of popularity. At one time, this was the women's liberation/feminist books. More recently, the Mommy War books. Those of us who went through the 1970s and women's lib to give women a choice of working or being

stay-at-home moms don't want to hear young women kvetching about that choice. Many mothers today, especially single mothers and low-income women, don't have a choice. If you do have a choice, do it or don't do it, but hush about it.

3. I now feel like the Madame Curie of literature, because I think I have identified a new genre of women's literature—Old Dame books.

That is not a derogative term, like "old biddy." Old dames have lived lives of substance, courage, and merit. They have achieved wisdom, and they can share it with a sense of humor and humility.

Most of my mentors have been old dames. At church, Jane Cleveland Bloodgood was one of them. After raising a family, she received her PhD at age seventy-two and became the first Episcopal female priest in Oklahoma when she was seventy-eight. She got a hip replacement in order to process down the aisle for her installation. When *Tulsa World* editor Jenkin Lloyd Jones wrote a column about her, he said, "She's as tough as a $1 steak." She has humor, too, he said.

One Sunday after church, she and I went to her tiny apartment for lunch. She cooked us a small steak, and as we talked long into the afternoon, we drank so much wine we got tipsy. She told me Episcopal jokes. "Episcopalians are known as drinkers," she said. "They say that wherever three or four are gathered, you'll find a fifth."

She also told me that both of her adult sons had committed suicide—both by hanging themselves. It takes a strong old dame to live through that, continue on with a life of purpose, and keep a sense of humor. Her favorite scriptural passage was from the Apocrypha: "Hew the wood and you will find me; turn but a stone and I am there." The more I ponder this through the years, the more depth I find in it and the more meaning it adds to my own life.

One thing I admire about old dames is their straightforward truth telling. They don't mince words, and they don't evade with a verbal dance. They tell it like it is, direct and plain. When Bloodgood and I were finishing a priest-parishioner conversation about theology, she asked if I had any other questions. "Yes," I said. "Tell me about prayer. How to pray." "Ah," she answered, "now you've asked the hard question, the one I always have trouble with."

Historian and writer Angie Debo is famed for her research into Oklahoma's Indian tribes, but when I grumbled about not knowing how to find some information I was looking for, she said, "That's what I always had the most trouble with—finding the information." She found it the hard way, with long hours in archives and libraries writing out notes by longhand. She was proud of the knot on the first knuckle of the second finger on her right hand, the mark of thousands of hours writing by hand.

I like old women for their courage as well as their wisdom. What a treasure trove to discover life-shaking memoirs written by women. First, I found books by May Sarton. My favorite may be *Plant Dreaming Deep,* about her house and garden, a woman coming to terms with living alone. She wrote into her brave old age.

I have read all of the nonfiction books by British late-life author Diana Athill. She writes about her career as an editor, her romances, and her personal tragedies. Describing Athill, Canadian writer Alice Munro says, "She's got her teeth into life!" In her mid-nineties, Athill spoke and wrote about her loss of sex drive—"a kind of freedom"— and about dying. It's silly to be afraid of being dead, she said, but the process of dying is another matter. "Death is an inevitable end of an individual object's existence," she said. Not "end of life," she clarified, "because it's part of life." Everything begins, develops, then fades away, she said. Everything—rocks, mountains, even planets.

The late Irish writer Nuala O'Faolain wrote an extraordinary memoir titled *Are You Somebody?* Part of it is her bleak, penniless childhood in North Dublin. Part is her rebellious life with many love affairs. And part is what she learned, as a woman of a certain age, when youth was gone and passionate love affairs were gone. What she learned is that the world is filled with new things to love—things as ordinary as gardens, dogs, music, and walks in the country. When he reviewed her book, the great Irish writer Frank McCourt said, "She stirs love with a long spoon."

I realized I had become a woman of a certain age one Valentine's Day when I was positively thrilled to have—a new mop! And I'd bought it for myself.

And so, my discovery: Old Dame literature.

Penelope Lively at age eighty published a new memoir written from a country she calls "old age." Fay Weldon at age eight-three wrote a *New York Times Book Review* column about the difficulty an older woman has finding a publisher if she is writing about the sexual and social predicaments of her own age. Publishers want protagonists in their twenties or thirties.

Several male friends of mine seem stressed—frightened almost— by approaching retirement age. And why not? In a society that identifies us by what we do, retirement seems to be another word for worthless. Hence, a new surge of websites and books about "being, not doing," about inventing our later years as a second act, and about becoming a Human Being, not a Human Doing.

Absolutely right. And who explored this country first? Old dames. When I interviewed Tulsan Norma Eagleton, now eighty, for a magazine article, we talked about her active life and political career. Then I asked her what she is doing now.

"Trying to grow old with dignity and worth," she said.

A great philosophy for all of life. Women were right all along.

The Learning Curve

The title I wanted for this essay is "How We Learn What We Learn If We Learn It at All," but that is too long.

"Learning Curve" seems too gentle. A learning curve suggests an accompaniment of encouraging comments such as "That's the way, but let's try it again."

Much learning seems to be not a curve at all but a straight line. Sometimes the line is flat. That's what a restaurateur meant as he saw his fifth restaurant go broke. "Do I have thirty-five years' experience in this business," he asked me, "or have I made the same mistake for thirty-five years?"

Sometimes the learning line is a sharp incline. That's when we learn something the hard way and say, "Wow. I won't be doing that again." Such as have a couple of glasses of wine and color your hair yourself.

The learning line can be a steady decline. That's when people shake their heads sadly and say, "She just doesn't get it, does she?" Some of us never learn.

Some of us don't want to learn. We are happy the way we are, flaws and all. I knew a pretty young woman with a slight speech impediment, a "w" for "r" substitution. Not as pronounced as Elmer Fudd's speech, more like a little girl's cute mispronunciation. This was back when I was in charge of fixing the world, so I arranged for her to see a speech therapist. Nothing changed. She liked the way she spoke, and I kept on trying to fix people.

Some of us are determined to change the answer and show the world we're the one who is right. These are the righteously stubborn who keep walking into a wall while trying to prove it's a door. This is not as entertaining to watch as some might think.

Learning can come in a happy eureka moment or over time, with age and experience. Harry Truman said, "The only thing I learned worth knowing is what I learned after I knew it all."

Some of the lessons we learn come too late.

What you learn when you're fired: You should have seen that coming. Take it as an opportunity to move on.

What you learn when you're dumped: You should never have chosen that person in the first place. Take it as an opportunity to move on.

What you learn when your mother dies: You want to contact everybody you ever sent a cursory condolence note and say, "I am really, really sorry because now I know what a loss that is."

What you learn when a friend betrays you: Stunning pain.

What you learn when a friend defends you: Deep gratitude.

What you learn when you fall down stairs, drive over a curb, back into the garage door, and lose the TV remote all in one week: You need to slow down, do less, and manage your stress.

What you learn when your new hair color is garish: It's only hair. It's not like you painted your house a ghastly color.

What you learn when you do paint your house a ghastly color: Say you like it that way and let some time pass before you repaint it.

What you learn when you hit ages forty, fifty, sixty, seventy, eighty . . . : Boy, I've wasted a lot of time. I'd better make hay while the sun shines.

The sun shines thinly in the month of November. I used to think of November as bleak. Our long summer and short autumn are over. All that lies ahead is the frenzy of the holidays and then snowstorms and ice storms.

(What you learn during an ice storm: You simply must remember to unhook the garden hose from the house before the faucet freezes.)

Over the years, I have learned to like November. No guilt about gardening when I'm lolling inside reading a book. Too late to worry about moving the big pots of plants before they freeze. No more getting up early on Saturday mornings to go to the farmers' market. No more stressing about how I look in T-shirts and shorts. No more having to see flip-flops on everyone.

T. S. Eliot called the month "sombre November." I've learned not to see November as dark and dull but to welcome it with an ahhhh of relief.

That's my current learning curve.

What Did I Ever Do to the Weather?

I don't want to sound like a crybaby, but the weather has it in for me. Here I am just minding my own business, but every time I turn around, it's something new with me and the weather.

I didn't take it personally when hundreds of pounds of limbs from my giant sycamore fell on my house. Twice. After all, those were bad storms and lots of people had tree damage.

I was saddened when wind snapped off my row of ornamental pear trees, but I should have known they were too fragile for Oklahoma weather.

I was more awed than offended when yet another storm drove a large limb straight into my roof as if a burly god on Mount Olympus had hurled a javelin.

No, those external effects of weather didn't defeat me. Over the years, however, the battle between Mother Nature and me has become internal. First, there were the migraines kicked off by changing atmospheric pressure. Pharmaceuticals and I licked that. Now, it's just one spot of pain in my left temple signaling that the weather is changing. Score one for me.

If rain is coming, my thumb hurts, the thumb I broke in high school. My thumb and I can predict rain better than any meteorologist. It's not a big bone or serious pain, so score two for me.

Obviously Mother Nature is a sore loser. She has brooded and stewed, wondering how to ratchet up the game. She has stared at me with a malevolent expression, searching for just the right weapon.

She found it: bursitis. This is an inflammation of the bursae, the pads of fluid around the joints. Sometimes it's caused by repetitive motion, hence the colorful names housemaid's knee, baker's elbow, and weaver's bottom. It may be exacerbated by certain foods or drink, making it akin to gout.

Lucky for me, not all of my joints are affected at once. I'm not frozen, like the Tin Man in *Wizard of Oz*. My bursitis is migratory, and the cause—my personal diagnosis and totally unscientific—is that it is caused by the weather. I now understand the full meaning of the term "under the weather."

With bursitis, we're not wearing a cast or bandages, so nobody knows how we suffer. Unless we carry on about it, which I recommend, with moans, groans, grimaces, and profanity. How else will people know that we are martyrs, going valiantly about our daily work?

Bursitis in the hip makes it painful to walk. Bursitis of the shoulder makes sleeping difficult. Bursitis of the ischium, the bony part of the hip we sit on, makes sitting uncomfortable. But bursitis of the knee, the worst of all, makes it hard to pray, garden, or shoot craps.

Rest is recommended as a cure, but I can't sit or lie down, so what am I supposed to do? Lean against a tree like an old horse? Being ill makes me depressed; pain makes me cranky.

Ice is also recommended. I prefer having my ice in a frosty mojito, but alcohol is not recommended. I'm forced to resort to the almost cartoonish image of an old-fashioned ice bag, which invariably leaks.

What did I ever do to the weather to deserve this?

Clearly I'm out of my league with the weather. I'm no match for her. Backed into a corner, I decided to take the higher path. I will not curse the weather, I will celebrate it.

I will remember the philosophy attributed to Abraham Lincoln: "Most folks are about as happy as they make up their minds to be."

Somehow I grew into adulthood before discovering the classic lullaby of a book *Goodnight Moon*. In the book's famous green room, a child drifts off to sleep saying goodnight to every comforting thing around him, including the moon. Now, instead of going through the day looking down, being negative, and noticing all the things I have not attended to—the garden not weeded, the floor not waxed, the fence not painted, the dog not brushed, the lamp not mended—I will greet the day looking up.

I'll look at the intricate spider's web overhead, the gaudy Oklahoma sunset, the red-tailed hawks patrolling overhead, the yellow leaves of the golden rain tree. Mother Nature, I'll think, you may be eccentric but you are an incredible artist.

While I was doing all of this positive gawking, the weather changed and my bursitis passed.

Hello, sky.

How I Adopted the Wrong Dog and It ____ My Life

Act I. Come on In

"How you do one thing is how you do all things," according to Zen wisdom. Gosh, I hope not.

And yet, when I look back, I see an alarming trend in how I have made decisions in my life. Impulsively. Irrationally. Insanely. This has applied to jobs, clothes, apartments, and men, as well as to important things. Eventually, it works out all right. Except when it doesn't.

My most recent impulsive decision was to get a dog. Why? I have pondered that question myself far into the night.

Peer pressure was a big factor. After my dog Bingo died, people came out of the woodwork with available dogs. "Have I got a dog for you!" they said. Now I know how eligible bachelors feel.

Sympathy was another factor. This particular dog's boarding time on earth was up unless some kindhearted person stepped forward and opened a door.

Attraction to showy talent was still another reason. This particular dog, sleek black with a white patch on his chest, came knowing how to sit, catch a ball, and come when I whistle. Not one trick, but three!

By comparison, my cats and I were content as we were, fat and lazy. The house was quiet.

And then—I opened the door to Bucky.

Bingo was a shepherd mix that grew old, fat, and lazy. Bucky may be a border collie mix. Adopting that breed as a house pet, I learned far too late, is like having a mountain goat in the home.

Bucky doesn't just jump the picket fence, he elevates over it. I would come home from work to find him bouncing around the rooms like a Ping-Pong ball. Border collies were bred to run like the wind over rugged Scottish hills and to herd sheep. In my house all he had to herd was the cats.

Besides being the wrong breed for me, he was the wrong age for me. He was barely a year old and had lots of puppy energy. He needed exercise, play, and training. What I needed was to sit quietly and read.

Bucky and me *(author's collection)*

Help! Immediately I scrambled for dog advice, dog books, dog day care, dog trainers, and sedating food and drink. Except for doggie day care, which is mostly for Bucky's benefit, the rest of it was for me. I am not a commanding dog person. Instead of ordering "Sit!" all of my commands were in the interrogative case. "Would you like to sit?" or "How would you feel about sitting?" When that didn't work, I recognized that Bucky and I needed professional help. The dog trainer I chose advocated a benevolent training style using body language, a clicker, dog treats, and a calm and quiet voice. This is all harder to master than you might think.

At the first class, I was thunderstruck at all I do not know about dogs and dog training. How can I be so ignorant when I've been around dogs all my life? But then, I've been around electricity all my life, too. I've turned light switches on and off every day, but I don't know how to take a screwdriver and fix one.

Joe Ely sings a song that begins, "Now that I know everything I know is wrong." That's me. First, I had to learn the differences between people and dogs. Here are some of the things I've learned:

Stop Talking. Humans are verbal, dogs are physical. We communicate with different languages. A cartoon shows one dog saying to another dog, "Hi. My name is No No Bad Dog, what's yours?" I need to keep my voice low and use one-word commands, not lengthy requests or explanations. When I call Bucky, I need a smile in my voice, not anger or volume. Makes sense; I wouldn't want to trot over to pat a dog that is snarling and barking loudly.

Get Physical. Body language is more effective with dogs. A better way to dissuade him from jumping up on me is to behave like a snob: turn my shoulder away from him, lift my head slightly, and look away. Body blocking him by standing in front of him is more effective in teaching him not to bolt out the door than is yanking on his collar. Repetition and gentleness are the keys to dog training.

It's Not All about Me. I was astonished to learn that dogs don't like being patted on the head. A great way to stop a dog from begging is to say "Enough," pat him twice on the head, and look away.

Patience and Compassion. In dog class, I have learned what it is like to be the stupidest pupil in the room. I mean me, not Bucky. The animals the trainers are really teaching are the humans, and I seem to be a slow learner. At a particularly frustrating class—"Walk. Click. Treat. Walk. Click."—I couldn't get the sequence right. Every time I made the same mistake, I said, "Dammit." I wasn't talking to the dog, but Bucky began to bark uncontrollably. The other class members—humans and dogs—edged away from us.

Bucky and I were dog class dropouts. His earsplitting barking continued at the veterinarian's office and to visitors at my door, to people walking past our house, to a vase he suddenly noticed on the mantle, and to a car driving by. We went through two more trainers before we found the right one for us, a dog whisperer who made house calls.

I bought a stack of dog training books to learn how to communicate to a dog and to understand what he was trying to communicate to me. I bought chew toys for him to keep him occupied.

I had an Invisible Fence installed.

One day, I realized that our life has settled into a pleasant companionship. The change had taken place slowly over several months. We have both learned new skills, but mostly me. I have learned new ways to communicate, not only with dogs but also with people. I have learned that after we learn one lesson, life gives us another one, usually harder. I have learned there's not always a quick fix to problems. I have learned that I have less energy than I once had. I have learned to be more patient and compassionate with myself.

Something I already knew was the importance of commitment. Some people recycle dogs or cats when they feel they have made the wrong choice, and that may be the right decision for them. I can't do that, although commitment is hard work.

After one particularly disappointing dog class, I came home and collapsed for a nap. I don't know which was lower, my spirits or my faith in myself as a successful dog owner. Failure is exhausting. Bucky hopped up on the bed beside me. Just as I dozed off, I started to pat him. Then I remembered that dogs don't always like to be patted, so all I did was put one hand over his paw. As I fell asleep, I felt him slide his other paw under my hand. And then the tip of his nose. "Good woman, good," he was saying. After that, we moved forward side by side.

Act II. So I Said to the Pet Psychic . . .

I knew I had not yet shaken off the sloth of winter when I realized that the most aerobic exercise I'm getting these days is trying to put on my panty hose in the morning.

When the days are short, cold, and gray, and when the nights are colder, my inner toad wants to burrow lower into the soil and sleep longer.

Suddenly, spring jumps in and a switch is flipped. I wake up and I want to do something. No, that's not accurate. I want to do everything.

I want to plant something. And then plant something else.

I want to paint something orange.

I want to clean the closets until only about a dozen items are hanging in them, unwrinkled and spaced widely apart.

I want to drink an icy cold beer.

I want to dump out those drawers that are stuffed with unidentified parts and pieces, candle stubs, inoperable pens, old lipsticks, and mascara, and a single chopstick. Those drawers that qualify me as a candidate for *Hoarders*. I want to outfit the clean drawers with neat dividers.

I want to drink another icy cold beer.

I want to give most of my clothes and almost all of my stuff to Goodwill.

I want to repaint the little cement backdoor step and paint a tic-tac-toe puzzle on it.

Then I remember that warm weather means that my new dog, Bucky, will spend more time outside in the yard. Or, more accurately, outside and over the picket fence. Barking loudly at strange and frightening persons and things. Oh, the efforts Bucky and I have made to modify this behavior.

We took dog training classes. Not very successful. For Bucky or me. We called in a dog whisperer. She observed and counseled us, separately and together. This was semisuccessful. For me, not Bucky. She swore to God that she would come back. She didn't. Bucky and I moved on.

We installed an Invisible Fence that came with more dog training and counseling. Very successful, until Bucky persuaded the cat to spray the fence's transmitter unit, which shorted it out.

When Bucky's barking was so loud and incessant at the veterinarian's that it shook the clinic's windowpanes, she began to murmur something about Xanax. I think she meant for all three of us.

I read that effective dog training can be personalized and improved by understanding the dog's breed. Little problem here. Bucky is a rescue dog assumed, but not proven, to be a border collie mix. Uh-oh. This breed needs lots of exercise; border collies can run like a racehorse and jump like a gazelle.

So, to accurately ascertain Bucky's breed, I sent off for a canine DNA kit. The results told me that Bucky is a cross of Australian shepherd, German shepherd, and mastiff. The key characteristics of these dogs are intelligence (Bucky and I could have told you that); active, energetic, and watchful natures; herding tendencies (the cats and me); eagerness to learn and responsiveness to rewards; enjoyment of dog sports such as agility and competitive obedience; and protectiveness around strangers.

Some less positive characteristics were listed, but Bucky and I chose to ignore those.

Hungry for yet more information, we consulted the celebrated local pet psychic Pam Case. This was more for me than for Bucky. I have known about her work for some time and was anxious to meet her. She met the two of us, closed her eyes for a moment to tune into Bucky, and then told me what the dog was thinking. He told her

- He is the most amazing dog I have ever had.
- He is very smart and talented and has remarkable poise, much like Sir Laurence Olivier.
- He finds our daily routines comforting.
- He would like to have more specialized training, such as search-and-find classes because he has such a great nose.
- His favorite food is chicken.

All of this helped pass the winter when we were indoors a lot. Not all of the time, because while I go to work, Bucky goes to a doggie day care to burn off some of his energy.

Now it really is spring, not just those disappointing false starts. I have eliminated some of the items on my ambitious to-do list. In fact, I have eliminated most of them, although I did paint one small table orange and I drew a hopscotch course on my front walk.

As for Bucky, once the Invisible Fence was repaired, he stopped jumping the fence. We cannot report equal success with loud barking at scary people and objects. One morning at 3:00 A.M., he discovered the killer ceiling fan in the bedroom. Thanks to his loud vigilance, we are both alive to tell the tale.

We're considering additional training for him—scent classes, agility competition, search-and-find training. Despite what he told the pet psychic about loving chicken, he now refuses to eat it.

Everything changes with spring. Some of it for the good.

Act III. Starting Again

Wasn't it Dorothy Parker who wrote, "Everything is always worse than you thought it was going to be?"

Bucky and I are a testament to the truth of that.

We signed up for an agility class for him at a new dog shop. The registration fee included our interview and two classes. This was exciting, as we both imagined him sailing over and under and through obstacles and then flying home like a barrel racer. We talked about where we would put the blue ribbons and medals.

We never got that far. We failed the interview. Both of us.

Bucky failed because he wouldn't stop barking at the trainer. She stamped him as an aggressive dog and a danger to other clients. I failed because I had not properly taught him to Leave It. She said that both of us would have to have lots of basic training before being considered for the agility class.

Few things are as defeating as failing a dog interview. Bucky and I slunk home, ate comfort food for supper, and went to bed early. When I had recovered enough to talk about it, I related the event to the owner of Bucky's doggie day school. It was humiliating, as if confessing to a child's kindergarten teacher that you know the child will never be promoted to first grade.

"Nonsense," said Nancy Gallimore, the doggie day school owner. "She doesn't know what she's talking about. Bucky's not aggressive; he's fearful. He wasn't trying to bite her, he was trying to make her go away."

That made sense to me. I remembered that every time Bucky barked at her, she flinched and jerked backwards. So he barked more. That reminded me of the actress Ronnie Claire Edwards's book *The Knife Thrower's Assistant* about how she got her start in show business. She became the replacement assistant after the first assistant had developed the bad habit of flinching every time the knife was thrown.

So Nancy, whom I now think of as the Good Dog Trainer, explained that since Bucky had spent his first year in a crate, he had missed two important periods of socialization. He loves all of the other dogs at doggie day school; what frightens him are humans he doesn't know. He's not a mean dog; he has some developmental challenges.

"Bucky is just afraid," I explained to one man cowering against a fence. Bucky was barking at him maniacally, neck straining at the leash. I planted my feet and pulled back on the leash with both hands, "He thinks that if he behaves like an ass, people will go away from him."

"He's right," the poor man said, the whites of his eyes visible at six feet.

"I'll work with you," Nancy said. "We'll go back and teach him those skills he missed."

Thank the Lord. If you only knew all of the bad, amateur advice I've had from friends and relatives: Swat him with a newspaper. Lock him in the bathroom as a time-out. Sharply yank him back beside you.

Sometimes they took it upon themselves to try to discipline him with loud shouts and commands.

All of that is wrong for him, Nancy said. What I do that is right—and perhaps the only thing I do right, although she had the good manners not to say that—is stay calm and not yell at him. If I get agitated, he will become even more agitated. It is a lucky break that my instinct as a dog trainer is to look quizzically at him when he behaves badly and ask him, "Why in the world did you do that?"

"We'll build up his self-confidence," Nancy said. "It's no fun going through life being afraid."

So, back to dog books and dog training. Nancy recommended a book about helping cautious dogs overcome their fears. Right at the beginning, the book said, "This program takes a commitment of time and energy."

Oh, no, not that again.

I saw results right away. Not with Bucky but with myself. I wrote the Evil Dog Trainer a letter saying Bucky and I would not be returning for the two trial classes and demanded—asked politely, actually—for a refund of half of our registration fee.

She replied with a sharp letter about the danger of aggressive dogs, but she returned half of the fee.

Bucky and I did a high five.

He and I have made great behavioral strides, but we choose to maintain a courteous relationship. I have advanced to one-word commands. Two words, actually. "Sit, please," I command. Followed by "Thank you." Being a polite dog, he replies, "You're welcome." Not in people words, of course, but I can see that he is thinking it.

So this is the story of how I adopted the wrong dog and it changed, improved, and enriched my life.

Up Jumped Spring

I was lolling in bed one Sunday morning, listening to public radio and trying not to open my eyes or get up, when I heard Abbey Lincoln singing "Up Jumped Spring."

That's all it took. Within minutes I was sitting in my back garden with a cup of coffee and the newspapers. This is what I look forward to all year. This is why I spend every penny and every minute working in my yard—so I can have spring mornings like this.

The rest of the year I roar through life in high gear, barely hanging on to the earth as it hurtles and tilts and spins through space. But suddenly—up jumps spring.

The first section I read in the local paper is the obituaries. All too often there is someone I knew. That obit comes like a little pinprick of memory: "He was so funny." Or "I'm glad she had a good life." Sometimes, "Why didn't I call her?"

Strange word, "obituary." From a Latin root variously translated as death, departure, going to meet or to fall. Since the 1700s, "obituary" has meant a notice of a death. Not that you would know it in the paid obituaries written by the deceased's family or loved ones. Especially the religious among us search for comforting euphemisms such as "gone to his heavenly father," "has been called home," "sleeping in the bosom of Jesus," and "now wears angel wings." Perhaps this style is more common here in the Bible Belt than elsewhere. This is comical to me as an Episcopalian accustomed to the unsentimental realism of the funeral service in the *Book of Common Prayer* with the poetic but blunt sentence "In the midst of life we are in death."

I saw a question on the Internet about that. A woman asked what that phrase means: "In the midst of life we are in debt."

No, Roseanne Roseannadanna, not debt—death.

The word "death" is being edged further and further away from our mainstream vocabulary. Even some newspapers that once were the standard-bearers of good English usage now substitute the word "passed" for "died." "Passed" is a word I associate with a kid named Rollo I went to school with. Rollo was always in danger of being held back a grade. We all liked Rollo, so every year at the end of school term we'd ask one another anxiously, "Did Rollo pass?"

I'm not the first to notice that as people fall away from organized religion with its ceremonies, we so crave ceremony that we invent new ones. We build makeshift shrines at the site of automobile crashes. We pile flowers and mementos at the location of tragedies. And we rewrite funeral services or cobble together new ones with a personal twist. An Anglican priest in England lamented publicly how today's bereaved reject traditional hymns. He said the songs they request most frequently are "I Did It My Way" or, even more curious, "Nobody Does It Better."

And so, in the midst of life is death. And even in the midst of spring comes calamity. My cat Jesse caught a cold. Sneezing, watery eyes, stuffy nose.

At the risk of sounding sexist, I must report that he took it like a man. Which means, he went to bed for three days. My bed. He slept on a pillow, and I took him his meals on a tray.

All is well now. My cat is well. Only strangers listed in the obituary column today. And as a cherry on a sundae, I bought a new pair of yellow shoes. That's what life is like when up jumps spring.

The Summer Game

When the ball game went into extra innings, the cat and the dog and I decided to turn off the TV, go to bed, and listen to the rest of the game on the radio. The next day was a workday, and we needed our rest.

I hadn't listened to a baseball game on the radio in years. The late *New Yorker* editor and writer Katherine White had a farm in upstate New York. This was before TV was popular, so in October, she would listen to the World Series on the radio as she polished gourds from her garden. I love that image.

A baseball announcer is a special artist. He has to describe enough to make it come alive—the pitch, the swing, the action, the reaction—but not talk us into a coma. Traditionally, his vocabulary is an art unto itself. That's the way it was that night I listened to the ball game on radio. When one inning ended, the announcer said, "And that retires the side. Some were lookin' and some were swingin'."

Is that not a summary of life? Some of us stand around looking, some of us are out there swinging.

At a craft bazaar, I was immediately attracted to a booth selling gauzy, hand-painted jackets. The booth was empty except for the artist. I put on one of the filmy kimono jackets, and other women swarmed around. A woman from another booth said, "Oh, I've been looking at these all day and just waiting for someone to put one on." We all chattered about the jackets—how fascinating, how artistic, how fanciful, how fun.

"I'd love to have one," a woman said, "but I wouldn't know what to wear it with."

"With anything," I said. "For a dressy occasion. Or with jeans— that's what I have on. Get one," I said. "They're not expensive."

She looked longingly at the jacket. Finally she said, "I just can't. My husband would think I was crazy." And she walked away.

Isn't that one of the saddest stories you've ever heard?

An important book for me is titled *What Do You Care What Other People Think?* It was written by the great physicist Richard Feynman, an intellectual with an unquenchable curiosity and an appetite for adventure. I like the book, but I love the title. Great question: What *do* I care what other people think?

Not that we shouldn't live within boundaries of kindness, civility, and manners set by society, but also not that we shouldn't think for ourselves. We don't have to be nice all the time. We don't have to shape ourselves to please other people. And we should be able to wear a frivolous, fanciful jacket if we want to.

It's not easy to get out of our comfortable ruts. I pondered for years over a line from C. S. Lewis: "It is pain that drives us out of the nursery." I think I finally got it. Most of us don't change anything when we're fat and comfortable. It's only pain—loss or grief, perhaps—that makes us venture into change.

I'm intrigued by the question "What would you do if you weren't afraid?" I have written that in purple sidewalk chalk on a wall in my house. I think that quote comes from the book *Who Moved My Cheese?* but it has grown legs of its own. It has come to challenge us to think of what we really want to do personally and professionally—if we aren't afraid of change, money, security, other people's opinions, or aren't too timid about stepping out of our comfort zone.

What would I do if I weren't afraid?

I won't be standing there lookin' at life—I'll be swingin'.

Meditations in the Grocery Store

"Random acts of kindness" is a philosophy that suits me. I may be inconsistent, but I can always be random.

If I see a paper towel thrown on the floor of a public bathroom, I pick it up. Sometimes. I can rescue lost dogs and cats. Usually. I try to remember to compliment store clerks on the color and style of their hair. The more outlandish it is, obviously the more thought they have put into this personal expression. They're working at low-paying, boring jobs with complaining customers; the least I can do is acknowledge their presence by praising their two-tone green hair.

When I was that age, to display our nonconformist, creative personalities we wore black like Beatniks and smoked French cigarettes. Nowadays, young people wear strange hairstyles, startling hair colors, multiple piercings, and tattoos. Tattoos are so alien to me, I am uncertain how to react to them. Do we stare, or should we peep? Do we ask for their meaning, or ought we to ignore them? Do we acknowledge them and say, "Nice ink," or do we act blasé and indifferent? I don't understand why someone would want an image of Mickey Mouse tattooed on her foot or a poem tattooed around his neck or any other design displayed on public skin.

This is where the Internet is useful. I looked up "tattoo etiquette" and came upon a piece by a young woman who said, among other things, "Don't assume the person with a tattoo is unemployed." I had not assumed that, but what should I assume? I am no more enlightened than I was before my Internet search.

On a recent Saturday afternoon in the neighborhood grocery store, an elderly lady wearing strong perfume kept crossing my path. More accurately, blocking my path. She was like a squirrel in the road, except a squirrel with a grocery cart and so much perfume it made my eyes tear. Luckily, I was just up from a nap and feeling mellow, so I just smiled at her—aisle after aisle—and went on with my shopping.

At the checkout line, the new policy is to ask anyone buying beer for an I.D. The man across from me, in his fifties, threw a two-year's-old fit. I was buying beer, too. I laughed and told him I was so flattered I was going to show my I.D. again, voluntarily, before I left.

"I'm not flattered," he snapped. "It's harassment, and I'm sick of it." The checkout clerk with green hair whispered to me, "Last week he cussed me out."

Luckily for the rude and angry man, my Avenger Cloak was in the laundry, so I ignored his tirade. Instead, I turned to the young woman in line behind me. She was piling fabulous food on the conveyor belt.

"I want to go eat what you're making," I told her.

"It's a special dinner," she said. "My best friend's boyfriend died last week. On her birthday. So I said we need a special dinner."

The woman was so young, I asked, "How old was he?"

"Thirty," she said. "He had an eight-year-old daughter. The really bad thing is, her mother died in January."

When I'm trying to remember to do my random acts of kindness, I think of Emily Dickinson. She was right. We are all bandaged souls.

In the grocery store, the old woman had dressed and perfumed herself for an outing. Perhaps her only outing of the day. I could be patient with her.

The angry man was a boiling teakettle needing a spout to let off steam. I could ignore him.

Some people need to declare themselves with brightly colored hair, elaborate nails, or tattoos. I can notice them.

Some people make special suppers for a grieving friend. I can admire that.

As I was leaving, the grocery clerk whispered to me again, "Thank you for being nice."

She had caught me on a good day.

Memories and Opinions

Memories and opinions are interesting because both can be deliciously wrong.

My opinion of children is that they are all adorable. My opinion of most parenting is less favorable. Yet if I were to tell them, "You're raising your children as if they are the center of the universe," they would reply, "Thank you."

My memory of my own childhood is that we were raised with what one writer called "benign indifference," being sent outside to play for eighteen hours a day. We were not the focus of our families, we were little spies and spectators.

And yet . . .

Miscellaneous memories belie that fact.

I grew up in a small Oklahoma town. When I look at it in the rearview mirror, I can see that life there was slower and safer for children. I lived on a street right out of *To Kill a Mockingbird,* complete with a haunted house. Down the block was the small, dark house of River Jordan, his wife, and his brother. They were tiny, ancient people (German, we thought), about the age of my great-grandparents. When they walked to town, they walked single file. River Jordan was first, followed by his brother and then his wife. All three wore dark, old-fashioned clothes.

Some bored afternoons, I drifted down to their house to visit. Inside was dark and smoky, since the house had wood stoves and kerosene lamps. I watched the brothers smoking their pipes and silently playing chess while I chatted with Mrs. Jordan as she baked. She didn't talk much either, just quietly handed me small plates of heavy cake as I told her about my wondrous seven-year-old life.

"Leave those people alone," my mother would say. "Don't bother them."

Some days after work, my father walked down to the Jordans' house to ask if I were bothering them and to help them chop wood for their stoves. The old brothers talked some to my gregarious father. Mrs. Jordan only came out of the kitchen to give me a cookie. "When you get tired of her," my father told them, "send her home."

Years later when I asked my mother about River Jordan and his family, she laughed. "Their name was Jordan," she said, "but it wasn't River Jordan. That's something you came up with from Sunday school."

After we moved to another house on another block, I didn't see the Jordans. My parents were busy with projects that involved lots of volunteer help from family and friends—digging a storm cellar, laying a hardwood floor, building two additional rooms.

When my parents decided to get a piano for me—who knows why—that became a group project, too. Someone in the country had an upright piano for sale for one hundred dollars, and someone else had a pickup truck to go get it. Nobody thought about having the piano tuned after the gut-jolting drive over country roads. The more I plunked on it, the more often my mother sent me outside to play.

Once a week I rode my bicycle to have a piano lesson with elderly Miss Pierce. The lessons cost fifty cents each. She sat beside me on the piano bench, her hands veined and dry as she showed me how to curve my fingers gracefully. Lucky for my mother and sadly for Miss Pierce, I did not practice much.

Miss Pierce lived with her elderly mother, who stayed in a back bedroom while lessons were being given. Their house was dark inside, too, the furniture covered with crochet work. Drapes were closed and the house was stuffy, smelling of dried roses. I thought it was the smell of old people.

Once when home from college, I went back to visit Miss Pierce, chattering about my life and friends. Suddenly she said, "I could have married. I had a beau. But he was goggle eyed and looked like a frog."

Piano lessons for an untalented child, freshly baked cake for a neighborhood chatterbox—another child in another time being raised as the center of the universe.

These are my tender memories and that is my sweet opinion.

Our Quaint Ancestors

It seems to me that at one time or another, many of us become fascinated by our own family tree. We want to know more about our ancestors. We may want to do genealogical research. We may even want to write a family history.

I'm sure there are deep philosophical reasons for this—the need to leave a footprint on the earth or the dread of time's winged chariot circling us like something out of *Harry Potter*. Maybe it's just that we finally have time to take a breath in life and wonder how we got to be as we are.

Most of our family histories are interesting only to us—like photos of our vacation or the dream we had last night. However, I read a journalist's family history that is as fascinating as a novel. The author is Lee Sandlin, and the title of the book is *The Distancers,* which refers to his family's being noncommunicative. They didn't want to talk about themselves or any family history.

But boy, does Sandlin tell their stories, generations of them. I particularly like the story about an uncle, a quiet man whose long-suffering grievances with his brother-in-law erupted into a fistfight. The two men never spoke to one another again, although they lived together in the same house for seventeen more years. Now, there are people who can sharpen a grudge to a razor edge.

I like the book so much, I'm toying with the idea of writing one myself about some of my own family. Especially my great-grandmother Eliza Young.

I knew her and my great-grandfather—tiny, quiet people. I have a black brooch that belonged to her and an antique light fixture from their home. I remember my great-grandmother, her gray hair pulled into a bun, always wearing a black dress. Turns out, that memory isn't accurate. All of the photos show her with a sweet little smile and wearing a springy, flowered dress.

Long after everyone involved was dead, I discovered a scandalous secret about her. I think I was the last to know. My great-grandparents and three of their children were living on a farm in Missouri when Eliza began a romance with a neighbor man. More than a romance, an affair. Relatives say they used to meet down by the creek. I imagine new grass and spring flowers on the bank of a clear stream, maybe a romantic weeping willow tree.

When her husband found out, he yanked the family out of Missouri and moved to Oklahoma, and that is where the fourth child, my great-uncle Vernon, was born. No wonder he didn't look like the rest of the family, people whispered; he was the love child.

Another relative said, "Oh, no, it wasn't a neighbor. It was her husband's brother she had an affair with. That's the father of Uncle Vernon. There was a big blowup and the brother moved to California and was never heard from again." Or did he move at all? His disappearance was so sudden. And so mysterious. Could there have been foul play by a husband scorned?

This lurid history didn't match the old people I remember. This story has all the makings of a colorful novel or movie. But then I took another look at the family genealogy, and Uncle Vernon's birth date didn't jibe at all with this tale.

So maybe none of this is true. Maybe because Uncle Vernon was taller than the rest of the family, that is what ginned up the whispered story. Then again, in 1889 my great-grandmother had named her first child, a daughter, Nellie Bly. This was my own grandmother: Nellie Bly Young. She was named after the most famous woman journalist and adventurer of the time, who had traveled around the world in less than eighty days.

So maybe my great-grandmother Eliza had a private fantasy life of dreams and aspirations. Maybe on a farm with small children and a dour husband she couldn't live her dreams, but maybe she hoped her children would. And so she named a child Nellie Bly in the hopes that the daughter would live a life of adventure.

Maybe that's the story.

Postscript

My grandmother did not sail away to adventure. She married a handsome, older man she first saw wearing a purple shirt and riding a good horse. They had six children and lived in a small town. It became an unhappy marriage. My grandfather had several failed businesses. He became withdrawn, angry, and hurtful. I suspect he suffered from clinical depression.

During the hard days of the Depression, it was my grandmother who patched together little jobs to provide food for the family. One summer she hoed strawberries for a neighbor. During World War II she worried about her three sons and two sons-in-law in active military service. It was a close-knit, almost clannish family. Two sons never married and lived with my grandmother all their adult life. At bedtime, she turned down their beds. I knew my grandmother to have only one friend who wasn't a relative, and when that woman moved away, my grandmother grieved sorely.

Except for family deaths, I never knew my grandmother to be sad or complaining. She made a quiet, loving family for her children and grandchildren. She crocheted and quilted for all of us. She had her own strawberry patch in the backyard, and she made the best strawberry shortcake I have ever tasted. And yet, she often sang an old, sad song about two poor little babes who were stolen away on a bright summer's day and lost in the woods. The song ends this way:

> And when it was night, so sad was their plight
> The sun it went down and the moon gave no light
> They wept and they wept and they bitterly cried,
> Then the poor little babes, they laid down and died.

> And when they were dead, the robin so red
> Brought strawberry leaves and over them laid
> And that is the end of my sad little song
> For the babes in the woods are now gone.

Art, Literature, and the Glorious English Language

I love Art. He's the mechanic who keeps my Volvo running. I also love art, lowercase. I've been in college and community theater productions. I was a member of a poetry-reading quartet, The Tyger's Eye. For fifteen years I managed a ballet company. That was a great job for a writer. Ballet is a nonverbal art form, so I got to do all of the talking.

I can't sing, dance, draw, paint, sculpt, weave, or create any of the visual arts. Words are my medium. They are puzzling little beasts to work with. Sometimes when I'm writing, it seems they dance in *grands jetés* across the page. Other times, it's as if I'm trying to carve granite with a Popsicle stick. I can identify with the Shakespeare phrase "Zounds! I was never so bethump'd with words."

Whether I'm writing them or reading them, words can bethump the bejesus out of me.

A Prayer for Language

Whenever a new school semester begins, I sense on the prevailing wind the sound of sincere schoolteachers working diligently to teach the use of proper grammar.

I have been the student. I have been the teacher. And as the teacher of grammar, I often felt I was the wind itself, just blowing air.

And so, on behalf of all those students and teachers—and for language itself—I have crafted this lyrical prayer.

A Prayer for Language

O God, who has demonstrated a love for language through your preachers and prophets who use it so enthusiastically and even, on occasion, excessively,

Look with favor, we beseech thee, on thy lowly creation—the objective case, the which suffers so grievously in this current American culture.

Let not the compound pronoun of the objective case be lost and fade from this beauteous earth, tromped underfoot by carelessness.

Let not the sluggard tongue of mankind (also womankind and childrenkind) obliterate entirely the tiny words "her," "him," and "me." Rather, let these pronouns continue to be beautiful in Your sight in the objective case.

To wit, I humbly offer the correct example, "Give the albatross to her and me," and not "Give the albatross to she and I." Hear my plea when I ask you to smite all of them—note that I did not say "all of they"—who speak such abominations.

And speaking of "they" and "them," O God, turn Your brooding eye over the pagan use of "they" and "their" in reference to singular subjects. To wit, this incorrect example: "The women's club is holding *their* meeting today." O Lord, you know how evil that is to the ear. Strike down the secretary of that women's club, O Lord, for not saying "The woman's club is holding *its* meeting today."

And not just club secretaries, O God, but unleash the full fury of your linguistic wrath on mass media, print, and especially television reporters, who defame the English language so atrociously. Suffer the little children of this nation not to hear such errors.

Neither let *us* adults hear it either, and please note, O Lord, that I did not say, "Neither let *we* adults hear it." That pronoun misusage would be a dagger to thy ear.

Dear God, we are the sheep of your pasture, and you recall the pain and suffering we endured in Mrs. Simpson's sixth grade English class to learn the enduring lessons of subject-verb agreement. How we were made to let the pronouns, yea, even the compound pronouns in the objective case, leap like lambs among our little sentences. Even until the ends of time.

Visit, we ask you, other Mrs. Simpsons—or like English teachers—on these heathens of the language of the King James Bible. Correct them. Guide them along the right grammar path. Or strike them mute. At least when they are in my earshot.

All this we ask you in the name of all that is Right and Holy and Grammatically Correct.

For as we were taught, in the beginning was the Word, and our supplication is that we not live to hear the ending of the correct Word as we know and love it.

Amen.

So This Guy Walks into
an Accordion Shop . . .

I do not play any musical instruments. But if I did, the instrument heading the list I would not play is the accordion. Give me something easy like the gong or the triangle.

Accordions are for Lawrence Welk, sturdy women with big bosoms, and jolly fellows at polka festivals wearing leather knee breeches.

That was the wisecrack I made to my friend Warren Houtz, who, it turns out, does play the accordion.

"Accordions don't play 'Lady of Spain,'" Warren told me coolly. "People do." Being a smarty-pants can shorten a friendly lunch. With time on my hands, I went home to sit alone at my computer, and there the Internet introduced me to "accordiona." A plethora of information exists about this musical instrument, first patented in Vienna in 1829 and sometimes irreverently referred to as a squeezebox.

One website listed accordion jokes:

"If you drop an accordion, a set of bagpipes, and a viola off a twenty-story building, which one lands first?"

"Who cares?"

And

"What's the difference between an Uzi and an accordion?"

"The Uzi stops after twenty rounds."

With a mighty restraint, I did not forward these jokes to Warren. Instead, I remembered an accordion shop that I drive by often. How many accordion players are there in Tulsa, I wondered? Evidently enough to warrant a shop for repairs, sales, and lessons.

Fired with curiosity, I phoned for an appointment and went to visit the Cottingham Music and Accordion Shop. There I met proprietor and teacher Mary Cottingham, age eighty-seven, with a southern accent you could spread on a biscuit.

She first discovered accordions at a jam session when she was in college in Nashville. For twenty-six years, her family has been in the accordion business in the same location. Every room of the home business is lined, stuffed, and stacked with musical instruments—pianos, organs, and guitars but mostly accordions. She has Cajun accordions, concertinas, and accordions of all styles and sizes from Korea, China, Italy, and Mexico. They range in size from toy accordions to instruments that weigh thirty pounds and cost thousands of dollars.

Like an old-fashioned schoolmarm, she used a long wooden pointer to show me the different parts of the instrument: keyboard, buttons, bellows, bass, shoulder strap, bass strap, shift for the treble, and reed block. A student having a lesson, a retired woman, demonstrated the instrument by playing an achingly slow version of "Shortnin' Bread." Mrs. Cottingham's students range in age from six to seventy.

I had taken a friend along to the accordion shop, an accomplished organist. "Could he try one?" I asked Mrs. Cottingham. "No," she said, ever the professional. "He wouldn't do it justice."

I have since learned of the Oklahoma Accordion Club and its monthly newsletter, *Oklahoma Squeezins*. The newsletter lists upcoming accordion festivals and conventions, from Florida to British Columbia.

Accordionists are like stray cats; once you notice them, you see them everywhere. Tulsa has an active group of eight or ten musicians who perform in the area. My hairdresser wants to learn to play the accordion. A volunteer at my branch library played the accordion as a girl. I saw a notice at a community center announcing the rehearsal of an accordion band.

A national organization called Closet Accordion Players of America (CAPA) has its own website and is dedicated to "improving the image of the accordionist and fighting accordion abuse." With a better sense of humor than my friend Warren, CAPA dreams of having a glamorous accordionist role model: Johnny Depp, perhaps, or Julia Roberts.

Accordionists seem to be social creatures and like to gather in groups. One August in Newfoundland, more than nine hundred accordionists signed up to set a world's record in the *Guinness Book of Records* for the largest number of people playing accordions simultaneously.

Not long ago, an Air Force recruiter attended a New York accordion festival looking for just one good player. The accordionist for the Strolling Strings military band had retired and a replacement was needed. One little string was attached—six weeks of boot camp is required.

Yet another reason I won't be taking up the accordion.

Happy Birthday, Scarlett

Hard to believe, but Scarlett O'Hara is more than ninety years old. *Gone with the Wind* was published in June 1936, in the depth of the Depression. Some say the romantic novel with its defiant and resilient heroine helped save the nation. And yet. An article by Evgenia Peretz in *Vanity Fair* magazine said this about the book: "*Gone with the Wind* won the Pulitzer and inspired comparisons to Tolstoy, Dickens, and Thomas Hardy. Now it's considered a schmaltzy relic read by teenage girls, if anyone." So says *Vanity Fair*. That highbrow, literary journal.

I have a far higher opinion and a deeper respect for *Gone with the Wind*. The book is often considered a Civil War novel, but author Margaret Mitchell said the theme of the novel is survival.

"What makes some people come through catastrophes and others, apparently just as able, strong, and brave, go under?" she asked. "Survivors used to call that quality 'gumption.' So I wrote about people who had gumption and people who didn't."

Mitchell was born in Atlanta to a quiet, attorney father and a fiery, suffragist, Irish Catholic mother. She grew up among Civil War veterans and heard the stories of battles and hardships so often, they became a visceral part of her.

She was a chatterbox tomboy who loved to ride and read, grew into a flirtatious flapper, and was a nonconformist who occasionally shocked the grand dames of southern society. She called herself Peggy and became a newspaperwoman known for her lively personality and storytelling talent. She said she liked her "likker."

Her first marriage was a disaster. Of all her beaus, she chose a rogue, a sometimes bootlegger called Red who had strong sex appeal and a bad temper. Once he beat her so badly she was in the hospital for a week. Two scandals followed: she divorced him, then went back to court to regain her maiden name. Her second marriage was to John Marsh, a gentle man, former English teacher, and journalist who worked in marketing for the Georgia Power Company. He continued to work full time at the power company, but he devoted himself to her writing, was her lifelong private editor, and, after *Gone with the Wind* was published, became her business manager.

After her marriage, she resigned from the newspaper to be a conventional stay-at-home wife. The couple lived modestly on his salary. She said she wore four-year-old cotton dresses and drove a nine-year-old car. While she was recovering from a broken ankle, he brought her stacks of books from the library and finally plunked her in front of a typewriter and told her she could write a book better than any of those she had been reading. So she did.

While she wrote it, she wore baggy men's overalls and a green eyeshade. Actually, she wore baggy *boys'* overalls, because she was so tiny, just 4'9".

That diminutive size was not unusual in the South, I learned recently, while touring a Creole sugarcane plantation outside New Orleans. Antebellum people were small. Men frequently stood no taller than five feet. I saw custom-made dining room furniture scarcely more than child size but a table set with oversized cutlery because wealthy Southerners were prideful of their table silver. The combination reminded me of a child's tea party.

Mitchell wrote most of the book in three years but spent seven more years refining and embellishing it. She worked to write in a style so simple a child could read it. She said writing was hard for her, so hard that the only things she hated more than writing were Wagnerian opera and tap dancing.

Like some other writers, Mitchell wove the straw of her life into the gold of fiction: Ashley Wilkes was inspired by her own quiet fiancé killed in World War I; Rhett Butler with his hyper-masculinity and charisma was based on her first husband. The child Bonnie Blue dies of a fall from a horse, and Mitchell herself wore heavy orthopedic shoes as the result of two serious riding accidents. Scarlett, sixteen years old when the book opens, is based partly on Mitchell, the southern belle who flouts tradition.

In the movie version, Vivien Leigh is a stunning beauty, but in the novel, Scarlett is known more for personality than appearance. This is the way the novel begins: "Scarlett O'Hara was not beautiful, but men seldom realized it when caught by her charm." Mitchell originally named her protagonist Pansy, not Scarlett.

The movie casting caused a national frenzy. Almost every female star in Hollywood was considered for the role, including Paulette Goddard, Jean Arthur, Joan Bennett, Bette Davis, and Katharine Hepburn. Unknown starlets and nonactresses across the country wanted to audition. Mitchell tried to distance herself from the turmoil, but she was deluged with letters, interviews, and inquiries about casting and production. She voiced a private opinion that her choice for

Scarlett would be Miriam Hopkins and for Rhett, Charles Boyer if he didn't have a French accent. Finally, frustrated by the clamor, she said she thought Donald Duck would be wonderful as Rhett.

Pat Conroy said he became a southern novelist because his southern mother so loved the book she reread it every year. That book set his mother's imagination on fire when she was a young girl in Atlanta, he said, "and it was the one fire of her bruised and fragmented youth that never went out."

Conroy once considered writing a sequel. His book would have been about Rhett Butler and the kind of war that created the kind of man who would marry Scarlett O'Hara.

Mitchell published her novel under her maiden name. She was thirty-five when the novel was published. It was an immediate best seller and won the Pulitzer Prize. She tried to live a quiet life avoiding publicity, but the novel and movie generated public and media turmoil that consumed her life, affected her health, and drained her talent. She did not write another book. She died in Atlanta at age forty-eight after being struck by a speeding car while crossing the street with her husband to go to a movie.

Gone with the Wind is an epic, romantic novel about the home front and the people who lived through the Civil War, Reconstruction, and the loss of the only world they knew. Although everything around her died, Scarlett survived. No wonder our mothers and our aunts loved the book. They had survived the Great Depression and World War II. Inspired by them, some of us, their daughters of gumption and survival, also came to love the book.

This is what Margaret Mitchell gave us. I'm sorry she could not survive her own book.

My Soapbox du Jour: Books and Women

The Mommy War books make me cross. This is the genre of books proclaiming the virtues of stay-at-home moms and decrying the difficulty of being a working mother.

Both of those concepts are true. I don't contest that. Families are lucky when they can afford for a mother to not work outside the home. I don't envy them the time they spend at the gym, the beauty salon, and the manicurist. I admire their doing volunteer work.

It's just that I know how rough it is for a mother to raise children and hold a job. I salute the single mothers who usually have no choice; they raise children and work one or two jobs, usually low-paying jobs at that.

But the others, the ones who do have a choice, the upper-class young moms who choose to have children and choose to have a job and then whine about it—they are the ones who annoy me. These are women who summer at Sissy-Pants Ranch, which is, of course, located on the banks of Crybaby Creek. A new wave of literature on this subject reports the difficulties of rejoining the workforce after time off to raise children. Lower salaries when they return, many moms lament, but worth it for the family life they have had, others say.

In contrast, I think about the generations of women before them: the suffragettes and the women's libbers. The right to hold a job outside the home was a long, hard-fought process. Along with it went the right to an education, to vote, to own property, to get a credit card, and the many other rights that 90 percent of the world's population of women long to have. In that context, I consider the Mommy War mentality an affront to them and to all of us who went through the sneering and jeering of the 1970s women's movement.

I was barely over this ill mood when I read a list purporting to be the best American fiction of the past twenty-five years. The best book, the judges declared, is Toni Morrison's *Beloved,* a novel by a woman. Only one of the twenty-four runners-up is also by a woman, Marilynne Robinson's *Housekeeping.*

That's it. Only two books by women proclaimed to be great American fiction. Yet some of the most popular books have been by women: *Gone with the Wind* by Margaret Mitchell, *The Good*

Earth by Pearl Buck, *Peyton Place* by Grace Metalious, and *To Kill a Mockingbird* by Harper Lee. I'm not saying all of these are great literature, but they have been enormously popular books, and they were meaningful books reflecting the changing society of the times. They feature strong women. They addressed important issues. They took on controversial subjects.

Bartlesville, Oklahoma, selected Betty Smith's *A Tree Grows in Brooklyn* for its One Book–One Bartlesville program. The book was chosen, I was told, because it fits these criteria: it has lasting, proven viability; and both a movie and a play were written from it.

My book club chose this book too, recently, but not for such high-minded reasons. We chose it because it was on the buy-two-get-one-free table at Border's. Still, we're on the bandwagon.

A Tree Grows in Brooklyn was a best seller in 1943 when it was published. It featured strong women, and it revealed the squalor of turn-of-the century Brooklyn tenements. It was partially autobiographical.

Betty Smith was the daughter of German immigrants, lived in Brooklyn, left school at age fourteen to work in factories, married, and raised two daughters before she finished her education and went to college and the Yale School of Drama for Playwriting. She was fifty-seven when she wrote *A Tree Grows in Brooklyn*. (Personal note: I am particularly fond of late-starter stories, since I hope to be one myself.)

When I checked the list of books chosen by all of the states since the One City, One Book program was introduced in Seattle in 1998, I discovered that the book selected most often is *To Kill a Mockingbird*. Second is *Fahrenheit 451* by Ray Bradbury, and third is *October Sky/ Rocket Boys* by Homer Hickman. Many of the books chosen were contemporary best sellers: *The Life of Pi, The Kite Runner,* and *Seabiscuit*. Authors most often chosen were John Steinbeck, S. E. Hinton, Willa Cather, and Sue Monk Kidd. These books feature a mix of male and female authors and protagonists. As it should be, in my opinion.

The biggest surprise to me was the choice of Malibu, California. That city chose *Gidget*, a 1950s book by Frederick Kohner. Defenders of the book say the choice isn't as outrageous as we might think. *Gidget*, a neologism combining the words "girl" and "midget," was based on the author's daughter Kathy, a fifteen-year-old, petite Jewish girl who was something of a rebel when she broke into the outcast, surfer subculture. They say it is an important book because it is a portrait of that specific time and place. And it popularized both surfing and Malibu.

Women writers seem to have a tougher time of it. Before Judith Viorst became a psychoanalysis researcher and writer (*Necessary Losses*) and before she wrote children's books (*Alexander and the Terrible, Horrible, No Good, Very Bad Day*), in the late 1960s and '70s, she published sharp, funny poetry books (*It's Hard to Be Hip over 30 and Other Tragedies of Married Life, People and Other Aggravations*).

Viorst knows what modern life and love is like. "It's true love because if he said quit drinking martinis, but I kept on drinking them and the next morning I couldn't get out of bed, he wouldn't tell me he told me."

Oh, she also knew the double daggers facing women writers. In one poem, she kvetched, Did Emily Dickinson have to write poetry with baby diapers around her? (I'll tell you something else that's not easy to do—writing with cats around the house. They lie on the printer, walk across the keyboard, and pee on the manuscript.)

Whether female or male, literary figures always seem to be swimming upstream. They're on a quest or in a struggle. They're fighting either against something or for something. Sometimes they are young female characters: Mattie Ross in *True Grit*, Dorothy in *The Wizard of Oz*, Ree Dolly in *Winter's Bone*, Frankie Addams in *A Member of the Wedding*. Whatever it is they're after, it is not easy to do or get or be, and so we pull for them.

In *A Tree Grows in Brooklyn*, what young Francie Nolan yearns for is no less heroic than slaying a seven-headed Minotaur: "Let me be something every minute of my life. Let me be gay; let me be sad. Let me be cold; let me be warm. Let me be hungry . . . have too much to eat. Let me be ragged or well dressed. Let me be sincere—be deceitful. Let me be truthful; let me be a liar. Let me be honorable and let me sin. Only let me be something every blessed minute. And when I sleep, let me dream all the time so that not one little piece of living is ever lost."

....

Here's something I love about America: Name something—anything—and someone's against it.

Take reading. How could anyone be against reading? Easy.

As soon as Seattle introduced the One City, One Book project, someone began carping about it. And someone has been sharpening that complaint ever since.

The purpose of One City, One Book is generally explained as supporting the culture of reading and as a way of bringing together diverse cultures in discussion. Seattle started with Russell Banks's book *The Sweet Hereafter*, a powerful book but a strange choice, since it is about a fatal school bus accident. I think I would have chosen something more jolly.

But see, there I go joining the pundits—I've always wanted to use that word—who are complaining about the book choice. Complaining is easy; creating is what's hard. I used to work at an advertising agency. After the criticizing clients were out of earshot, we grumbled among ourselves, "Where were you when the paper was blank?"

When *To Kill a Mockingbird* was chosen for Chicago, the book was checked out of the library 6,500 times. Dublin chose the book *Dracula*, by Irish writer Bram Stoker. Pasadena was more high-minded in choosing the book *Gardens of Water*, about one Muslim Kurdish girl and one American Christian boy in Turkey. Galveston County, Texas, tried to select Mark Haddon's fine book *The Curious Incident of the Dog in the Night-Time*, but that unleashed an uproar because of the obscenities in the book. I quite understand. We don't want Texans learning to swear, by golly.

I am delighted to report that one community in Oklahoma chose a book that hits on all cylinders. It is by an Oklahoma author, it is well written, it is historic, and it is down-to-the-ground accurate. Stillwater chose Angie Debo's book *Prairie City*, which was first published in 1944 and has been reprinted three times since then.

Debo is known as Oklahoma's "first lady of history." She was a female historian with a PhD at a time when no university would hire a female professor, so she became a writer instead. She lived in the tiny town of Marshall, Oklahoma, and she wrote thirteen books, including the groundbreaking histories of the Creeks and Choctaws, *A History of the Indians of the United States*, and her most powerful book, *And Still the Waters Run: The Betrayal of the Five Civilized Tribes*. She died in 1988, but her books are still found in libraries around the world.

She was a woman of great personal integrity, in her work and in her life. She planned to leave her papers to Oklahoma State University, but when she discovered that the university was thinking about acquiring the papers of Richard Nixon, she put a codicil in her will that if the Nixon papers came to OSU as a memorial to him, her papers would go elsewhere. And she told OSU that. In the end, Nixon's papers went elsewhere, and so there is an Angie Debo room at the OSU library, including her papers.

In conjunction with choosing her book for One City, One Book, Stillwater scheduled more than a month of activities celebrating Debo.

Dr. Angie Debo in 1940 *(courtesy of the Western History Collections, University of Oklahoma Libraries [OU Press 14])*

I was invited to be on a panel of writers and scholars who had known her. It was good to see how she is revered and how librarians are keeping her work and her memory alive. The activities culminated with the unveiling of a statue of Debo at the Stillwater public library. Aptly, the statue shows a young Debo sitting with a book and a pen.

Prairie City is the story of a small Oklahoma community from the land run of 1889 to World War II. The book is particularly important to us in Oklahoma because it is the story of Oklahoma. The historian Mari Sandoz reviewed *Prairie City* in the *New York Times* when the book first came out. She quoted the Sioux and said, "A people without history is like the wind on the buffalo grass."

Prairie City, though, is more than the story of one small town. It is a social history of almost all small towns, America in microcosm. It is a love song to our history and to small towns. Debo closed the book this way: "As for me, I live in a small town where I am willing to continue, lest it grow smaller."

That is a quote from Plutarch.

Breakfast at Tiffany's—
Half a Century Later

If Holly Golightly were a real person instead of a literary character, she would be a senior citizen. She would be on Medicare and drawing Social Security.

The heroine of Truman Capote's classic *Breakfast at Tiffany's* was not quite nineteen when the book was published in 1958, now more than fifty years ago. A few critics dismissed the book as "frivolous fluff" and a "romantic Valentine," but more considered the novella a masterpiece. Norman Mailer called Capote "the most perfect writer of my generation" and said he would not have changed two words of the book.

Capote may be best known for *In Cold Blood,* the true account of a Kansas family's murder. With that book he invented a new genre, the nonfiction novel. With *Breakfast at Tiffany's* he created a new kind of heroine—a quintessential American free spirit with a yearning heart. Holly Golightly is a poor country girl who reinvented herself in the big city. Since 1958, readers and critics have tried to define Holly. She is a survivor, imperfect and fascinating. She is the sophisticated flip side of the Beat Generation, a glamorous image of New York in the 1950s. She represents the emerging sexual freedom and demographic mobility of post–World War II America. Holly is a cosmopolitan looking for home.

Don't think about the popular 1961 movie starring Audrey Hepburn. As good as that is, it is a different medium and practically a different story. I saw the movie before I read the book, and it had a strong influence. Like Holly, I began to wear big sunglasses, eat Melba toast and cottage cheese, and wear slim black dresses with black alligator high heels.

The movie is a romance with a happy ending complete with kisses in the rain. The book is a different enchilada. The book's story is rawer. It was slightly racy for its time, featuring a girl with easy sexual morals but high personal standards. It gives us unorthodox characters and subjects, some taboo at the time: homosexuals, mobsters, models, millionaire playboys, marijuana smokers, Latin lovers, ethnic neighbors, wild parties, and the allure of nonconformity.

This was exactly what we thought New York was, so different from Hometown, U.S.A.

Fun facts about *Breakfast at Tiffany's:*

- Holly's full first name was Holiday. In an earlier draft, Capote named her Connie Gustafson.
- Her real name was Lulamae. Capote's mother's name was Lillie Mae.
- She had short, pixie-styled blond hair that she colored herself.
- Capote wanted Marilyn Monroe to play the role. He hated the movie.
- Her sunglasses were prescription.
- The title came from a story Capote heard about an older man's one-night stand with a young Marine. "Where do you want to have breakfast?" the man asked. "Pick the fanciest place in town." The younger man, who knew nothing of New York, answered, "Let's have breakfast at Tiffany's."
- *Harper's Bazaar* cancelled plans to publish the novella in the magazine because Capote wouldn't omit four-letter words or change the way Holly made her living. (She accepted a hundred dollars from elderly escorts for "trips to the ladies' room" and cash for carrying "weather reports" from the Mafia's Sally Tomato in Sing-Sing.)

Whatever you do, don't just read *about* the book. Read the book. Study guides I consulted show a surefire way to squeeze the juice out of it. Students are asked to consider whether Holly had abandonment issues or if it is a story about misguided love or about sexual, asexual, homosexual, or even spiritual love. Where does it stand in women's literature? What does the cat represent? And the horses? Sample essay questions include "Do you feel that Holly's unorthodox behavior is a way of protecting her uniqueness from the conformist demands of American society, or is it a symptom of her inability to achieve stability and maturity in her personal life?"

Dear God. Talk about wrestling a work of art to the ground and wringing its neck. George Plimpton, who wrote a very good, oral biography of Capote, said one theme of *Breakfast at Tiffany's* is that the special, strange, and gifted people in the world must be treated with understanding. This is probably how Capote—diminutive, tiny-voiced, precocious, outlandishly gay in a time when the closet was firmly shut—saw himself.

Half a century after it was published, I still consider *Breakfast at Tiffany's* a small masterpiece of American literature, with a memorable heroine, a storyline with a twist of mystery at the end, and pure, polished prose. Like this: "If you let yourself love a wild thing," Holly says in the book, "you'll end up looking at the sky." Still, she says, "it's better to look at the sky than live there. Such an empty place, so vague. Just a country where the thunder goes and things disappear."

Much like Holly herself, whose calling card read: "Holiday Golightly, Traveling."

Pretty Is

Let's see a show of hands of everyone who believes the proverb "Pretty is as pretty does."

That's what I thought.

Some variation of "Pretty is as pretty does" has been around forever. A Chinese inscription from 200 B.C. says that an attractive heart is revealed in an attractive face. In the fourteenth century, Chaucer wrote it in his *Canterbury Tales.* We say it. We repeat it to naughty children. We want to believe it ourselves. We know that appearances can be misleading. We spend billions on products and services to make us better looking.

And still . . .

What pain and anguish it causes us to not be pretty. Or not to be as pretty as we want to be.

However noble our intentions about preferring pretty behavior, we betray our real thoughts with our words and actions. Here's an example. In a popular book titled *My Life in Middlemarch,* author Rebecca Mead writes about the book *Middlemarch,* which was published in the 1870s, and about its author, George Eliot, which was the pen name of Mary Ann Evans. Eliot was not pretty. In fact, she was once described as "magnificently ugly." The author Henry James commented on her unattractive appearance but went on to say, "In this vast ugliness resides a most powerful beauty." So far, so good. But then this book was reviewed on NPR's *All Things Considered* with host Robert Siegel. I suppose he was trying to be witty when he commented on a photograph of George Eliot by saying, "What a horse."

That unleashed—in me and others—a rash of outraged responses. One woman wrote, "Henry James looked like a toad, but nobody mentions that."

So the question is, are women the only targets for potshots about their looks? Even—or perhaps especially—brilliant, talented women?

My admiration for Queen Elizabeth I bounced off the charts after reading Anna Whitelock's *The Queen's Bed: An Intimate History of Elizabeth's Court.* She had a country to run, plots and assassination attempts to foil, and ambitious suitors to stall, yet much of her energies—and those of the women in her court—were spent on demonstrating her health and beauty. It was not all vanity; the queen's person personified England itself, so she had to look young and fit.

I learned that the queen was not a morning person—my soul sister. She liked breakfast in her bedchamber, then often started the day reading. She spent considerable time on her daily toilette, washing her face with castile soap made with olive oil and keeping it wrinkle free with a milk-based posset curd. Although bathing wasn't popular at the time, she bathed regularly, at least once a month.

Elizabeth paid particular attention to whitening her teeth but to no avail. She had such a love of sweets, her teeth yellowed, then decayed and blackened until many fell out. She suffered from severe toothache and late in life had so many missing teeth, some courtiers had trouble understanding her when she spoke.

Her ivory complexion was a particular conceit; it was kept white by cosmetics her ladies mixed laboriously from egg whites, powdered eggshell, alum, and, unfortunately, mercury. Her lip salves contained lead carbonate and lead hydroxide. In short, the queen's quest for beauty poisoned her, pocked her skin, and perhaps contributed to her hair loss. By the time she was seventy and at the end of her life, the pale-skinned, russet-haired girl had become a bewigged fright, almost completely bald, with a face grotesquely painted and a shrunken body weighted down by jeweled robes and gowns often open to display her breasts, as was the custom of unmarried women. Whether for self or country, she went to her death chasing after beauty. She lost the race, but she was never less than a queen. She was regal in bearing and short tempered. She "swore much," a contemporary said, and boxed the ears of any who annoyed her. That's the Elizabeth I like.

An extraordinary biography of the Brontë family—almost a thousand pages—is titled *Wild Genius on the Moors: The Story of a Literary Family.* One of the saddest things the book told me was how Charlotte Brontë suffered because she was plain. All of the Brontë girls—Emily, Anne, and Charlotte—were small and shy to the point of paranoia or reclusiveness. They were as rough-hewn as the north country where they lived and wrote about people and customs they knew, which made for salacious reading and some public contempt. The Brontë sisters were certainly not as refined in person or in fiction as the more genteel Jane Austen.

Charlotte was the most sociable of the sisters. Sadly, she had no social conversation skills, and on the few London social occasions she attended, she rarely spoke, so her brilliance did not shine. She liked men, handsome men, and they admired her mind and her talent, but they married beautiful women. She saw this and it hurt her. She was so unattractive she considered herself repulsive. She was small, almost gnome-like, with beautiful, large, hazel eyes but a prominent nose and mouth. As with many of the women of that age with a poor diet, she was missing some teeth. Her hair was thin, and she wore a bad, cloth hairpiece, which made her look even more countrified. At one London gathering in her honor, she was so visibly uncomfortable among the chattering, lovely, society women that her contemporary William Thackeray said, "I realized that in that moment, she would have traded her genius to be pretty."

Which brings me to a wonderful story I remember from an oral storyteller. A man set out on a quest to find Truth. He said he would search the world until he found her. He crossed seas and oceans, deserts and forests, and finally he was told that Truth lived in a large, dark cave near the top of a rugged mountain. The man climbed and climbed until he found the cave on the mountaintop, and then he crawled inside. At the back of the cave he found an ancient, haggard crone crouching near a small fire. He asked her, "Have I found you? Are you, indeed, Truth?"

She nodded slowly that she was. And he asked her, "Is there a message that you want me to take from you out into the world?"

Again she nodded yes and with a gnarled finger gestured for him to come closer. She whispered, "Tell the world that you have found me. Tell them that you have found Truth. And tell them that I am beautiful."

Postscript: Mary Ann Evans/George Eliot's grave is planted with hellebores, one of my favorite plants. I hope the ones on her grave bloom green, as mine do, because at a glance the plant seems to have no blossoms at all, only leaves. A lingering look reveals a lovely, cup-shaped bloom of five calyxes. The flower lasts a long time. That's why I hope Evans/Eliot's grave has the green-blooming *Helleborus odorus*—simple, deceptively beautiful, long lasting, but with dark qualities. Some species are poisonous, and perhaps one of these was the cause of the death of Alexander the Great. Also, according to lore, hellebores can cause women to go mad and run naked in the streets. I have not experienced this urge myself. Yet.

Road Trips by the Book

Remember when summer vacations automatically meant road trips? Nothing quite like piling the whole family into the car and driving to Colorado or New Orleans. Now, according to federal highway data, American motorists are driving fewer miles for the first time in three decades. For a while, this was because of the high price of gasoline, as well as hotel, motel, and campground costs. Another factor is changing times and demographic shifts.

The golden age of the automobile is said to be the 1950s, when *Traveling by Car: A Family Planning Guide to a Better Vacation,* published by Shell Oil, offered planning, budgeting, packing, and other helpful information for halcyon road trips. The length of a car vacation was assumed to be two weeks.

Women were advised to take one 26-inch suitcase and an overnight case. They should pack a "travel suit . . . a two-piece after-driving dress . . . a spectator sports ensemble . . . [and] a rugged-life costume. In many resort areas," the book said, "slacks are frowned upon—more in the East than in the West."

For children, "dungarees shouldn't be worn in the car." Although comfortable, "they're not suitable for wear even in a roadside restaurant."

The dawn of the car trip might be dated 1935, when gas was seventeen cents a gallon. That was also the year Congress approved the Works Progress Administration (WPA), a program to help relieve the Great Depression by funding the employment of more than eight and a half million people. In colloquial terms, it was part of Franklin Delano Roosevelt's New Deal and an effort to get Americans back to work. One of those projects was the Federal Writers' Project, the most ambitious government-funded arts program in American history.

During 1935–43, some seven thousand writers were hired to write the *American Guide Series,* guidebooks for every state in the union. To my mind, they are the greatest American travel and history books ever produced. I think the best ones are the original versions. I collect them.

Top writers of the day were hired to write about states' history, art, industry, agriculture, and geography. They were the best writers of the time, doing top-notch research and reporting: Conrad Aiken, John Cheever, John Steinbeck, Studs Terkel, and Zora Neale Hurston. They were paid about twenty-five dollars a week. In Oklahoma, the editor of the guidebook was Angie Debo, who had won the John H. Dunning prize for best U.S. historical book in 1933. Incredibly, her essay was so botched by another editor that she withdrew it from the guidebook. That essay is restored in the 1986 reprint, which is why I own both this version and the original.

The collection of guidebooks—and they are highly collectible—has been described as "a vast panorama of our land" and "the finest contribution to American patriotism of our generation." The original books sold for two and a half dollars; today a first edition of the Oklahoma book can sell for seventy-five dollars.

The books, with maps included, laid out road trips and provided colorful historical and cultural detail along the way. They explored the ordinary and found magic there—a Whitmanesque portrait of the American scene. The purpose of the guidebook series, the director of the project said, was to assemble the data the inhabitants possessed about their country, "boil it down to convenient size, and put it into the hands of people who don't realize that wonders exist at their own door."

Historian and University of Oklahoma (OU) professor Edward Everett Dale wrote the essay "The Spirit of Oklahoma" for the Oklahoma Guide. He wrote that Oklahoma was the "last American frontier" and that Oklahoma "has made greater material progress in a single generation than has any other area of comparable size in the United States."

The academic and professional relationship between Debo and Dale, who had been her mentor, is a story in itself, and the full story is told in Shirley Leckie's biography of Debo. Dale considered himself to be her "academic godfather" and recognized her as his outstanding student. Still, he would not hire her when a teaching position was open at OU. Male professors, even with lesser academic qualifications, were preferred. Besides, Dale was not comfortable with her blunt, academic style or what he considered the explosive nature of her research. To her death, the turn of their professional relationship was hurtful to her. To me, a sister of the women's lib movement of the 1970s, it is a shameful, repetitive verse in the history of women's struggle for equality.

The Oklahoma guidebook was the last volume of the series. It was 1930s Oklahoma throbbing with life. The *Saturday Review of Literature* said, "This is the most exciting of the lot. Nearly every page contains material for a novel."

Here's what the Oklahoma Guide says in part about Tulsa:

In 1879, Tulsa was a post office on the pony mail route through Indian Territory. Into this primitive section, unknown to many whites . . . came the Atlantic & Pacific Railroad in 1882. Originally the builders planned to stop in the Cherokee Nation about a mile from the riverbank, but since Cherokee laws prohibited trading except by native, intermarried, or adopted Cherokee citizens, the rails were extended into the Creek Nation. There on the site of the present Tulsa business section, the railroad established a terminal with a roundhouse and a large loading pen [for] vast herds of cattle [to be shipped] to the stockyards in St. Louis and Chicago. . . . Main Street was made 80-feet wide because the early settlers felt that 100 feet was too far to wade the mud.

Norman, we learn, was named for a government engineer who pitched camp south of the present site of Oklahoma City in 1872. When the Atchison, Topeka and Santa Fe Railroad built tracks through the territory years later, a boxcar named Norman Switch was set near the spot he had camped.

In early-day Lawton, famed town marshal Heck Thomas chased Lon Chaney, a town photographer turned actor, out of town for speeding on horseback.

In 1930, wheat replaced cotton as Oklahoma's principal crop.

The Great Salt Plains in western Oklahoma are probably the remains of a prehistoric sea.

Woodward in the Cherokee Outlet became a town between noon and sunset, September 16, 1893. Activity was so chaotic, a volunteer committee tried to establish law and order by passing the word, "If you must shoot, shoot straight up."

The book is chock full of historic nuggets like this.

For an illuminating road trip, find a copy of a collectable WPA guidebook. Luckily, costuming for car travel today is more casual than it once was. Today, wearing dungarees is practically dressing up.

Me and The Egg and I

I have such admiration for writers who can take the dreary straw of their life and spin it into golden stories.

My favorite may be Betty MacDonald and her book *The Egg and I.* It was written more than seventy years ago, but I reread it every few years because it is so funny and written well. *The Egg and I* is the story of her saga as a newlywed living on a remote chicken farm in Washington state with her rugged back-to-the-earth husband, Bob. Her neighbors include Ma and Pa Kettle and two Indians named Crowbar and Geoduck.

The book became an immediate best seller when it was published in 1945, and it stayed on the best-seller list for three years. The movie starring Claudette Colbert and Fred MacMurray was equally popular. The public so loved Ma and Pa Kettle, several movies and a TV series were spun off featuring them.

One reason for the popularity might be the era, right after World War II. People wanted an innocent story about a young, self-sufficient couple on a farm for the same reason a wartime audience loved the sweet musical *Oklahoma!* about a young couple going to a picnic basket party.

Betty MacDonald was a saucy writer for a woman in the 1940s. Pa Kettle is notorious for mooching building materials or chicken feed and for trying to get someone else to do his work. At first the young couple found him charming, but "by the second year on the farm," MacDonald writes, her husband referred to him as "that lazy, lisping son of a bitch." That's saucy.

The real story is that *The Egg and I* is an airbrushed picture of the marriage. The farm had no electricity, phone, mail service, or running water. The couple worked from four in the morning until nine at night. The rain was deadening.

Here's a quotation from the book: "It rained and rained and rained and rained and rained. It drizzled—misted—drooled—spat—poured—and just plain rained. I became as one with all the characters in all of the novels about rainy seasons who bang their heads against walls, drink water glasses of straight whiskey and moan, 'The rain! The rain! My God, the rain!'"

MacDonald was tired, lonely, and depressed. And during the four years on the farm, she had two babies, which made life even harder. She said that she hated chickens and had married the wrong man. At twenty-three, she went home to Seattle, divorced Bob, and stayed there.

She was a single mother trying to support two children in the Depression. Then she caught tuberculosis and spent a year in a sanitarium. She wrote about that experience in another lighthearted book, *The Plague and I.*

When she was thirty-seven, she remarried and moved to Vashon Island. She and her husband commuted by ferry to work in Seattle. She wrote a book about that, too.

Three years later *The Egg and I* came out, sold a million copies the first year, and was translated into twenty languages, such as the French *L'oeuf et moi* and the Spanish *El huevo y yo.* She was famous, wealthy, profiled in *Life* magazine, and sued for libel by people who said she based the Kettles and the Indian Crowbar on them.

Her books are still in print, and *The Egg and I* is described as an American masterwork, although one section about an Indian picnic is painfully racist to read today.

For ten years, happy in her new marriage, she lived on the lush island writing books—funny memoirs and children's books. In 1958, she died of cancer.

Today their home on Vashon Island is a bed and breakfast. Betty MacDonald packed a lot of life into her short forty-nine years: some of it was hard, sad, and sick, but she saw joy around her and wrote her life as a comedy. Not much different than poet laureate Philip Levine, who died recently. He wrote poems about everyday life and cosmic wonder. That's how I want to live.

I'm a Believer

I am a child of American advertising. That means I believe everything. And anything.

I believe the purpose of life is romance, style, and a great smile.

I believe I can have these things if I buy the right shampoo, toothpaste, car, and mobile phone. If all of that fails, finding a good Christian online dating system will save me. A click of the mouse is all it takes.

I am not alone in believing big.

In high school, my friend Betty remarked one day that the sun had not come up. The rest of us thought it was a cloudy day. Not Betty. She believed that some days the sun came up in the east and some days that lucky old sun simply chose not to roll around heaven all day.

This prepared me for years ahead of living in Oklahoma, where many of us believe the unbelievable, especially about politics and religion. No use trying to debate or reason with us, just say "Hmm" and look for the nearest door.

And so it is that I believe in prescriptive reading. Reading the right book can cure what ails you, or at least it can ameliorate the symptoms.

Take one of Oklahoma's recent summer-long, Hasty-Bake heat waves. That ailed me. So I prescribed myself a series of cooling novels. I made a stack of Barbara Pym novels, moved a chair directly under an air-conditioning vent, and reread my way through them.

It's hard to believe that Pym, the English author considered the contemporary Jane Austen, was born a hundred years ago. Her slim, witty novels are set in 1950s English villages and suburban Anglican parishes. They feature women who wear hats and gloves, drink a great deal of tea, entertain the curate for supper, remember old beaus, and are bemused by daily life in their cool and damp climate.

"Ah," an English woman told me, "the England that never was." Light-years away from a hot Oklahoma summer, which is what I wanted.

I had just seen the play *84 Charing Cross Road* and realized for the first time the austerity and food shortages of post–World War II England. This gave me new insight into the frugality of Pym's characters. I understand now why they fussed over what to serve the vicar at tea, lamented the shortage of meat, busied themselves letting out the seams of an old dress, and noted the progress of the new buildings going up in the bombed ruins of the Blitz. Yet they pressed on, enjoying life and relishing the fussiness of the Anglo-Catholic Church of England. Pym called them "excellent women," endlessly burnishing church brass and decorating churches with flowers.

Pym's novels are social comedies but not as flashy as Noel Coward's. Although they are quiet, they are not trifles. She was shortlisted for the acclaimed Man Booker Prize, a supreme award for novels. She writes gently, with a clean style and clear observation of human behavior.

Time roars past so quickly, history seems left in the dust. One hundred years ago, when Pym was born, Woodrow Wilson was president, suffragettes were marching in the streets, steel was invented, Camels became the first packaged cigarettes, Hedy Lamarr was born, and the Philadelphia A's won the World Series.

Boy, does that sound like a long time ago. No wonder Oklahoma's glamorous chanteuse Lee Wiley sang naughtily in 1933,

> Don't save your kisses, pass them around . . .
> Who's gonna know that you passed them around
> A hundred years from today.

Since I believe everything, I believe history can be both informative and enjoyable. As autumn approaches, I have rediscovered a way to enjoy recent history. I'll make myself a plate of finger sandwiches, pour a glass of sherry, and reread my Pym favorites: *A Few Green Leaves, A Glass of Blessings,* and *Excellent Women.*

Then, thoroughly charmed, I'll move on to the British author—not the actress—Elizabeth Taylor, whose novels were published from 1945 to 1971. She is a soul sister of both Austen and Pym and, according to Kingsley Amis, was "one of the best English novelists born in this century." She said that "life is so untidy," and she wrote everyday-life novels that captured people with both wit and clarity. The children making brief appearances in her books are portrayed as deliciously naughty.

Discover Barbara Pym and Elizabeth Taylor and you, too, may believe there's no substitute for a cool book.

The Annotated Alice

This is a little story that just gets curiouser and curiouser. I read about a website titled—I'm not kidding—runpee.com. It is a website to tell us exactly when to dash to the bathroom during a movie so as not to miss much action.

I didn't believe it, but there it was—runpee.com—telling me that the best time in the new *Alice in Wonderland* movie is thirty-four minutes in, during the Mad Hatter's tea party.

That made me think of the quotation "The world is full of a number of things, I'm sure we all should be happy as kings."

And that made me wonder if the quote was from *Alice in Wonderland*. So I pulled out my tattered copy of *The Annotated Alice*, published in 1960. I was surprised to discover that the author of that book is Martin Gardner from Tulsa, born in 1914. That's when the story really got curious.

I love knowing about writers' lives, so how happy was I to learn that Gardner, then ninety-five, lived in Norman. Nearing the end of his life, he had moved back to Oklahoma to be near his son James, a professor at the University of Oklahoma. I interviewed him by phone. What a dope I am. When I called, I had no idea how internationally famous he was, not only for the Alice book—his most profitable book—but also for his expertise in mathematical games. He is the author of more than one hundred books and even more articles about recreational mathematics, puzzles, flexagons, tangrams, polyominoes, and hexaflexagons—all Greek to me. He also wrote about L. Frank Baum, the author of the *Wizard of Oz* books, and even founded the international Wizard of Oz Club. What irony. (Irrelevant aside: When I worked at the University of Tulsa, I listed my membership in the Wizard of Oz Club on my curriculum vitae as one of my professional memberships. It was my private little joke, because academics revere CVs oh so highly.)

Gardner was particularly famous for his column Mathematical Games in *Scientific American*. He was admired for his skill and knowledge of magic and wrote books about the magic trade. When he died in 2010, a couple of years after I interviewed him, the magician Penn Jillette of the duo Penn and Teller wrote a bouquet of an obituary of him for the *New York Times*.

In 2013, Gardner's posthumous memoir was published with the wonderful title *Undiluted Hocus-Pocus*. What I like most about this chatty and informal book is what he has to say about growing up in Tulsa. The book begins this way: "I have always loved colors. All colors. To me, the ability to see colors is one of God's great blessings." That love may be traced to his mother, who studied painting at the University of Tulsa with celebrated Tulsa artist Adah Robinson. An oil painting of his mother by Robinson is owned by Tulsa's Gilcrease Museum. Robinson was also the designer of the art deco Boston Avenue Church that the Gardner family attended.

The Gardners first lived in a small house with an outdoor pump in north Tulsa, but after the success of his father's business, Gardner Oil Company, they moved to the more fashionable south part of town. Their final home still stands at 2187 South Owasso.

Gardner was a student at Lee Elementary School, then Horace Mann Junior High, and finally Central High School, which he hated. He said it was like four years in prison. The only classes he liked were mathematics and physics. (He later dedicated some of his books to his geometry class teacher and his physics class teacher.) He particularly disliked history classes and believed the history of science was more important than anything kings, queens, and religious leaders did. His passions in high school were chess and magic.

Gardner went on to study philosophy at the University of Chicago, serve in the navy, and make his living as a writer. His first real job after graduation from the University of Chicago was back in his hometown as an oil writer at the *Tulsa Tribune*. It was a dull job, he said, and he was paid fifteen dollars a week. After about a year he was fired from that job by editor Jenkin Lloyd Jones. He left Tulsa for good and went on to greater things. For twenty-five years, he wrote magazine articles, columns, and books. Among other things, he became an authority on Lewis Carroll, who, like Gardner, was a mathematician.

Lewis Carroll's real name was Charles Dodgson. He taught mathematics at Oxford and was a quiet, slight man who stammered, unless he was speaking to small children. Both Gardner and Carroll were fascinated by magic tricks, especially card tricks and games. *Through the Looking Glass* is an actual chess game, and Alice is the pawn.

Gardner told me that his favorite character in the Alice books is Alice herself. "She's a wonderful little girl," he said. "Nothing seems to bother her, even when people are rude to her. She's bright and asks good questions. No wonder Carroll loved her."

What appealed most to Gardner about the Alice books were their puzzles, riddles, and allusions to mathematics, metaphysics, philosophy, science, and ethics. He is not alone in that. Bertrand Russell was another fan, and Gardner suggested that Russell write an annotated version of the Alice books, but the eminent philosopher said he was too busy with important works, so Gardner wrote it himself. It became his best-selling book.

An annotation is different from symbolic or psychoanalytical interpretations. Those are what we write for literature classes, amazing ourselves, one another, and sometimes the authors with the creative meanings we have ferreted out. Because, as some wag once said, sometimes a cigar is just a good smoke.

However, as Gardner points out, a joke isn't funny unless you see the point of it, and the jokes of the Alice books were written for British readers of the Victorian era. "It's a masterpiece," he said, "but we can't understand all of it without a footnote. So much of it is about cards and chess." To help us appreciate the wit of the parodies and puns, he included the original poems and popular songs.

Some of the characters Carroll created were patterned on his Oxford neighbors, such as the Mad Hatter. Hatmakers in the 1860s often went mad from the mercury they worked with to cure the felt, but the Mad Hatter is also a caricature of the Oxford resident Theophilus Carter. He always wore a top hat and was known for his eccentric inventions, such as the "alarm clock bed" that woke the sleeper by throwing him out of bed onto the floor.

The Annotated Alice book has sold more than half a million copies around the world and may be more popular today than when it first came out. Gardner had received his most recent royalty check just weeks before we spoke; it was for $25,000.

He wrote about mathematical games, card tricks, philosophy, pseudoscience, literature, puzzles, paper folding, linguistics, wordplay, and conjuring. Ironically, although he was good at math in high school, he never took a mathematics class in college. And yet mathematics is what he wrote about. His book *Mathematics, Magic and Mystery,* published in 1956, was the first in-depth book about mathematic card tricks for nonmagicians.

When he died, praise for him flooded the media. "He brought more mathematics to more millions than anyone else," said a British mathematician. Pulitzer Prize winner Richard Hofstadter said that Gardner was one of the greatest American intellects of the twentieth century. His editor at W. W. Norton said, "He was an Oklahoma boy who happened to be a genius. He was the opposite of pretentious. He was like something out of *The Wizard of Oz*."

Oh, Now I Get It

I'll explain the title of this essay before I'm finished.

The subtitle could be "If You Don't Read, You'll Stay More Ignorant Than You Have to Be." And that's because of how I got it; it came to me after reading—serendipitously—three books in succession about famous people. All three books are some of the most compelling books I've ever read.

The first book, written by a medical doctor named John J. Ross, is titled *Shakespeare's Tremor and Orwell's Cough*. Ross summarizes some writers' life stories—especially their illnesses and, oh, my God, the medical treatments of their days—and then gives us a contemporary diagnosis.

The writers include the Brontë sisters, Nathaniel Hawthorne, James Joyce, Herman Melville, John Milton, Shakespeare, and more.

My first thought was: "What a sissy-pants I am. To go to bed with a mere fever and vomiting." These writers lived their lives—their productive lives—with incredible illnesses and even worse medical treatment.

For his blindness, Milton was prescribed the moss from a skull of a man who had died violently. This was remarkably easy to find because of the decapitated heads on pikes. After his eye surgery, poor James Joyce had leeches applied to his eyes to reduce the swelling.

With the most advanced treatment of their days, the writers were treated with arsenic, morphine, lead, and mercury, which probably killed some of them.

Even more fascinating to me was the modern diagnoses of the mental illnesses that likely affected many of these famous writers: bipolar disorder, autism, Asperger's, depression, obsessive-compulsive disorder. Which they self-medicated with alcohol and drugs. It made their lives hell and was probably worse for their families—their wives and children, who cared for them day after day.

Still reeling from this, I read the powerful memoir by Carobeth Laird titled *Encounter with an Angry God*. Published in the 1970s, it was written when she was in her eighties, an age that gave her voice a forceful honesty. It's her talent and memory that give the book a great style.

She tells the story of her youthful marriage in the 1920s to John Peabody Harringon, a giant of American anthropology described—kindly—as an eccentric genius. He was obsessed with researching the languages of Indian tribes, and she was his faithful assistant. They lived a life of incredible deprivation—by his choice—existing usually on cold mush. Her life was so hard she often thought of suicide. The subtext of this memoir is "Why did he behave and live like that? And why did I put up with it for almost a decade?"

And finally, Gioia Diliberto's page-turning biography of Hadley Hemingway, the writer's first wife, titled *Paris without End*. It is a great love story that shows Hadley's total, unquestioning support and her husband's total, obsessive drive to become a great author.

Hemingway is not yet thirty years old when this story begins, young and excited about writing. Then he becomes successful and mean. And then, after their divorce and for the rest of his life, regretful.

And that's what brought me to the conclusion "Oh, now I get it." They were all barking mad. All of these great geniuses had some, however mild, form of mental disability. Which can stimulate creativity and accomplishment. Which the world has benefited from, but which was no picnic for the people involved. Which they tried to self-medicate in some way—alcohol, drugs, philandering, obsessive work.

And then I thought—just them? Just the talented and the genius? No. Modern research tells us that one in seventeen of us has a severe mental disorder such as schizophrenia and one in four has a milder mental imbalance.

Does that explain our behavior? What we usually think of as character flaws, laziness, rudeness, egotism, or self-absorbed or self-indulgent behavior?

And if it does—so what? Does it excuse hurtful behavior? Will that make us more compassionate? Will that help us think of mental disorders more kindly? More accepting of family and friends and colleagues who behave badly? If we equate physical health to mental health, would we say, "Oh, I wouldn't expect you to climb the stairs if I knew you had a broken leg?"

Here's the question: when is it an illness and when are they just behaving as jerks? When are *we* behaving as jerks?

All we know is what we know now. Maybe our current knowledge and treatment of brain chemistry is about on the level of applying leeches to the eyes after eye surgery.

Writing a Children's Christmas Classic

The two books I wish I had written—wish I had the talent to have written—are *To Kill a Mockingbird* and *The Best Christmas Pageant Ever.* Both are classics, both tell big messages from a child's perspective, and both are funny. The children in these books are not sugar and spice; these kids are tough, naughty, and curious.

Who would have thought that a story about "absolutely the meanest kids in the history of the world" would become a Christmas classic? *The Best Christmas Pageant Ever* features the Herdmans—six children who "talk dirty, hit little kids, cuss their teachers, and set fire to Fred Shoemaker's old broken-down tool house." And then they finagle their way into taking over the church Christmas pageant. In the midst of chaos, we, the readers—if not the Herdmans—rediscover the meaning of Christmas.

The book is classified as a children's book, but I did not discover it until I was an adult. I laughed aloud, I reread it every year, and I give it as gifts to my adult friends. I am such a fan of the book, I arranged to interview the author, Barbara Robinson. I wanted to know what it was like to have written a classic.

She and I spoke in 2002 as the book was celebrating its thirtieth year in print, had sold two million copies, and had foreign translations in France, Germany, Czechoslovakia, Italy, Sweden, Norway, and Japan. By now, the book's popularity has grown even more, and it has been produced as a play and as a movie.

Robinson created the six Herdman kids for a magazine Christmas story in 1972. The story generated so much reader mail, she expanded it into an eighty-page book. Students, librarians, parents, and ministers fell in love with the rascally Herdmans. *Publishers Weekly* described it as one of the best Christmas books ever.

Robinson was seventy-five at the time she spoke to me from her home in Berwyn, Pennsylvania. She told me about writing the book. "I had no idea it would do this," she said. Neither did she consider it a children's book. She wrote it as a family story. When she was commissioned to write a Christmas article for *McCall's* magazine, she flipped through a children's picture book for inspiration and was struck by the nativity's familiar language, "It came to pass . . ."

She wondered about kids who had never heard the nativity story or Bible stories. "I realized they would be fairly wild and woolly," she said. That was the beginning of the incorrigible Herdmans—six skinny kids who live over a garage, who grow poison ivy instead of grass in the yard, and who "emptied the whole first grade in three minutes flat" at show-and-tell.

Her books are not for very young children, Robinson says, and she advises her readers not to do what the Herdmans do, either in the Christmas book or in the sequel, *The Best School Year Ever.*

Robinson traveled extensively, visiting schools to talk about reading and writing. Students always ask her if the Herdmans are real or make-believe. "I never knew a whole family of them," she answers, "but like any other kid in school, there were people I avoided." She had never visited an Oklahoma school, she said with a laugh, but she was phoned by an Oklahoman writing an article about dysfunctional families.

She reported encouraging news from her visits with schoolchildren across the country. "Television or not," she said, "kids are reading. They're reading more than we think they are. And they are writing." There is no greater audience than boys and girls who read, she said. "They demand the most exciting, mysterious, touching, and funniest." She gave me a tip about speaking to classrooms of children—wear red, she said; they need a bright color to capture their attention.

Robinson was an only child whose father died when she was three. She and her mother, an elementary school teacher, lived with her grandparents in a southern Ohio River town. It was a small town where people sat on the front porch on summer evenings and drank lemonade while the kids played kick the can and caught fireflies.

She grew up in a reading family and began writing when she was in grade school. She did not try to sell any of her work until she had graduated from Allegheny College and was married. After five or six years of rejections, she became a successful short story writer with work published in *Ladies' Home Journal, Redbook, McCall's,* and others.

Robinson remained a lifelong, avid reader. "My idea of a wonderful day would be to finish the book I'm laboring over and not have anything I have to do but sit down with a whole sofa full of books."

When not traveling, she wrote every day, "slowly but steadily," from 9 A.M. until 2 P.M., on a manual Olivetti typewriter that she ordered from the Old Vermont Country Store catalog. When she got stuck, she picked up the typewriter and moved to another room. On lovely days, she pulled the shades to avoid distraction. Still, she said, working at home is difficult, especially for women. "That's where we do all the other stuff, so it's very hard to separate those two lives. Very easy, if the writing isn't going well, to say, 'I'll go put in a load of wash.' I need to resist that very strongly."

When we spoke, she was working on another book about the Herdmans. "It was supposed to be finished two years ago, but writing funny books is slow work. I wish I were a faster writer. I wish I were more prolific. I'm not. Humor is so fleeting. You have to catch it on the run."

Robinson died in 2013 at age eighty-five.

At home, she always had a stack of books at her side. When she travelled, she told me, the book she took with her everywhere was *To Kill a Mockingbird*.

Oh, We Are a Quaint, Merry Folk

Don't you just love how smart and good we are?

I do. I can't think of any species that is smarter. Or gooder. Take December. It is the month of wonderful, uplifting stories. Some are stories of transformation. Something small and simple—a broken nutcracker toy or a lame child with a crutch—conquers evil or brings goodness.

Some are stories of redemption. A reindeer with a big, red nose becomes a hero. Stories of secularized saints who leave candy and toys for children remind us what fun generosity can be.

We hear again miracles of a one-day supply of oil burning for eight days and of a great star guiding kings to a baby in a manger.

The story of a little match girl teaches us compassion. O. Henry's tender short story "The Gift of the Magi" shows us loving self-sacrifice.

These are stories and legends that inspire us, teach us, and enlighten us. They come during the shortest, darkest days of the year, the time we most need light and joy.

Banned Book Week got by me one recent September. Otherwise I would have been amazed anew at our ability to be ridiculous about the printed word.

Examples: A school in Menifee, California, pulled *Merriam-Webster's Collegiate Dictionary* off the shelf because it includes the offensive term "oral sex."

A couple of school districts in California banned *Grimm's Fairy Tales* because Little Red Riding Hood's basket held a bottle of wine for her grandmother.

One of my favorite books is *The Annotated Mother Goose,* which includes hundreds of nursery rhymes, songs, and jingles. The book reveals the deeper meaning in many of them. Some, like "Eena, Meena, Mino, Mo," are just nonsense games. Some were to help children learn to count ("This little piggy . . ."). Others were satirical religious or political jibes, saying in playful verse things that were too dangerous to say outright.

"Bah, Bah black sheep" was likely a rhyming complaint by the common people about how much of their wool was claimed by the king and nobility. "Hey diddle diddle / the Cat and the Fiddle" supposedly referred to Queen Elizabeth and carryings on in the royal court. And

"Little Tommy Tucker / Sings for his supper" pokes fun at Cardinal Wolsey, who was greedy and so lazy he had bishops tie his shoes. O welladay. These rhymes evoke a linguistic nostalgia in me. I hardly ever hear someone say "welladay" anymore. A lovely, archaic word. Means "alas!" Akin to "Woe am I."

Which brings me circuitously back to Christmas. Alack, it was not always celebrated as a holy day.

In Boston in 1687, the Reverend Increase Mather preached that the early Christians did not believe that Christ was born December 25. Nay, he said, over the centuries Christians adopted the pagan Roman Saturnalia festival and layered it with religious meaning. Originally the celebration honored the Roman god Saturn with widespread intoxication, merrymaking, and singing naked in the streets. Some of the old hey nonny, nonny has hung on. The singing part became Christmas caroling, albeit dressed in warm scarves and muffs. We hardly ever see naked carolers these days, at least in Oklahoma, where December is cold.

The Puritans banned Christmas in Boston, and all of Massachusetts, from 1659 to 1681 because of its heathen origins. We're over that now. December is a month full of musicals and dances and plays and stories and dinners and parties and religious services. It is a month imbued with celebrations and symbols that stir our souls. We surround ourselves with glimmer and twinkling lights and we celebrate. We move mankind forward, out of the darkness, with good intentions and sometimes silliness.

It's a time for wishes. Here are some of mine. I wish I knew someone whose first name is Increase. And I wish someone would bring me a bottle of wine in a basket.

The Duchess and Her Chickens

As the duchess said to me . . .

Actually, she didn't *say* it to me, since we didn't converse. She *wrote* it to me, in her own hand, from Chatsworth House, one of England's great homes.

Actually, she was the dowager duchess at the time, and when she wrote me, she wasn't living at Chatsworth proper but at the Old Vicarage on the Chatsworth property, having turned over the estate to her son, the 12th Duke of Devonshire.

I hope I am not a name-dropper by habit, but if any of us do drop names, I say drop interesting ones. Deborah Cavendish née Mitford, the Dowager Duchess of Devonshire, is one of the most interesting women I can think of.

She was the youngest of the six Mitford sisters, an internationally famous family in the mid-twentieth century: Diana, proclaimed to be the most beautiful woman in England, who married the Fascist leader Sir Oswald Mosley and spent time in prison; Unity, infamous for her friendship with Hitler, who tried to commit suicide; Nancy, best-selling novelist of *Pursuit of Love* and *Love in a Cold Climate;* Jessica, a communist who became an American citizen and wrote *The American Way of Death;* and Pamela, more of a homebody happy with her beloved dogs. I admit to having a small library of books about the fascinating Mitford family.

Deborah, the most entrepreneurial of the sisters, married the man who became the Duke of Devonshire and so inherited responsibility for the great Chatsworth House. He became duke when his older brother, the eleventh duke, died unexpectedly. That older brother—stick with me on this chronology, because it's coming to an American point—married Kathleen Kennedy, sister of President John Kennedy. Five weeks after the wedding, the groom was killed in World War II, and four years later, the widowed bride was killed in a plane crash.

That family alliance with the Kennedys is how the duchess developed a kinship with America. She made a grateful discovery of American pantyhose when she attended Kennedy's inauguration that cold January day in 1961. She had a special fondness for Elvis Presley, so she visited Graceland and collected Presley memorabilia.

Her head for business is credited for saving Chatsworth from stately decline into a popular tourist attraction. She did it with hard work, imagination, and a head for business. The 35,000-acre estate included tourism, retail shops, and a working farm. The farm had chickens, which she had begun raising for pin money as a girl. She loved her chickens, and that is how we happened to correspond—about chickens and weather.

I have friends who live near Chatsworth: Vilna Kembery and the Reverend Ralph Urmson-Taylor. I so liked the duchess's book, *Counting My Chickens,* that I had the audacity to send her (via Vilna) my own book of essays, *Light and Variable.*

The dowager duchess wrote me a short, handwritten note, saying how interesting she found my stories about Oklahoma—"all unknown" to her. She said she particularly enjoyed my description of August in Oklahoma, a month that goes on for so long it seems to include September.

She wrote the note in January and ended with a comment about her own weather at the time. "Darkest time. No daylight till 8:30 A.M. and dark again at 3:30 P.M. Nevertheless, my hens are laying, so I have no complaint." She signed the note plainly, "Deborah Devonshire."

The dowager duchess died in 2014 at age ninety-four, the last of the famous Mitford sisters. People said it was the end of an era. The Reverend Urmson-Taylor sent me a clipping from the *Daily Telegraph* about her extraordinary funeral. The thousands of mourners included the Prince of Wales and the Duchess of Cornwall (Prince Charles and his second wife, Camilla, to us Americans) and Deborah's granddaughter, the model Stella Tennant.

Standing along the road of the funeral cortege were the six-hundred-plus employees of the Chatsworth estate. The funeral, the *Daily Telegraph* reported, reflected her life and interests and "her sense of mischief." There was high ceremony, yet her coffin was wicker and topped with flowers from the Chatsworth gardens—and chicken eggs from her beloved hens. The service in St. Peter's church included the traditional hymn "Holy! Holy! Holy!" and Elvis Presley's recording of "How Great Thou Art."

Royalty, chickens, and Elvis—what a way to leave the building.

Haiku—It's Me, Connie

When I came from a small Oklahoma town to attend the University of Tulsa, one of my first classes was an advanced speech class with John Hurdle. We started with Shakespeare's sonnets. And then he introduced us to a poetry form I had never heard of—Japanese haiku. I was enchanted.

This—oh, this!—was the big-city sophistication I had dreamed of.

Haiku is the shortest form of poetry, a total of seventeen syllables in three lines divided this way: five syllables, seven syllables, five syllables. As taught by Hurdle, each miniature poem captures a moment in time, makes a reference to nature, and alludes to a more profound idea.

I think of haiku as a visual art form as well—three short lines bobbing in white space on paper. In the gabble of the language around us, this is a feng shui moment. The beauty and meaning—without clutter—reminds me of Emily Dickinson.

Some of the greatest Japanese haiku poets wrote in the seventeenth and eighteenth centuries. They created tiny works of complexity disguised with simplicity, like an emperor in a peasant's cloak. Such as this by Tan Taigi (translated from the Japanese):

> Now in late autumn
> Look, on my old rubbish heap . . .
> Blue morning glory.

Tan Taigi is one of Japan's most famous haiku poets. He lived in the 1700s and was a monk, overly fond of socializing and saki. His death from a brain hemorrhage is attributed to his saki addiction, not unlike some Western authors felled by drugs or alcohol.

Haiku is known as a poetry of sensation. Many hundreds are written about the Japanese heat, like this witty poem from the poet Seibi:

> A hot day:
> With silent Zen masters
> Glaring at each other.

It is also a poetry of sensuality, illustrating an emotion or an epiphany when we suddenly see something anew. Maybe this is called a "haiku moment."

I thought of haiku only as collected in small, elegant books until I learned of haiku websites, haiku journals, and daily haiku available online. Poets of many nationalities write in the form. Jack Kerouac wrote haiku, and so did Amy Lowell. Who knew that a woman from Ada, Oklahoma, named Marlene Mountain is something of a rebel haiku poet? She writes a version called haibun.

Yet haiku is not for everyone. I've tried for years to explain it to my ex-husband, who always says, "I don't get it. It doesn't rhyme." Well, there is that. It is like jazz. You either get it or you don't. A lot of the world does get it. In 1964 when the Olympics were held in Tokyo, Japan Airlines (JAL) held a haiku poetry contest for children; it was broadcast over a U.S. radio station. In that first contest, 41,000 haikus were submitted.

Now the JAL Foundation holds an annual world children's haiku contest. One year, the topic was "impression of the wind." Here are two of the children's entries:

Autumn wind
Please blow softly
For the stray cat.

The breeze
Peeks at the book
I am reading.

If you are counting and notice that those aren't seventeen syllables, remember they are translations.

Americans have jumped into haiku with exuberance and often with typical American humor. In 1981 an urban myth circulated that the Japanese had replaced the impersonal Microsoft error messages with haiku—reminding us that the brief poems are often wistful and yearning.

Here is one of the haiku computer error messages:

First snow, then silence
This thousand dollar screen
Dies so beautifully.

I have found American haiku books on all subjects. In my church bookstore I found a little book titled *Episcopal Haiku*. I discovered a book of dog haiku and cat haiku in a book titled *Catku*.

Americans love contests, so naturally we have haiku contests, too. Nashville has a Hot Tomato haiku contest in which all entries must be tomato related. Portland's haiku contests are about wine or beer. Philadelphia's haiku contest was about the city's controversial trash collection fee. Pittsburgh had a haiku contest on the subject of the Group of 20 industrialized and developing nations meeting there.

Inspired by these, my colleagues and I at Tulsa's public radio station launched a haiku contest of our own. We prepared ourselves for an avalanche of entries from our clever audience. Sadly, our contest generated such a small response that I entered the contest myself. I did not win.

I didn't let that get me down. We must soldier on. As Angie Debo told me, "We must keep writing books. Even if nobody reads them, we must keep writing them." I understand that advice all too well. I am among the multitude of authors who have marched bravely to our own book readings attended by only two or three people, or worse yet, to book signings with no people at all. The village pillory couldn't be more painful than sitting in a bookstore behind a table of books to sell, staring with puppy eyes at every person coming through the door. That experience gives me post-traumatic stress, flashing back to my wallflower Friday night dances at Teen Town.

Luckily, we don't have to create art to enjoy it; we can just rub up against it. That's why arts in public schools are important. It is like being exposed to poison ivy; once you catch it, you are always susceptible. Every April, which is National Poetry Month, I catch the poetry bug again. I am amazed that an entire month is still devoted to celebrating poetry. In this day, with the fine arts staggering through society like Dickens's waifs, the art form could very easily be relegated to National Poetry Long Lunch.

Does anyone still read poetry? Is poetry a dinosaur looking for a tar pit?

Just as we might despair at our unlettered state of affairs, guess who came to poetry's aid? Oprah. That's right: Oprah Winfrey. One April issue of her *O* magazine featured young poets modeling spring fashion. Hard to get your head around that, isn't it?

David Orr wrote an article for the Sunday *New York Times Book Review* about the shotgun marriage of spring fashion and poetry in a popular magazine. He was deliciously unkind and funny, acidly describing the effusive coverage of works by Mary Oliver—"About whose poetry," he wrote, "one can only say that no animals appear to be harmed in the making of it."

I admire Oliver's work, particularly her poems "Wild Geese" and "The Journey." Certainly she's not as witty as Billy Collins, who writes poems with titles such as "Another Reason Why I Don't Keep a Gun in the House," but her poems go straight from my head to my heart.

This poet name-dropping suggests that I read poetry as often as I read my horoscope, and who would believe that? Well, maybe a Sagittarius, but nobody else.

I used to read poetry. We all did. As a little girl, one Christmas I asked for—and was given—a book of Longfellow poems. Remember "Song of Hiawatha"?

> By the shores of Gitche Gumee
> By the shining Big-Sea-Water,
> Stood the wigwam of Nokomis,
> Daughter of the Moon Nokomis.

If that is not word perfect, it is because I typed that from memory. Do kids still memorize and recite poetry in grade school? Do they submit their poems to little journals as I did in high school?

When I was a student in community college, a literature classmate was a retired, white-haired man. He was an oddity among us. Older adults were rare in college classes then. For one assignment, he stood in front of the class and read Vachel Lindsay's

> Booth led boldly with his big bass drum—
> (Are you washed in the blood of the lamb?)

To illustrate the rhythm and musical cadences of this poem, he did the Twist while reciting the poem. We were shocked at his uncool behavior. I've never forgotten it. Or the poem.

When I was attending the university, my friends—guys and girls alike—read Rod McKuen's books. A birthday gift from a boyfriend was Carl Sandburg's book of poetry *Honey and Salt*. We read poetry not for class but for entertainment and because we were young and romantic and had oh-so-sophisticated conversations over cheap beer.

Now I read more *about* poetry than poetry itself. Sometimes, though, poems jump out of books or magazine articles—jump out unexpectedly like a kid in a Halloween costume.

That's how I discovered Elizabeth Bishop. I was reading *The Love Letter*, a light little novel by Cathleen Schine, and there was Ms. Bishop's poem "Casabianca":

> Love's the boy stood on the burning deck
> Trying to recite "The boy stood on
> The burning deck." . . .

I love that poem. One Valentine's Day I sent it to my friends. Some of them said, "What does it mean?"

"I'm not sure I know," I said. "I understand it about as well as I understand love. I just like it."

Luckily, we don't have to understand poetry. We just have to love it. Or, as Mary Oliver writes in "Wild Geese,"

> You only have to let the soft animal of your body
> Love what it loves.

Still, of all poetry, the one form that returns to tug softly at my sleeve is haiku. Maybe because I associate it with being twenty-one, starting classes at a big-time university in a real city, and the future so big I couldn't see around it.

So I was pleased to discover the book *haiku mind* by Patricia Donegan. The flat-footed subtitle, *108 Poems to Cultivate Awareness and Open Your Heart,* does not do justice to the small book. One haiku is presented on a subject, such as pausing, compassion, transience, and sorrow. This is followed by a few paragraphs of elaboration and then a tiny biography of the poet. I began to read it at bedtime as a daily meditation, a way to slow down from the hurly-burly day and to shift gears toward sleep.

I went from reading haiku daily to writing one haiku of my own. It was my haiku diary of the summer, a brutal summer in Oklahoma of record heat and drought. Like Donegan's book, for each poem, I made a note of what I was trying to capture.

In early August, as the Muslim holiday began:

> under the same moon
> crescent Ramadan for you
> slice of light for me.

Week after week of no rain and hundred-degree days:

> crape myrtle blossoms
> fall in a purple carpet
> covering parched ground

Traditional Japanese haiku is filled with images of plums, peonies, chrysanthemums, moonlight, snow, and cherry blossoms. Since haiku is about seeing what is around us, my Oklahoma images are plain and homespun.

One summer night under a full moon, I sat outside in my backyard and listened to a concert of tree frogs, crickets, katydids, and grasshoppers. First came the bass, steady as a drumbeat. Then the altos, followed by the tenors. Hums and trills joined in. They formed a nocturnal jazz band, making new music to their own beat.

> deep in my backyard
> a quartet of summer frogs
> sing "hotcha hotcha."

A musician friend identified the tree frogs' two notes for me. Now I know that my garden sings to me in A and A-flat.

My literature classes in community college were taught by a dapper former journalist named J. Henry Hedley. He wore suits with vests, parted his gray hair sharply in the middle, and might have just stepped off a 1940s train from Chicago. We adored him. Sometimes he taught us with mystifying Socratic questions.

"What is the difference between poetry and verse?" he asked us one day.

We looked back at him with blank faces.

"Anyone can write verse," he explained. "Only a poet can write poetry."

That is the way I think about my haiku diaries. I write them with joy and well-deserved modesty. I do not presume to be writing diaries in haiku. What I am writing, playfully, is a diary in entries of seventeen syllables.

As for my university speech professor, Hurdle, who introduced me to haiku, he literally ran away with the circus. He left university teaching to manage the Ringling Bros. Circus Museum in Sarasota, Florida. See what adventures can befall you when you discover haiku?

Not Poems, but Verses

Here's a verse by me. It's autobiographical.

> I loved you for what you were.
> Or what I thought you were.
> Or what you thought you were.
> Boy, were we wrong.

> Now when I dream of you
> I know it's a sign
> That I'm coming down with something—
> A virus or a migraine.

And here's a verse I like:

> God is great, he won't hurt us
> Because he looks like Tony Curtis.

Guess who wrote that? Curtis himself.

Writing about Food

For ten or twelve years, I was a restaurant critic. I wrote a weekly newspaper restaurant review column titled Eating Out. Sounds like a dream job, and it was. Sometimes. But like any job, there were the other times. The times I had to eat out and write about food when I was sick. Or the time I reviewed all the food on the midway at the state fair and couldn't eat anything fried for three months. And the time I reviewed a pizza place and ate—for some reason I cannot fathom—a double garlic pizza with extra garlic oil. To this day, I cannot eat garlic. And the time I was at an upscale steak house and pointed out a mouse to the waiter. His response was surprising. He leapt into the air and stomped the mouse, then discreetly covered its little corpse with a napkin. And left it there.

I no longer write about food, but I am a devoted reader about food. I have a small collection of vintage, regional, and Native American cookbooks.

I have long admired the work of M. F. K. Fisher, who I believe is the all-time best writer about food. Writing about food, she said, is more than rice in the bowl, it's about nourishment of the heart. She wrote about food with the art of a sensual poet. "The soufflé," she once wrote, "sighed voluptuously at the first prick of the fork."

She lets us know what the food and wine looked like, tasted like, the Spanish hillside where she ate it, and the lover she was with when they ate the ripe tomatoes.

So no wonder I rushed to get the first full-length biography about M. F. K. Fisher when it appeared a few years ago. It is a big book, almost five hundred pages, titled *Poet of the Appetites: The Lives and Loves of M. F. K. Fisher,* by Joan Reardon.

I learned long ago to separate the artist from the art, so my heroine did not fall from the pedestal when I read about the self-centered life she often lived. I was amazed that she could write so well while going through patches of a hard life, but I was not disheartened to learn that she was a complex person, like the rest of us.

She embellished her own history. She was no model mother, for sure. One daughter was born out of wedlock, and Fisher never, ever revealed to anyone—not even on her deathbed and not even to the daughter—the identity of the father.

The biography made me want to read less about her and more of the elegant food books she wrote: *Serve It Forth, Consider the Oyster, The Gastronomical Me,* and so many more.

....

And 180 degrees from the artistic work of Fisher comes a delightful food book with a very long title, *Being Dead Is No Excuse: The Official Southern Ladies Guide to Hosting the Perfect Funeral.* I thought this was going to be a cutie-pie, southern belle book, and it sort of is, but it is laugh-out-loud funny. The two authors, Gayden Metcalfe and Charlotte Hays, live in a small southern town in the Mississippi delta. They tell us that the three great social events in their town are baptisms, weddings, and funerals. The greatest of these are funerals and the receptions that follow. This is the backbone of the Mississippi delta society. "We're living in the past," they write. "It makes life more charming." Polishing silver, they say, is a southern lady's version of grief therapy.

Everything from the funeral food to the music in their community is determined by religion. When someone dies, the authors say, you automatically take a plate of stuffed eggs and a bottle of wine. Unless it's a Methodist funeral, then you just take the eggs. Methodist cuisine, we read, is a covered dish casserole.

Baptists put "little bitty marshmallows" on congealed salads; Presbyterians are more fun; Episcopalians in the South are snootier and spurn recipes that hinge on either a Duncan Hines cake mix or a can of Campbell's soup.

And although the liveliest hymn at an Episcopal funeral is "Oh, God, Our Help in Ages Past," Episcopal receptions are more fun because they include what the authors call "restorative cocktails." Often, so many restorative cocktails are served that the bereaved get "knee-walking drunk."

As an Episcopalian myself, I adore Episcopalian jokes. Episcopal jokes make fun of how fussy we are and how formal and acrobatic we are in worship—up, down, bow, kneel, cross yourself. Episcopal jokes often begin, "You know you're an Episcopalian if . . ." If, for example, you have ever had a parish committee meeting in a bar or if you genuflect to the movie screen automatically before taking your seat.

According to Metcalfe and Hays, nobody in the world eats better than the bereaved southerner. An absolute staple at a funeral reception is tomato aspic. So is pimiento cheese. Their book features several recipes for pimiento cheese because it is "the paste that holds the South together." Here's a quote from the book: "Nothing whispers sympathy quite like a frozen-pea casserole with canned bean sprouts and mushroom soup."

This book is full of southern recipes, most of them tacky, tasty, funny, or all of the above. The recipe for Vodka Cake begins this way: "We're embarrassed to death to tell you what's in this cake . . . [because] how many of the world's great chefs use Jell-O pudding?"

It is such a funny book, even the recipes are funny and call for cakes cut into "ladylike pieces." When I give book talks promoting my own books, I often talk about this book, even holding it up and reading out the title and authors. Make that past tense. I did hold up the book. All too often, the audience rushed up afterward for purchases and said, "Oh, no, not yours. We want the funny funeral book."

I say nothing. I simply smile a polite, Episcopalian smile. Then I go home and have a restorative cocktail.

. . . .

"Take two fresh coconuts . . ."

So begins one of my favorite recipes in the enchanting vintage cookbook *Spécialités de la Maison.*

You read that right. Cookbook. But oh so much more than a cookbook. It is also history, biography, culture, and recipes, written with as much charm as any novel I've come across.

A slender volume—I've always wanted to use that phrase—it was originally published in 1940. Oh, happy days, it has been reissued. It features recipes from Hollywood stars, Broadway celebrities, artists, and socialites of the day: Noël Coward, Tallulah Bankhead, Eleanor Roosevelt, Mary Pickford, Christian Dior, Charlie Chaplin, Fanny Brice, Pearl Buck, Vivien Leigh, and many more, some of whom are obscure now or simply unknown to me. Such is celebrity.

These are the dishes the celebrities cooked at home for their friends and families. They wrote the recipes in first person, making the book even more intimate.

Here is the history of the book. In the summer of 1940, as France began to fall under German's Vichy government, philanthropist Anne Morgan rallied her glamorous friends to raise funds for French evacuee relief centers. Morgan, then in her sixties, was the daughter of America's financier J. P. Morgan. The war-relief organization she formed was the American Friends of France and one fund-raising project was this book of recipes.

The crème de la crème of society sent their recipes to her. They were people of style, wit, and entertainment, and that is the way they wrote their recipes. "Spread each side of sandwich with just a suspicion of mayonnaise," wrote a socialite from New York. Musician Deems Taylor added these directions to his recipe for Quick Cheese Soufflé: "Eat very hot and very quickly, as it turns into morocco leather in about six minutes."

It was another time, when food was cooked in bacon grease or lard. Back then, they used a lot of double boilers, gelatin, and molds. Sardines were a popular ingredient, too, as in Cheese and Sardine Mousse, which is pressed into a mold and served with thin, hot toast.

It was another culture, too. Who among us cannot envy the leisurely start to Mrs. Douglas Ives's recipe for Bananas Flambé Kirsch: "When you sit down to luncheon, have cook put bananas in a copper saucepan in which there is butter."

What fun to think of Katharine Hepburn making Chicken Burgundy Style and Madame Igor Stravinsky cooking up a pot of Le Petit Borsch. Mrs. Stravinsky, we read in the biographical notes, had been the maestro's lover for two decades. They were married in 1940, after the death of his first wife.

The thumbnail biographies at the end of the book are as fascinating as the recipes. We meet Lucius Beebe, gourmand and author of thirty books, who was expelled from both Yale and Harvard for bad behavior. In one prank, he chartered a plane and toilet-papered J. P. Morgan's yacht.

Mrs. Charles Boyer submitted her recipe for Mulligatawny Soup. The ingredients are vague—"a few sliced onions, a little flour, a little curry powder" added to half of a fried apple and bouillon. The Boyers were married forty-four years, and when she died, he committed suicide two days later.

Even the original ads at the very, very end of the book are delightful. The St. Regis hotel describes itself as a sophisticated hotel and boasts of "a tickless clock in every room."

In the 1920s, the famed Round Table of literati such as Dorothy Parker and Robert Benchley gathered regularly at the Algonquin hotel in New York to drink lunch and match wits. When HarperCollins reprinted *Spécialités* in 2010, the Algonquin offered a special vintage menu from the book. The twenty-nine-dollar, three-course meal included Norma Shearer's Lentil Soup, Mrs. Vincent Astor's Eros Steak and for dessert, Helen Hayes's pancakes (at the time, spelled as two words—"pan cakes").

I like to read about cooking more than I like to cook. I have a little library of specialized recipe books reflective of geography and ethnicity, such as Amish country, New Orleans, and Native American tribes. My collection includes historical recipe books of movie stars, U.S. presidents and first ladies, and literary figures. What fun to read about famous people in such an intimate way. "Tell me what you eat, tell me what you drink, and I'll tell you where you're from." Is that a southern maxim or did I make it up?

I want to host a vintage meal with selections from *Spécialités de la Maison*. Perhaps I'll begin with Cecil Beaton's Tea Punch, include the Countess di Zoppola's Lobster Romance, and perhaps add Mrs. Samuel Goldwyn's Golden Gate Salad. It will definitely end with actress Constance Collier's Coffee Pie, because I like the name. And because it involves a double boiler.

Bon appétit and *toujours gai.*

Dancers—En Pointe *and* En Garde!

Good heavens, I have become Miss Marple. You know, the Agatha Christie character who solved crimes because everybody reminded her of somebody else.

Except the similarities I recognize are—rather twisted.

One evening I watched a TV documentary about salmon fighting their way upstream to spawn. Those who succeeded—the survivors—arrived physically transformed. They were tough, and they looked it with their torn fins, missing scales, and lower jaw protruding aggressively. They had sharp teeth like stilettos.

This was followed by a documentary on ballerinas. Not young, dewy, and aspiring dancers but tough old gals who had fought their way to the top of their art. Some of them even looked like salmon survivors.

Ballerinas can be a competitive and envious lot. Here's a classic ballet joke: How many dancers does it take to become a ballerina? One hundred: one to be center stage doing thirty-six pirouettes and ninety-nine to stand in the wings saying, "I can do that."

A dancer told me about performing with the Ruth Page ballet company when a ballerina—during a performance—fell and concussed herself. As she was being carted off on a stretcher, two other dancers fought to tear the headpiece off her head. Whoever got the sparkly headpiece got to finish the performance.

Page was no marshmallow, and although she was wealthy, she was infamously frugal. During a rehearsal, a violinist had a heart attack and collapsed over his music stand.

"Keep dancing. Keep dancing," Page shouted to the dancers.

"Miss Page," the ballet master said. "We can't dance with a corpse in the orchestra pit."

"Oh, all right," she replied, irritated. "Take a break. Fifteen minutes."

So with my own Miss Marple version of Everything Reminds Me of Something Else, I watched a starling working to get a bug out of the grass. A glossy black bird with bright yellow legs on the verdant green grass. I like starlings. I like how they strut like the vain Pooh-Bah from Gilbert and Sullivan. I like how sunlight catches a sheen on their feathers, black and multicolored as an oil spill. And I like how focused this one little starling was.

Zoom out. Here's the bigger picture. I was watching the starling from my car, sitting at a stoplight. The bird was on a very narrow strip of grass in front of a QuikTrip. On both sides of him were wide expanses of cement with cars and trucks zooming by, people coming and going. He was oblivious to it all. He was focused: get the bug out of the grass.

Then I thought, Margaret Thatcher.

I don't know enough about British government to have an opinion of Margaret Thatcher's politics. What I like is her focus. She seemed driven by her convictions of what she believed was good for her nation and the people. Not like too many of today's politicians, pandering to public opinion for reelection and lacking genuine convictions.

At Thatcher's state funeral, people lined the streets. Some threw flowers. Some hurled abuses. The funeral procession moved on through it all. The hearse, too, was focused on a goal.

Like a ballerina or a salmon. Like a starling getting a bug out of the grass. Here's the raw animal philosophy of success: Focus. Focus.

Christmas Was a Nutcracker

January was one of my favorite months when I was manager of a ballet company. *The Nutcracker* was finally over for the year. That meant the months of rehearsals, the grueling winter tour across the country, and the home theater run were all ended. The dancers were gone on break, and all of us, dancers and staff alike, could begin trying to recover from the ailments brought on by winter, close quarters, extended bus travel, stress, exhaustion, sinus infections, stomach flu, tendonitis, and hurt feelings. We had a few days off to heal our bodies. We could get serious about nursing backstage grudges.

With the *Nutcracker* tour over, that meant I wouldn't be getting emergency phone calls from the company manager at the airport saying, "You know the dancer with diarrhea? The one the doctor gave suppositories to? Well, she took them. But there's a problem. She didn't know she wasn't supposed to swallow them. The plane is boarding; what should I do?"

I wouldn't be standing at the box office in Guthrie, Oklahoma, ten minutes to curtain time with a local volunteer stagehand staggering into the crowded lobby dripping with blood. Mercifully they were superficial wounds, but there were a lot of them. He was a high school student intrigued with the dry ice used to make the fog for the "Forest of Christmas" scene. He put a piece of it into a soft drink bottle, capped it, and shook it to see what would happen. It explodes, is what happens.

With the home production run of *Nutcracker* over, that meant the three hundred children in the casts had gone home. I wouldn't be getting calls from parents saying, "My son is a toy soldier and I asked him what he learned at rehearsal last night and he said that he learned that a royal flush beats a full house." No more dress rehearsals with mice screaming in fear of the Seven-Headed Mouse King or refusing to ride on the giant cheese. No more baby angels falling over their hoop skirts and crying, no more little rabbits with broken arms in a cast, not a single bunny tiptoeing across the stage during the Sugarplum Fairy's solo. No more Sugarplum's being cautioned about appropriate language when correcting naughty bunnies.

Throughout the ballet season, backstage drama rivals the wonders of the performances. I worked for a company in the Ballet Russe tradition, and I met great artists who came to set ballets, choreograph, coach, observe, perform, or be honored: Alexandra Danilova, Freddie Franklin, Rosella Hightower, Marjorie Tallchief, Arthur Mitchell, Yvonne Chouteau, Fernando Bujones, and others. I found the dancers to be lively storytellers who love to cook, eat, drink, laugh, and talk. They love to dish about other dancers, and they love to tell funny stories—the more dramatic the better.

The Ballet Russe was a mix of nationalities and languages. In her Russian accent, Madame Danilova told a dinner story about meeting the young child of two dancers.

"I said to the child, 'Do you speak Russian?' No answer. So I said, 'Do you speak French?' Again no answer. Then I said, 'Do you speak English?' And still no answer. I said to the parents, 'What language does this child speak?'"

"'None, Madame Danilova,' they said. 'He's only two.'"

She laughed until her famous false eyelashes almost came off.

One season, we had a new receptionist in the office. The first phone call of her first day went like this:

"Good morning, this is Tulsa Ballet Theatre."

"Hello, this is Ludmila Dokoudovsky. I'm calling for Anthony Zelinsky and Nina Nijinska. We want to speak to Roman Jasinski about *Les Biches*."

"Oh, whoa," the receptionist exclaimed. "You're going to have to spell some of that."

We frequently did mixed repertoire productions, the old Ballet Russe bread-and- butter evenings. These were surefire crowd pleasers and particularly good for people new to the ballet. The

classic pattern was to open with a white ballet, such as *Swan Lake,*
Act 2, premier a ballet in the middle, and end with a lively closer,
often *Gaîté Parisienne,* with high-kicking cancan girls. That was the
pattern the evening we debuted *Billy the Kid.* Since it was new, *Billy*
was the most promoted, highly hyped ballet. At the first intermission
a young woman in the mezzanine turned to her date.

"Well," she said, "how did you like it?"

"Okay, I guess," he said. "But I don't get it. Which one was Pat
Garrett?"

"No, no," she said. "That was *Swan Lake. Billy the Kid* is coming up."

"Well, hell," he replied.

That's the way it is sometimes with ballet in Oklahoma.

Miss Larkin

It seems fitting to me that Moscelyne Larkin died at 11:30 at night in
late April. Eleven-thirty would be about the time dancers are leaving
the theater after a performance. Late April is about the time the ballet
season is over and dancers are off for the summer.

Larkin was a consummate ballerina, artistic director, and ballet
teacher, so 11:30 at night in late April seems the right time to close a
life in ballet.

I worked closely with her and her husband, the late Roman
Jasinski, for the fifteen years I was general manager at Tulsa Ballet
Theatre. We seemed to work round the clock. We traveled together,
toured together, had dinner, parties, and galas together. It was one of
the most fascinating times of my life.

She is renowned for being one of Oklahoma's famed Indian ballerinas, for performing with the Ballet Russe, for operating the Tulsa
School of Ballet (where she taught little girls to dance "with bluebirds
in their fingertips"), and for cofounding Tulsa Ballet Theatre, where
she and Jasinski spun straw into gold. They were experts at doing a
great deal with nothing. At the finale of *Coppélia,* the dancers carrying a huge, golden papier-mâché bell across stage had to be careful
to keep the bell's side with a huge hole in it upstage and out of view
of the audience. A national review of the early company referred
to the "corn-fed corps de ballet," a phrase that wounded the local
dancers for decades.

In the early days of Tulsa Ballet Theatre, she helped sew the costumes and paint scenery. For many years, the costume department
was in her garage. She cooked the seamstresses' lunch every day,
then went to the studio to teach class and conduct rehearsals.

Moscelyne Larkin in *Swan Lake* *(courtesy of Roman Larkin Jasinski)*

In her performing days, the Ballet Russe tours were more grueling than glamorous. They often danced in wretched conditions, so she was sourly amused at contemporary dancers' demands for specially built dance floors. She said that dancers of her era walked the stage before a performance to learn where the holes and nails were so they could dance around them.

She had danced all of her life, from the powwows with her Shawnee-Peoria father to dance classes with her Russian mother, Eva Matlogova. Larkin had retired from dancing when I knew her, so mostly I saw her behind the scenes and in the studio, where the hard, gritty, sweaty work is done to make the ballet productions look beautiful and effervescent. She worked hard, then she played. She loved to watch *Gunsmoke* on TV and go to the beach in the summer. When she did perform—speaking to an audience or a class—she commanded attention like a force of nature.

She was petite and always immaculately dressed, and she had the greatest sense of joy of anyone I've ever known. On our way to a ballet conference in Laguna Beach, California, our rental car broke down. She and I sat on a curb for almost two hours waiting for a replacement. She considered that, and every hardship, a great adventure. At another conference in Kentucky, after a long and tiring day of meetings, she jitterbugged half the night with Alun Jones, the artistic director of Louisville Ballet, while I yawned and longed to go back to the hotel.

One spring, the Jasinskis' home was on a garden tour. They didn't have much time for gardening, so the day before, they rushed out and bought flowers and plants for their garden. When garden tour visitors asked them the names of the plants, Larkin had no idea, so she would say, "I don't know what it's called in English, but the Russian name is . . ." and she made up something. Everybody was happy—her, too. She had a creative solution to filling out the empty spots in her garden for the tour; she stationed costumed dancers standing in classical ballet poses.

She was extraordinarily beautiful and charismatic. Her radiant smile could light up a city. And did. No wonder in her performance at London's Covent Garden Theater after World War II the English press said, "She is the first ray of sunshine this war-torn nation has seen."

Yet in her demands for precision she could be terrifying to young dancers. At dress rehearsal she sat in the middle of the empty theatre making corrections with a microphone. At one rehearsal, she yelled out to the corps of about eighteen girls, "Will the *stupid* girl get in line!" Every girl on stage took a step forward.

Larkin's mentor was the great Russian *prima ballerina assoluta* Danilova, equally tiny, charismatic, and fierce. Larkin was called Miss Larkin; Danilova was called Madame Danilova. In her lovely memoir, *Choura,* Danilova wrote, "In Russia we were taught never to touch our knee on the floor when taking a bow unless there was royalty in the house. We were to kneel only to royalty and God. But at my farewell performance, I spread the roses that had been sent me on the stage in front of me, and then I went down on my knee—in gratitude to the audiences who had given me my career."

At 11:30 at night in late April, Larkin made her farewell, not on stage but in a nursing home while suffering from Alzheimer's. In Tulsa, in Oklahoma, and in the ballet world, the curtain came down. Quietly.

Brava, Miss Larkin. Brava.

YIKES! Vampires!

Whew. At the last moment, I have yanked myself from the jaws of cultural embarrassment.

"From the jaws." That's a bad pun you will soon understand.

Until just recently, the current phenomenon of vampiremania, a word I just invented, passed me by. Vampire books, TV series, films—I knew nothing of them. I wasn't interested.

Or didn't think I was until I saw an interview with Anne Rice, queen of the vampire cult, who said that all of us know real-life vampires. They are people who try to drain us of our lives, she said. They suck us dry of our money, our time, our energy.

That was a creepy revelation. I know several people like that.

But what about fictional vampires? What is it about vampires that fascinates us? The thrill of being scared? The excitement of brushing against danger, like children running to touch a haunted house? Is it the titillation of dancing with fear or evil or the supernatural or death? Whatever it is, it has been around a long time.

Dracula, the most famous vampire, was introduced in 1897 by Irish author Bram Stoker. In that book, Dracula cannot enter a house unless he has been invited. So the victims bring their fate upon themselves. From the earliest time, much vampire literature has had an erotic edge to it. One person loses herself (or himself) entirely. She even, dare we say it, surrenders to another?

Bela Lugosi may be the most memorable movie Dracula, but current TV and movie vampires are steamy, romantic heroes. Usually they are portrayed as handsome, sensual, impeccably dressed, wealthy, and often conflicted by both lust and conscience.

Still, Dracula was not the first vampire in literature. The concept appeared in the 1700s. Then in 1819 came a vampire book inspired by the life of Lord Byron. And in 1872 there was a book about a lesbian vampire named Carmilla. Some say that the vampire literature of the Victorian era is a veiled reference to disease, blood, and death, especially from tuberculosis and syphilis, which were rampant at that time.

Now, the vampire genre has exploded with young adult fiction. A surprising number of vampire book authors are Oklahomans or have set their books in Oklahoma. That's what lured me into the genre.

I was standing in line at a neighborhood bookstore when I over-heard a teen girl talking on her cell phone to a friend about a book about a vampire school remarkably like a private school in midtown Tulsa. "No kidding," she told her friend, "you can recognize places in Utica Square." (Utica Square is an upscale shopping center in midtown Tulsa.)

Surely she didn't mean the books by Richelle Mead about a vampire academy—that is in Montana. I bought one of them, but it was so ghoulish I could not finish it. Neither was she talking about a vampire series by Tulsan Michele Bardsley, set in a town called Broken Heart, Oklahoma. Isn't that a perfect name for the home of a vampire? Nor was she discussing the series by Stephenie Meyer, the Mormon mother of three whose books about a vampire boyfriend have sold more than 25 million copies and have been released as the movie *Twilight*.

No, she was talking about Tulsa mother-daughter authors P. C. Cast and Kristin Cast. Their lusty vampire series for young adults begins in Broken Arrow and moves to Tulsa, where the vampire fin-ishing school has purchased—are you ready?—Cascia Hall, a private school located near Utica Square in midtown Tulsa.

The Cast books are the House of Night series, which I like a lot and not just because I like the authors. P. C. is a former high school teacher who knows something about Oklahoma, Indians, cats, and teenagers. Kristin was not much older than a teenager herself when they began writing the series. I asked P. C. if her characters spoke with an Oklahoma accent.

"Depends on which character is speaking," she said. "Like real people, some speak with more of an accent than others." And the character with the most pronounced Oklahoma accent?

"Stevie Rae Johnson from Henryetta," she said.

I certainly am not alone in liking the Cast books. Last time I checked, the series had sold 12 million copies in forty countries. That is equivalent to the entire population of New York or Paris or, closer to home, about 122 sold-out University of Oklahoma football stadiums. The series is so financially successful, for a while Cast bought homes, ranches, island vacation places, and jets like collect-ing charms on a bracelet. She left schoolteaching far behind and became a glamorous redhead in Jimmy Choo shoes. Then she left the state and moved to Oregon. There the vampire writer—or, rather, the writer about vampires—became a vegan. I love that twist.

Dedicated vampire aficionados may remember the 1979 German children's book titled *The Little Vampire*. Author Angela Sommer-

Bodenburg said her child vampire wasn't a monster at all but an affectionate little vampire with fears and foibles of his own.

About the same time in the United States, Deborah and James Howe introduced their Bunnicula series of children's books. The series features a vampire bunny that sucks the juice out of vegetables—maybe.

Since the current vampire phenomenon is most popular in America and since our nation is notorious for the way we love our pets, I wondered if anyone had combined the two passions. Sure enough, for $8.99 you can buy a ten-inch-high, talking vampire dog toy. Squeeze it and it says, "I've come to suck your blood."

Books for Boys

I could see the economic writing on the wall. More literally, I could see it in the *Wall Street Journal* when I read that the very wealthy in New York were starting to pinch pennies.

How? They were buying smaller yachts. Not buying much jewelry over twenty thousand dollars. Getting Botox injections instead of full face-lifts. And looking for less expensive nannies.

Ah, yes, we're all tightening our belts. It's certainly going to be leaner around my house this holiday season.

Even before I made this decision, I was thinking about gifts for children. Like an elderly, maiden aunt from a bygone era, I thought, books! Books are good gifts for children. Fosters literacy. Encourages reading. Supports the book business.

But this noble thought is complicated by the fact that the main children in my life are boys, Nicholas and Harry. And worse, they are boys who are not as interested in reading as they are in say, Legos, baseball, football, golf, lacrosse, and computer games.

I immediately eliminated as a gift any children's book on my shelves, especially *The Book of Virtues: A Treasury of Great Moral Stories,* edited by William J. Bennett. This is a collection of classic poems, fables, stories, and nonfiction pieces to "help children under-stand and develop character." That is a phrase from the book jacket. This is exactly what children need, and it is exactly what the boys in my life don't want. They would have to be tricked or bribed into reading things to instruct them in responsibility, courage, compas-sion, or loyalty. The boys in my life are good at throwing footballs, baseballs, basketballs, and, I have not one tiny doubt, a hefty book titled *The Book of Virtues.*

To heighten my concern, I've been reading about how the educa-tion system is going in the famous handbasket direction. This puts even more pressure on us adults when selecting educational books and toys.

I came across a book published in 1958 titled *One Hundred and One Famous Poems—With a Prose Supplement,* and at the back of this book were instructions for parents about choosing books for children. The rules were written by an author of books for boys.

Who would have thought that 1958 was antiquity? Here are a few of the rules for choosing wholesome books for children:

"Does this book lay stress on villainy, deception or treachery?

"Are all the incidents wholesome, probable, and true to life?

"Does it show young people contemptuous toward their elders and successfully opposing them?

"Do the young characters in the books show respect for teachers and others in authority?"

With these guidelines, Nicholas and Harry wouldn't touch any of the wholesome books recommended. Luckily a trip to the nearest bookstore shows me that help has arrived. Something new has appeared since I was last in the children's section picking out Nancy Drew books and *The Secret Garden, The 500 Hats of Bartholomew Cubbins,* and *Goodnight Moon.*

The something new (to me, at least) is a popular genre of books written especially for boys and based on the "yuck factor." I was so intrigued, I bought some and read them myself. Definitely yucky.

The most highly recommended in the article was the Wicked History series. None was available at my local bookstores. They are "library bindings," whatever that is—for schools, I guess—and cost thirty dollars each. But two bookstores offered to order them for me. They are written for middle schoolers, and subjects include Vlad the Impaler and "Bloody Mary" Tudor. Blood and gore flow in these books.

The books I did read, for slightly younger audiences (I would say fourth and sixth graders) include

- From the popular Captain Underpants series, *Captain Underpants and the Attack of the Talking Toilets,* second in the series by Dav Pilkey, a Scholastic book
- The equally popular *The Day My Butt Went Psycho! Based on a True Story,* by Andy Griffiths, also a Scholastic book
- By the same best-selling author, *Just Disgusting,* about a kid who is on a quest to gross out everyone around him (the blurb on the book says, "You'll laugh so hard, you'll lose your lunch")
- *101 Ways to Bug Your Parents,* by Lee Wardlaw, winner of several awards including readers' choice in five states including Oklahoma and Best Children's Book of the Year (Wardlaw also wrote *101 Ways to Bug Your Teacher*)
- And a favorite of the young boys in my life, *Oh Yuck! The Encyclopedia of Everything Nasty* by Joy Masoff, which

lists yucky things alphabetically from acne and ants to vomit and worms

What Nicholas and Harry really want—and about the only thing they do want—is another Lego set. They are obsessed with Lego sets, those miniscule building bricks and figures. Until a recent marketing campaign, not many little girls played with Lego materials, but boys are crazy for them. I don't know how they do it. They can't always get their shoelaces tied or buttons pushed through buttonholes, but they can assemble tiny, complex Lego bricks.

So I did some research to see if Lego products are wholesome, respectful of teachers, and adverse to villainy and treachery. That little piece of research sent me into an alternate universe; that's how big the Lego phenomenon is.

The first little Lego wooden toys were built in 1932 in Denmark by a master carpenter. Today, the company is owned by his grandson. The play materials are so popular, children around the world spend five billion hours a year playing with them. Seven Lego sets are sold every second. So many Lego minifigures have been produced—four billion—it's the biggest population group on earth.

There are Lego family parks in Denmark, England, Germany, California, and Kansas. There are Lego clubs, leagues, and tournaments. But Lego play materials are not just for children. An army of adult fans are active out there with websites and blogs and events. In fact, the Lego company tells us, the bricks are not to be considered toys; they are educational and considered playful learning. Lego websites especially for educators exist.

A mathematics professor using a computer figured out there are 915 million ways to combine six little Lego bricks. Good heavens. This makes our old Tinkertoys and Lincoln Logs sound like games from the Stone Age.

What Nicholas and Harry want most of all is the newest Lego set that won't be out for months. How do they even know about it? They subscribe to the Lego newsletter. I guess that counts as reading.

Where Are You, Virgil Cole?

When a writer dies, we grieve twice. Once for the writer and again for the characters who die with him.

I'm sorry that Robert B. Parker has died. I'm such a fan of his Spenser for Hire books with the smarty-pants private eye and his cooler-than-ice sidekick Hawk.

My deeper grief is that there will be no more Westerns from Parker. He had just started the series featuring Virgil Cole and his partner Everett Hitch, two guns for hire, but honorable guns for hire.

He wrote only four books in the series: *Appaloosa, Resolution, Brimstone,* and *Blue-Eyed Devil.* These four modern classics are the best Westerns I've read since Larry McMurtry's *Lonesome Dove.*

What is it about Westerns and the Western hero that have such allure? They're fictional, we know that. Was anyone ever that brave and strong and good? The lone Western hero intrigues us with his nomadic lifestyle and slightly mysterious past. But in real life, would we want to spend much time with a strong, silent type? A man who doesn't talk much? Communicates best with his fists and his gun?

Any woman who has had a husband sick with a cold longs for a John Wayne. Longs for a man who says, "Put the boot back on me. Lace it up tight. Get me back on my horse." Not a man who wants more than anything to have a little bell to ring so you can bring him more soup and NyQuil.

Probably the Western hero is more idealized than fictional. He is someone who protects the weak and stands up for what's right against all odds. He is someone who knows instinctively what is right and what is wrong.

In Westerns, the land itself is also a character. The great, beautiful, untamed land facing the namby-pamby civilization creeping forward to tie us down. In Westerns, nobody pampers the lawn like a newborn kitten. In Westerns, nobody has a lawn. What they have is barbed wire and prairie.

The railroads and the new towns in Westerns remind us that change is always nipping at our ankles like an annoying little dog we'd like to kick if we weren't so good and kind. Westerns confront change with all of its complications and the uncertainties of the future. Don't give me Blu-ray and apps and digital doo-dads. Give me land, lots of land under the starry skies. But also give me a cheap Chinese laundry on the corner in every Western town.

Give me Westerns with a clear code of honor, a quick sense of justice, people I can identify as good or bad. If there's a villain, give me Victor Jory or Gene Hackman—a bad guy I can spot a mile away. Don't give me the bucket-butt neighbor who is a contractor and says he'll build a room on my house but cheats me out of thirty thousand dollars and leaves town. (Hypothetically speaking, of course. Nobody like that ever appears in my own life.) If I do get a cheating contractor, please give me Clint Eastwood or Virgil Cole to go get him.

Cole is what's described in Western language as the kind of guy you want to ride the river with. That means he can take care of himself, and if worse comes to worse, he can take care of you, too.

So what if the Westerns are fiction? So what if I've never been able to ride a horse without falling off? So what if I'm allergic to Texas cedar, goldenrod, and everything else that blows on the west wind? The Western heroes are my ideals.

Oh, where are you, Virgil Cole, when I love you so?

. . . .

At some point, little children are keen to distinguish between what is real and what is make-believe. It's important for them to know the difference. I'm not sure we ever lose that interest. For adults, it's the blurring of history and legend.

That blurring and balance is much of the focus of the fine book by Glenn Frankel titled *The Searchers: The Making of an American Legend*. That title refers to the 1956 movie directed by John Ford and starring John Wayne.

John Wayne worked long and hard to create the persona of John Wayne. He was influenced by the Western actor Harry Carey but also by the great stuntman Yakima Canutt. When I interviewed Canutt for a magazine article I wrote about him, I asked him if it was true that Wayne imitated his rolling walk and drawling talk. Yes, he told me, it was true. "One day on a movie set," Canutt said, "I finally turned around and asked him, 'Why the hell are you following me around?'" When he told me that story, he was speaking in the same slow cadence of Wayne's speech. Except Canutt was the original.

I bought the Frankel book to read about the movie, which got a tepid reception when it was released. Now *The Searchers* is considered one of the great movies of all time and perhaps *the* greatest Western movie. The first half of Frankel's book is about the history that inspired it, and that (what is real) became more fascinating to me than what was legend (the novel and the movie).

Here's the history. Before Texas was part of the United States, it was part of Mexico. It was also the homeland of several Native American tribes, notably the Comanches and Kiowas, who knew nothing about landownership. What the tribes knew was that this was their ancestral hunting ground and the white settlers trickling in were destroying their lives' balance. The Indians so fiercely defended their hunting grounds, the Mexican authorities encouraged even more white settlement as a buffer between them and the tribes. Indian raids and white retaliation escalated into the Texas-Comanche War, which lasted for decades. Both sides were equally brutal. Indians scalped and disemboweled, whites beheaded and stuck Indian heads on posts.

One extended family of settlers was named Parker, a poor, crude, fanatically religious clan. One family of this clan was the victim of a Comanche raid in 1836; during that raid, a nine-year-old girl named Cynthia Ann was captured.

Taking captives was a common practice among some of the Great Plains tribes. Sometimes the captives were adopted into the tribe, sometimes they became wives or slaves, and sometimes they were bartered or sold. Cynthia Ann grew up to become a wife of the Comanche warrior who captured her, and she bore him three children. One legend says she was his favorite wife, a love match, but more likely, she was a chore wife and spent her days in hard work, especially cleaning and curing buffalo hides.

Unbeknownst to her, one of her uncles spent seven years searching for her before he gave up. And then—twenty-four years later—white soldiers attacked her camp and rekidnapped her. They reunited her with her family.

Another disaster for her. She had become Comanche and spent the rest of her life miserable among a white society she didn't know, longing for her two sons left behind. The white society didn't want her either, because she represented "a fate worse than death." She was a white woman who had known—in the biblical sense—a dark-skinned man. She was, therefore, unclean. The infant daughter captured with her died as a child. Cynthia Ann died lonely, yearning for her sons.

Meanwhile, the Comanches were conquered, not in war but by the American government's sanctioning the slaughter of their one source of food and shelter. With the approval of Generals Sherman and Sheridan, buffalo hunters slaughtered four million buffalo.

Cynthia Ann Parker's eldest son spent years searching for her. His name was Quanah, and in an extraordinary gesture he took her name. In a time when most Native Americans had one name, he declared himself to be Quanah Parker. He was tall and handsome with gray eyes. He wasn't the tribe's primary candidate for leadership, because he was half white, but he was such a self-promoter and diplomat he became known as the last great chief of the Comanches. Much of his story takes place in Oklahoma. I got out my state atlas to follow it. Quanah Parker was among the Indian captives at Fort Sill, then built his grand house, called the Twelve Star House—so no general would ever outrank him—in Cache, Oklahoma.

Flash forward. In 1954 Alan LeMay wrote a western novel titled *The Searchers* based on the historical story of Cynthia Ann Parker. Then came the movie, filmed not in Texas and Oklahoma, where it happened, but in Ford's favorite Monument Valley setting.

In the movie, John Wayne portrays his darkest character, a hard man driven by hatred, vengeance, and his own sense of right. It becomes clear that when he finally does rescue his niece—the character based on Cynthia Ann—he intends to kill her because she is unclean. And yet there is a tough, relentless, odd love about him that we admire. He is a Western hero.

One of the bit actors and stuntmen in that movie is Yakima Canutt. His most famous stunt was in the 1939 movie *Stagecoach*. We see a stagecoach with galloping horses. Canutt portrays an Indian attacking the stagecoach. He walks along the tongue of the wagon to release the horses from the wagon, falls to the ground, and the wagon passes over him at full speed. He sent me an autographed action photograph from the film.

I asked him how much he got paid for that stunt. One hundred dollars, he said.

"Mr. Canutt," I said, "that's a lot of money for the 1930s."

"Little lady," he drawled, "that was a lot of stunt."

That's history *and* legend.

As for Robert B. Parker, I was wrong. His books will not die with him. Other authors have been approved to write more books featuring his characters. I tried one of them, a Western. Didn't work. Wasn't Parker.

To me, selling an author's name and voice to another author is neither history nor legend. It isn't even a great stunt, it is just strange.

Who the Heck Is Lynn Riggs?

You cannot be from Oklahoma and not know who Lynn Riggs is. It's a state law, I think.

Lynn Riggs wrote the play *Green Grow the Lilacs,* on which the mega-musical *Oklahoma!* is based. I've been leery of learning more about Lynn Riggs, because I thought he was responsible for Carmen McRae and Shirley Jones and everyone else saying "anythin'" and "everythin,'" as in "Oh, what a beautiful morning, everythin's going my way."

That is wrong. Nobody says "anythin'" and "everythin.'" I'll get back to this later.

A collection of Riggs's plays published by the University of Oklahoma Press (*The Cherokee Night and Other Plays*) and a posthumous honor at the Oklahoma Writers' Hall of Fame shamed me into reading more about him.

His biography, *Haunted by Home* by Phyllis Braunlich, tells us that Rollie Lynn Riggs was born in 1899 near Claremore, near where Will Rogers had been born twenty years earlier. His mother was one-eighth Cherokee and died of typhoid when he was about two. His father, a prominent rancher and banker, remarried a woman who became a prototype of a cold-hearted stepmother. She locked young Lynn in the doghouse when he misbehaved.

He was a slight, fair young man—bright, articulate, but not quite manly enough for his father, who refused to pay his tuition to the University of Oklahoma. So Lynn mortgaged his Indian allotment and paid the tuition himself, augmented by money he made writing. He flourished artistically at the university. He wrote poetry, short stories, and plays. In a campus literary club he met another talented young Oklahoma writer, John Joseph Mathews. Riggs taught freshman English and sang on the Chautauqua circuit. Then he had something of a nervous breakdown over a girl. He relocated to Santa Fe and was reborn as an artist and a gay man.

Riggs's working career was as variegated as a calico cat. He worked as a cowboy, at the *Wall Street Journal,* at Macy's in New York, and as an extra in cowboy movies. In the late 1920s, he won a Guggenheim Fellowship and spent a year in France, where he wrote

Green Grow the Lilacs. It was produced in New York in 1931 starring handsome Franchot Tone as Curly and June Walker as Laurey.

Produced by the Theatre Guild, *Green Grow the Lilacs* made its Broadway debut with solid literary credentials. In theater, Tone's colleagues were stage luminaries such as Lee Strasberg and Stella Adler. In Hollywood a few years later, he married Joan Crawford and starred with her in several films.

Walker had appeared on Broadway five years earlier as the original Lorelei Lee in *Gentlemen Prefer Blondes.* Decades later, her son, John Kerr became an actor and appeared in the role of Lieutenant Cable in the film version of *South Pacific.*

The play's heavy was Richard Hale, named Jeeter in the play and renamed Jud in the musical. One of Hale's later film roles was Boo Radley's father in *To Kill a Mockingbird.*

Riggs's play and the musical are two sides of the moon. Both are set in Indian Territory, near Claremore, in 1900, and both tell the tug-of-war love of two young men for the same girl. The musical, however, is far brighter, with its sunny Rodgers and Hammerstein music that celebrates romance, parties, and happy endings.

For period authenticity, Riggs filled his play with traditional folk tunes he heard in his Oklahoma childhood, including the title song. Tex Ritter sang in the original production. Riggs let his characters talk about the hardships, loneliness, and fears of their pioneer lives. Aunt Eller talks about sicknesses, deaths, being poor and hungry, and being left alone in old age. Surely in his youth Riggs heard similar stories from his family and neighbors; he was writing about a place and a people he knew, down to the food they ate and the songs they sang.

Aunt Eller and Laurey rightly were worried and afraid. They were two women alone on the hard prairie, relying on men for farm help and protection. In the musical, Jud is a dark and ominous figure. In the play, Jeeter is genuinely threatening, hinting at murders he may have committed and houses he may have burned down. He lives in a dark smokehouse, brooding and looking at French postcards, pornography of the time. At night, he prowls around the women's house. Laurey is terrified of him and blocks her door with furniture.

A 2015 staging of *Oklahoma!* in upstate New York emphasized the dark and disturbing undercurrent of the musical as personified by Jud. His sinister tone reflected the time and place, the producer said; Oklahoma Territory on the edge of statehood was boiling with social and political upheaval.

"Could be," we polite folks in Oklahoma might say noncommittally, not wanting a fight. But what frontier has not been lawless and hard, won at the price of hunger and heartache? Yet Riggs's original play celebrated the endurance of the strong pioneers, building a new life by the strength of their own hands, and celebrating their work. Riggs wrote about the rough beauty of this time and this place that his relatives had known. He said that he wanted to recapture the place and characters with "their quaintness, their sadness, their robustness, their simplicity, their hearty or bawdy humors, their sentimentalities, their melodrama, their touching sweetness" and paint them with "a kind of nostalgic glow."

He plants that intent solidly with his playwright's introduction to scene 1, describing an "unearthly sunlight," and says, "It is a radiant summer morning several years ago, the kind of morning which, enveloping the shapes of earth—men, cattle in a meadow, blades of the young corn, streams—makes them seem to exist now for the first time, their images giving off a visible golden emanation that is partly true and partly a trick of imagination focusing to keep alive a loveliness that may pass away."

In the 1930s and '40s, Riggs was in Hollywood writing movie scripts, including Cecil B. DeMille's *The Plainsman,* a couple of Sherlock Holmes films, and *Garden of Allah,* starring Marlene Dietrich. He wrote to a friend, "Charles Boyer is superb. Dietrich, the bitch, is sometimes ravishing." He was best friends with Bette Davis and Joan Crawford, lived back and forth between California and New York, danced and dined at the Coconut Grove. His visits to Claremore were not happy.

He was one of the most distinguished writers of his time and wrote twenty-one full-length plays, twenty-four film and TV scripts, and several books of poetry. He was often mentioned in the same breath as Eugene O'Neill. Still, his father never approved of his work. When his father died, Riggs did not come back for the funeral. He died himself of stomach cancer in 1954 at age fifty-six. For the first time in state history, the governor of Oklahoma sent a state flag to be draped over the coffin at his funeral in Claremore.

In his plays he was fastidious about duplicating Oklahoma dialect. Literary dialect used to be more popular, such as in the Uncle Remus stories and *Huckleberry Finn. Green Grow the Lilacs* is so thick with phonetic spellings it can seem off-putting at first glance: "purty," "anywhurs," "skeered to death," "jist," "tetch," "orta." But slow down and read it aloud, and it is down-to-the-ground authentic Oklahoma speech.

I particularly admire how Riggs captured rural Oklahomans' pronunciation of words that end with an "a" sound. In phonetics, this is called a schwa, a short vowel, as in "America." It's not that we can't say it—we say "Havana," "Savannah," "Anna," and "banana"—but plain folks often substitute an "er" or "ie" sound for the short "a." In *Green Grow the Lilacs,* "Catoosa" becomes "Catoosie," "California" is "Californie," "tomatoes" are "tomaters." My farmer uncle Bus talked like this. One dry summer, his garden was so bad, he told me, "I didn't have no tomaters a'tall." (Riggs's characters also say a'tall.) We do this with names, too. My mother's name, Ina, was "Inie" to her siblings. And so I imagine that Riggs's Aunt Eller was really Aunt Ella and Laurey was probably Laura.

He wrote phonetic spelling for words like "doin,'" "kissin,'" "purty," and "cain't." But this poet had an accurate ear for language, and he did not write "everythin.'" It's a linguistic thing. Words with an "e" sound in the middle do not drop the final "g." We say "somethin'" or "nothin,'" but we don't say "anythin'" or "everythin.'" It was Hollywood and Broadway that said that. Tryin' to be Oklahomans. And failin.'

Again into Osage County

Just as we were all abuzz and agog about the play and the movie *August: Osage County,* I discovered another famous Oklahoma author who wrote about the Osage prairie.

Tracy Letts set his drama inside a house, but John Joseph Mathews went outdoors. And there he laid his heart.

It takes a special gift to write well about place and geography.

In her book *The Egg and I,* Betty Smith says the mountains of the Pacific Northwest made her uncomfortable, as if someone were always looking over her shoulder. Has anyone ever written better about fly-fishing in Montana's Big Blackfoot River than Norman Maclean did in *A River Runs Through It?* Has another writer portrayed west Texas with such love and appreciation as Larry McMurtry in his memoirs?

Their equal is John Joseph Mathews, who wrote eloquently about an Oklahoma prairie. It is a harsh place that he described tenderly. Perhaps because he was writing to heal himself.

Mathews, part Osage, was born in 1894 in Pawhuska, Oklahoma, and grew up in the Osage Nation across the street from the Osage Indian Agency. As a scholar, Mathews is renowned for his books about the Osage people and history. As a gentleman, when he wrote the biography of Oklahoma governor and oilman E. W. Marland, he was discreet about Marland's scandalous marriage to his adopted niece.

Mathews's early life and career were exciting. He was a World War I fighter pilot, got a degree in geology from the University of Oklahoma, studied at Oxford, and married in Europe after a whirlwind romance. Back in the States, the marriage failed, and the Great Depression knocked the wind out of his finances. It knocked the wind out of him, too. In the 1930s, he went back to Osage County to live in solitude. He built a little sandstone cabin he called the Blackjacks, and he wrote. Mathews in Osage County is compared to Thoreau on Walden Pond. Mathews said he went to Osage County to live, "as one climbs out of the roaring stream of civilization onto an island, to rest and to watch."

And how he watched. He watched the land, the seasons, and the animals so closely, he found his natural place among them. He captured this in his memoir *Talking to the Moon.* It was published in

1945 and sank in the clamor of World War II. Thanks to the University of Oklahoma Press for republishing it and letting me discover it. Each chapter describes a month and is titled with the Osage name for that month's moon: Yellow Flower Moon, Deer Hiding Moon, and so forth.

When Mathews describes an Oklahoma summer before electric fans or air conditioning and temperatures of 113 degrees, we swelter with him. When hunting season arrives and the first cold rain comes from the north with flocks of ducks on the wing, even the pacifist-vegetarians among us can appreciate his soul-deep joy. He takes the time to see truly the insects in the grass, the birds in their nests, his rough cowboy neighbors, and the Osage elders with their dry humor.

He writes in a style that is both unadorned and yet musical. Some of his old hunter friends "have nothing but keys and a knife to jingle in their pockets," he says. When he watches a coyote hunting field mice, "it stands on its hind legs like a fox in a fable." Butterflies, he writes, "float like the thoughts of a lively child."

Mathews died in 1979 at age eighty-five and was buried beside the sandstone cottage that he loved. On the mantle of the stone arched fireplace in his cottage, he had painted a motto in Latin. It had been the motto of a Roman legion on the North Africa frontier in the first century. Mathews said it was the motto of his life in the blackjacks.

Translated, it says, "To hunt, to swim, to play, to laugh—this is to live."

....

On an ordinary day in late June recently, I spent one of the truly great days of my life. To me, Oklahoma prairies are the most beautiful place on earth. They look like home to me because I was born in Nowata County, which is on the eastern edge of the Osage prairies.

This day, I had a private tour of the Tallgrass Prairie Preserve near Pawhuska, in the same place Mathews was born and died. My special guide was Harvey Payne, an employee of the Nature Conservancy, but so much more than that: local rancher, lawyer, municipal judge, photographer, naturalist, historian, philosopher, and storyteller.

I had made arrangements to meet Payne in Pawhuska because he is the person who could show me the sandstone cabin that John Joseph Mathews built in 1932, when the author was retreating from the world to reconnect with his lifelong love of wildlife. Mathews said he wanted to get his feet on his own piece of earth, to feel the harmony with the natural flow of life, to engage in physical activity, and "to live to the very brim" with life around him every day.

The little cabin—and it certainly is little, no more than fifteen by thirty feet—is so isolated I never could have found it by myself. It is solidly built of two layers of native sandstone. For the first years Mathews lived there, the cabin had no running water or electricity. I saw the pump near the house and the outdoor shower. A space remains where a screened porch stood, and there is where he slept, summer and winter. Inside the cabin was a fireplace. The bathroom, I understand, was the grove of blackjacks out back.

To be inside that cabin—the walls not quite square, the new roofers said—I felt the need I myself have felt when knocked off my own plumb lines and wanting a tiny space to feel secure. I've been in that fragile emotional place where I needed to pull in the world close around me. I wanted to be able to reach out and touch all the walls of my safe, snug place. The cabin was a cocoon for him to write and heal. When I put my hand on his historic fireplace, the cabin's only source of warmth, it felt reverent.

The sounds from the surrounding prairie and hay meadow were the soft buzzes and chirps from insects and birds. The solitude was peaceful, but the intense isolation seemed a little odd to me.

"If you have enough money," Payne said, "I guess it's called eccentric." And for much of Mathews's life he had plenty of money from his Osage head right. And from the sale of his books, especially his first book, titled *Wah'Kon-Tah*, about the Osages. It was published in 1929 and was a best seller.

Then we climbed back into Payne's white pickup and drove through the great Tallgrass Prairie Preserve on a magic tour. Once the nation's tallgrass prairie covered 142 million acres spread over fourteen states. Today, less than 10 percent of that original prairie land exists. We were on land that was once the great Chapman-Barnard Ranch, which covered more than 100,000 acres. Oklahoma's Tallgrass Prairie Preserve was begun in 1989 when the Nature Conservancy bought 29,000 acres of the ranch land, then expanded the preserve to 39,100 acres. The weather was pleasant, and after a month of rain, the land was so green and lush even the ditches by the road were full of wildflowers.

Payne showed me tall, yellow compass plants, so rare they grow only on that prairie, he said. They look like tall, knobby sunflowers. Cattle eat them like candy, eat them right to the ground, but bison don't touch them, because they don't eat broadleaf plants. Deer and a coyote crossed our path, and a brave jackrabbit with big, black-tipped ears stood motionless for a long time to have a look at us. We saw a herd of bison in the distance.

We talked about the famous tallgrasses—big bluestem, Indian-grass, and switchgrass—and how some can grow eight feet tall in low-lying areas. We talked about what the local people thought about the play and film *August: Osage County*. "It's about a dysfunctional family," Payne said, "and some people around here say, 'I think I know the family he's talking about.'"

As we drove along, he told me about Osage history, the extinction of elk in the area, and the near extinction of bison until they were reintroduced by the Nature Conservancy. We talked about the group of men who created the preserve, especially Joseph H. Williams. "He casts a tall shadow," Payne said with both fondness and admiration. "When he pees on a tree, he pees high."

Mostly we talked about John Joseph Mathews, his large family home on the Big Hill in downtown Pawhuska, the family genealogy from great-grandfather Old Bill Williams and his full-blood Osage wife to Mathews's two unmarried sisters (who lived in Pawhuska until their death), his books, and his cabin, which is being restored by the Conservancy. Like Thoreau, who didn't live far from his mother, Mathews wasn't entirely alone at the Blackjacks. After a few years, he remarried, and his second wife lived there with him. That's probably when they added a second sandstone room to be a kitchen.

"I can relate to him," Mr. Payne told me, "especially his love of wildlife."

Mathews was an avid hunter but also a dedicated naturalist, in the same company with Rachel Carson and Aldo Leopold. He was ahead of his time in his respect—almost veneration—of wildlife. This can be seen in his autobiography *Twenty Thousand Mornings* and espe-cially in the newly released book of his short stories, *Old Three Toes*. He does not anthropomorphize animals: no jacket-wearing rabbits or talking toads for him. He wanted to see wildlife as it is. That is clear from the rest of the title of the short story collection, *And Other Tales of Survival and Extinction*. When he writes about the sandhill crane or a big mule deer buck, it is with such close observation, we readers can see the world as the animal itself sees it. Mathews identified so closely with the animals around him, he once described himself as a sandhill crane. He was a slight young man when he played football, built like a sandhill crane, he said, with one important difference. "The sandhill crane had the advantage of wing, and I had to remain on the ground."

Another Pawhuska-born poet and author is Carter Revard. Although considerably younger than Mathews, Revard is also an Oxford graduate, and the two writers talked together about their different days at Merton College in Oxford. Revard remembers his Osage Reservation childhood in his book *Family Matters, Tribal Affairs*. He became a linguistics scholar and recalls the day he realized that his Osage grandmother, Josephine Jump, didn't have just an unusual speaking pattern, she was speaking English with a foreign accent—an Osage accent.

Revard taught and wrote about medieval British literature, but he also wrote about Osage County. He was honoring his Aunt Jewell, who sang him a Ponca courage song, when he wrote a poem about the mockingbird. How brave, he thought, for the little mockingbird to sing through the night when the owls were hunting by ear. In his poem he was also honoring the mockingbird, "our American singer that takes all the other songs and shouts them at the moon and to hell with the great horned owls."

Yet another poet, writer, and scholar from Pawhuska is the late University of Tulsa professor Winston Weathers. In his book *Indian and White* he wrote—as a poet—about the lessons of life and human spirit in the southwestern history, legend, and scene. I was a graduate student in his class when he told us something important about writing. "We do our work sincerely," he said, "but we don't take ourselves seriously." Perhaps he learned that on the great, open Osage prairie.

"And when the future finds us," Weathers wrote in his poetic prose, "let them say, 'They were a magic people in this ordinary place.'"

Perhaps the place is magic, too. Twenty-two miles west of Pawhuska is the little town of Fairfax, birthplace of the Indian ballerina sisters Maria and Marjorie Tallchief. Ree Drummond, famous as *The Pioneer Woman* cook, lives on an Osage County ranch with a herd of wild horses visible from her windows.

On the way home from my tour through the Tallgrass Prairie Preserve, I stopped at a Pawhuska restaurant named The Greek's. I saw no Greek food on the menu, but I had a nice chicken-fried steak. I read the local newspaper: problems in the oil patch and with the federal government, the Ben Johnson Memorial Steer Roping. That's Ben Johnson, Sr., longtime foreman of the old Chapman-Barnard Ranch and father of actor Ben Johnson, who was known as Son. Small-town papers often print the police blotter, so I read that. Mostly misdemeanors but one felony described as a "prisoner placing body fluid on government employee." Good information. Who knew that was a felony?

Some of us are ordinary people in a magic place.

The Great, Wild, Adventurous Backyard

The painter Grant Wood said that all the really great ideas he ever had came to him while he was milking a cow.

Not as silly as it sounds. We have to turn off our thoughts sometimes to let thought—and creativity and ideas—squeeze in.

I have just enough Cherokee blood to believe that the earth is full of holiness. Some experience this marvel in earthly majesty—the Grand Canyon, the Tetons, the oceans. I am a timid mouse. I find it in my own backyard.

My Summer Vacation

Oh, wow. Crazy busy summer. I'm not only following my bliss, I'm following it at a dogtrot. I'm seizing the day like a drowning woman. I'm grabbing my dreams with fists of steel. First, I'm off to the Himalayas. Ever since seeing the 1937 movie *Lost Horizons*, I've wanted to go to Shangri La. Not the Oklahoma one, the Himalayas one. So I'll be biking for three weeks this summer through the Himalayas. Rigorous? Heck yes, but that's how we live life to its fullest.

Then, since I have developed a real passion to help people, I've joined a volunteer group digging a village well in the Republic of Chad in central Africa. I get to take my own shovel! This will be two weeks of hard labor in harder conditions. What could make my heart fuller?

Then, since we have to put play into our lives, I'll be zip-lining across the Amazon. Whew! Takes my breath away.

I'll need to get centered after this vigorous activity, so I'll spend ten Zen-like days on the island of Little Corn—a pristine (read primitive)—place off the Caribbean coast of Nicaragua. (Note to self: pack mosquito net.)

Quickly revived by the sandy beach, blue ocean, and cheap seafood, I'll be on my way to South America, where I've been lucky enough to land a gig—through the son of a friend—with an animal-free circus. My job will be riding a unicycle and playing the cymbals. (Personal reminder: Learn to ride unicycle. Also, learn to play cymbals.) Wacky? Sure, but we've got to dance like nobody is watching.

Back in the U.S.A., I'll be fly-fishing in the Bitterroot River outside Missoula, Montana, featured in *A River Runs through It*. Then I'll commune with Mother Earth by spending a few nights camping near the sacred Blue Mountain in Navajo land. I'm composing a special mantra for the occasion.

In truth, I'm not doing any of that.

What I am doing for my summer vacation is fussing around in my garden, reading in my garden, and napping in my garden room. Inside or outside, my snoozing cat Muriel will be beside me (or lying on top of me), and I'll be surrounded by stacks of books bought especially for summer reading. My idea of a perfect summer vacation is inspired by books, films, and gardens.

The back door will be open all day so Muriel and I can wander in and out. Leaves and grass will blow in, too, reminding me that in the summer holiday, livin' is easy and relaxed.

In the morning we'll have mugs of coffee outside. In the afternoon we'll drink chilled drinks outside. Throughout the day we'll eat sandwiches and light meals in the garden. We'll eat strawberries and grapes and throw strawberry hulls and grape seeds onto the lawn. When we make fresh salads, we'll dump the vegetable scraps into the flower beds.

At sunset we'll sit on the front porch and watch the neighborhood parade of people and their dogs. (It's true, they do look alike.) When the first star comes out, we'll make a secret wish. Then we'll fall into bed to read until the Dewdrop Fairy sprinkles sleep dust over us.

This is just between you and me.

Every day it seems someone asks me, "What are your summer travel plans?" Nobody wants to hear that my perfect summer vacation consists of a reading list and deadheading the roses like Miss Marple. Instead, I give them this made-up, adventurous vacation plan.

What I want out of life, at this stage in my life, is a clean, well-organized house and a tidy garden. Without obsessive work. Here's my new plan for housekeeping:

> First, I refresh all the vases of cut flowers. Ideally with flowers from my own gardens.

> Then I'm through for the day. Reading and naps follow.

Let others climb the highest mountain. As for me, I love what Joan Plowright says in the movie *Enchanted April:* "I will sit in the shade and think of better times and better men."

Ahh, my perfect summer. And what are your plans for this summer?

A Quintet about Cats

Cats Can Make You Crazy

Oh, brother. As if I don't have enough to worry about, here comes another scientific hobgoblin to keep me awake at nights. I'm already worried about the pronouncement that the sun is slowly but surely shrinking and that a great black hole is munching its way toward earth. What does this mean? That I'll wake up some morning under an ice cap? Or discover that the black hole has taken a bite out of Kansas?

As scary as all of that, this new fear is closer to home—cats. That's right: cats. I read an article in the *Atlantic* magazine titled "How Your Cat Is Making You Crazy." Well, I knew that. Anybody who has a cat knows that.

To prove it, take this simple multiple-choice quiz.

Question: You have company coming for dinner, so your cat throws up
   a. The day before, so you have time to clean it up
   b. As the doorbell rings
   c. When you sit down for dinner
   d. All of the above
Cat people know the answer is "All of the above."

Here's the second question. The reason your cat throws up is
   a. A change in the weather
   b. Something she ate
   c. Just for something to do
   d. Who knows?
And again the answer is "All of the above."

Yet more reasons why cats are fascinating. Who knows what goes on in their little heads?

This magazine article doesn't address feline mysticism; it's all about cat physiology. According to the pioneering work of a biologist in the Czech Republic, house cats can carry tiny parasites that creep into our brains and change our personality. This eensy organism has a big name, *Toxoplasma gondii,* and the scientist claims it can cause everything from mental disorders to car wrecks. People who tested positive for *Toxoplasma* were two and a half times more likely to be in a car accident.

The evolutionary biologist is Jaroslav Flegr, who lives in Prague, where he has been a lone pioneer in the research. He has been studying the parasite in the protozoan family since the 1990s. Now other neuroscientists are joining him, saying this crazy-making cat bug theory isn't so crazy, after all.

The parasite messes with our neurons, alters our brains, and affects our personalities. It can turn introverts into reckless, trusting extroverts. Shy women might find themselves in bars flirting with strange men. It can even change the way we dress; men become sloppier, women grow more meticulous. It can cause mental disorders such as schizophrenia.

Just before I dismissed this as too nutty for words, the magazine article cited a slew of other parasites that change behavior in fish, ants, caterpillars, wasps, bats, and dogs.

Here's one example: a flatworm invades an ant's nervous system. Most ants go underground in cooler temperatures, but the infected ant goes the opposite direction. It climbs *up,* onto a blade of grass where it takes a big bite and locks its jaws. There the ant stays, swaying in the breeze until a grazing sheep eats the grass and voila! the worm gets into the sheep's gut. The little worms are excreted, find other ants, and around and around we go. The bottom line is that the parasite has a powerful survival instinct.

Here is how the cat parasite works: in developed countries, humans pick up the parasite from the litter box. Not all of us, but some of us. And then, Katie bar the door. Anything can happen. We might go barking mad, we might behave badly, we might start hanging out at honky-tonks, we might find ourselves playing the penny slots at the casino. It's okay. We have an alibi: my cat made me do it.

Comfort Me with Macaroni

What a foolish sight I must have been to some people. A grown woman with a red nose, eyes bloodshot and swollen from crying—all because my cat had died.

How can we grieve so over a cat, they must wonder, when there is so much larger grief in the world? And I would answer that every grief is part of a great grief. Just as every little love is part of a great love. It's all connected.

So when my calico cat Phoebe died, I wept. The grief was as sharp as a blade. It wasn't unexpected. She was nineteen. She had a heart condition and renal failure. And still I cried.

Anyone who has a pet knows that there are pets we love, and then there are special pets—a cat or a dog or a hamster—that forge a special connection with us.

That's how it was with Phoebe and me. She always behaved as if she deserved all the privileges I had as a human—and more. I believe she thought she was part kitty, part little girl, and part fairy princess. And that's the way I treated her for almost two decades. A special place on the pillow beside me at night. Special kisses throughout the day.

Always there is guilt, isn't there, when there is a death? I had to go to work early that day and I worked late. I was employed at a church at the time, and that day was particularly hard. In the afternoon, we held the funeral for a family of four—a young mother and her three children—killed in a plane crash. That morning, I had gone to the funeral at another church for the mother's friend, who had been piloting the plane. I knew all five of these people very well. It was a hard day, physically and emotionally, but that does not salve the fact that I was not with Phoebe the day she needed me most.

When I came home from work, Phoebe was curled in the bathtub crying out with a sound I had never heard from her before. It was if she asked me, "Where have you been when I needed you?"

The day had been so dark, it was almost black with a pounding rain that flooded streets. That night, with the wind still blowing fiercely, a smoke alarm in my house shrieked off and on all night. I couldn't defuse it. There was so much death in my life that day, it was if the heavens had sobbed and then at night the air screamed.

Phoebe leaves such a hole in my life—the little antique water bowl she won't visit again, the white pillow by the window where she will no longer nap. And such sweet memories: how I made up little rhyming songs as I brushed her, how she licked my nose in the middle of the night. How she romped through the house with Abigail when they were both kittens, in a great galloping game of chase—oblivious to the breakage they left in their wake—or to my shouting at them to "stop it this minute!" How she and I both grieved when Abigail died. Phoebe never again bonded with another cat and was never again as innocently joyful.

She died at the time of the hunter's moon, the full moon nearest the autumn equinox. A full moon is symbolic of completeness and the time of powerful love. Astrologers say when the hunter's moon is in Taurus, as it was that day, it is "a sign that reminds us that life is beautiful, warm, soft, loving, and sensual, filled with the pleasures of family and friends, good food, beautiful surroundings, great music and art, and all things that help soothe and heal anxiety and worry."

Phoebe died just as leaves began turning and autumn sunlight came on a slant. The natural things of the earth were taking new form, and I had the strong feeling that Phoebe, too, was taking a new form. Relieved to be freed of that old, sick body. Romping through the heavens with her soul mate, Abigail.

And in the meantime, friends console me and bring me flowers. And chocolate. And macaroni and cheese. Very comforting, my friends with their gifts, to a woman with a red nose.

I tend to my grieving myself, planting bulbs that will bloom in the spring. I will see them and think of Phoebe and of Wordsworth:

> And then my heart with pleasure fills,
> and dances with the daffodils.

Fleas

Remember that week of false spring back in January when the afternoon temperatures were high and the sun was bright and hot? The sunny weather grabbed me by the arm and threw me into a spring cleaning froth.

First I tidied the linen closet. Then—zero to eighty—I borrowed a steamer mop and bought a can of wax stripper and a hand scrubber. Two days later I had a shine on my kitchen floor so intense I had to squint to find my way to the refrigerator.

Confession. It wasn't the weather that inspired house cleaning. It was my cat Ellie.

"Fleas," the veterinarian diagnosed cheerfully.

Actually, she sang it out: "Flee-ees." Two syllables, which translated to "Fleas again."

This wasn't our regular vet, it was a substitute who happened to be an expert on fleas and on cats, and a quick study of Ellie's medical records, which showed repeated clinic visits for flea allergy.

The substitute vet gave me a tutorial on the life cycle of fleas from eggs to Ellie. "Your house is probably infested," she said merrily. This was a bright Saturday morning, a Saturday full of happy plans.

Scratch that.

"Go home," she told me. "Get yourself fueled up on coffee or wine and start vacuuming. Get your crevice tool and your upholstery attachment and vacuum. Vacuum under all the chair and sofa cushions. Vacuum the bottom of the bed. Vacuum the baseboards. Vacuum . . ." She stopped when she saw my stricken expression. "I know just how you feel," she said. "I once had two kids with head lice."

No, she didn't know how I felt. She didn't know that I was thinking, "Crevice tool? Upholstery attachment? I haven't seen those in years."

However, anyone who prescribes strong coffee or a bottle of wine is my kind of medical consultant. I did everything she said. On the way home I bought personal fuel, a new vacuum (with attachments), and a spray bottle of something to kill flea eggs. Then I vacuumed like a woman possessed.

I tried to make the best of the flea infestation by turning it into a learning opportunity. However, I found the bloodsucking little vampires too grotesque to study. All I learned is that we have more than two thousand species of fleas, including special fleas for cats, dogs, humans, moorhens, northern rats, and Oriental rats. Rabbit fleas can detect when the rabbit is about to give birth and jumps into the procreation itself, producing flea eggs.

I learned that fleas can jump seven inches high and thirteen inches horizontally. I learned that Borax, baking soda, and table salt help kill fleas. So does drowning. (That seems laborious, doesn't it? Drowning one flea at a time?)

Today, Ellie and I are both happier and cleaner. I admire people who keep their homes, their lawns, and their cars spotless. I am in worshipful awe of people who can cook like chefs. I am not any of those people.

Once I was invited to bring a dessert of my own making to an English tea at my church. I was proudly delivering my specialty—a plate of lemon madeleines—when I froze at the door of the fellowship hall. Those good churchwomen had laid tables with baked fantasies that put a Venetian pastry shop to shame. The priest came by about that time, look at my sad little plate of flat, brown pastries, and said, "Bless your heart."

I am a woman whose electric range has only two working burners and who owns an electric hand mixer with only one beater. Both appliances are fine with me. My current philosophy is that we must know our own strengths. We must celebrate our selves for who we are.

I can't cook or clean, but I don't have fleas. And thanks be to God for that.

My cat and dog are superior to me in so many ways. I wish I could jump, climb, and run like they can.

I wish I could purr, growl, bark, scratch, and nip with little needle teeth.

I wish I could ignore people when I feel like it. My face would be as blank as a stone statue, especially when people cooed and gooed over me.

If I had their talents, I'd leap over the picket fence in a single bound to greet people and dogs I like. If anybody passed by that I didn't care to speak to, I'd bark so loudly and lunge so fiercely, they would cross the street.

I would jump to the top of the bathroom cabinet, where it is warm, and ignore anyone who ran inside and outside all night long calling for me.

Sometimes, a gal just wants to be alone, so rarely, but oh so importantly, I'd crawl into such a secret hiding place—perhaps up behind a dresser and into a drawer—that newspaper ads and fliers would be posted begging for my return.

The hair on my head would bristle and stand straight up when I'm agitated. I would throw up effortlessly, just for entertainment. When alarmed, I would arch my back more elegantly than the Gateway Arch in St. Louis. Cross me and I would silently bare my teeth. Sometimes I would hiss.

Unless I really like you, and then I would lick your face when we met.

I would always sniff you to know—truthfully—where you've been and who you've been with.

Once in a while I would languish and be rushed to the doctor for expensive tests that revealed that everything was A-OK. Attention is such a good medication. Especially on weekends or holidays.

Sometimes I would sneer at my supper bowl and stand motionless until it was refilled with something more appealing.

I would know how to combine righteous selfishness with comfort, claiming the biggest and best part of the bed.

If you offended me, I would glare at you though slits for eyes, emoting malice sharp enough to slice salami. Clarity of communication would be my goal. I would simply yowl when I wanted attention and puddle on things I don't like. That would be so much simpler than writing discreetly worded memos and sharp e-mails. If I could rub my face against objects I want for my own, I wouldn't have to use a credit card.

I would turn my ears—together or singularly—in every direction to pick up sounds and vibes. I would hear things like music in the wind. I would smell secrets in the grass.

If I had whiskers, I could find my way in the dark without stepping on toys and swearing. I'd never bump into tables or trip over rugs.

Mostly, I would glory in my tail, an appendage humans no longer have. I would revel in my tail for clear, non-verbal communication. All I'd have to do is wag it and people would call me cute and smart.

My tail would wag briskly when I was happy, lower when I was sad or frightened or ill, thrash back and forth when I was angry, curl upward when I felt friendly, wrap around me when I was napping safely, point up like a dune buggy antenna when I was feeling really excited (or about to spray) and stick straight out (with my ears flattened) when I was about to attack.

Oh, boy, if I were a scorpion or a lizard or a monkey or a bird or a fish or a kangaroo, I'd have a tail with even mightier powers.

When I was an embryo I had a tail, so I understand, but it was absorbed into my body, and now I only have a tailbone, or coccyx, which is attached to my sacroiliac. Even that is inferior to a tail, thanks to bouts of bursitis.

I wouldn't worry about tricky grammar or techie gadgets, if only I had a tail.

Lola and me *(author's collection)*

A Cat's Life

My cat Lola is a climber. The first time I let her out of the house, she scampered up onto the roof of the house and scaled the chimney. There she stood, a small tabby cat on the tallest point of the property. Passers-by stopped their cars and took photos—of her with head back breathing the fresh air and her tail straight up. And of me on the ground, hopping from one foot to another like Rumpelstiltskin, crying, "Oh, my God!"

Since then Lola has been up on several roofs—mine, the neighbor's, the garage—and up into countless trees. She is such a high-wire act that her son William assumed he had inherited the climbing gene. Nope, it must have skipped a litter. On one of his first ventures outdoors, William got stuck in a small pear tree, and I had to fetch a ladder to get him down. It was such a traumatic experience that William went back inside and let it be known that henceforth if anyone wanted him, they could find him on the kitchen counter. There he stayed. Other cats may scale Mount Everest if they choose. William will watch out the window and nibble tuna treats.

I admire this self-knowledge in my cats. They know what they like and they stick to it. They are not pressured toward self-improvement. No one tells them to walk an extra mile a day or learn another language. No new recipes for them. Give my cats a tried-and-true can of fish and let some other cat sample the sautéed veal simmered in gravy. My cats' motto is this: If you are already happy, why try to be happier? Or the happiest? Life isn't a contest when you're a cat. Those who want to stay inside and shed on the furniture, do so. Those who want to go out to the garden, go out—and in and out and in.

The single objective of every cat and dog that has crossed my threshold to live here is to sleep on the Big Bed. No matter how or where they lived before, despite whatever wretched conditions, even if this is the first time they have set foot inside a home, they all have the same reaction when they spot the Big Bed. They stop in their tracks with their eyes glued on this ordinary, quilt-covered, double bed paradise and think, in cat language, "I have discovered Nirvana."

From that point, they are single-minded in gaining access to this homey paradise. The dog stakes out a place at the foot of the bed. The cats manipulate an elaborate caste system, from the exalted pillow beside me to a small corner under the covers. Whatever space they choose, they do not rest until they have achieved it. Some cats are fiercely territorial, loudly proclaiming themselves king of the mountain. Others are sly and cunning. These are the cats that creep into the bedroom in the middle of the night as softly as a breeze. I awake to find them packed alongside me like sandbags or draped around my head resembling a wool cap with the earflaps down. Some choose to be treetop cats and some to be countertop cats, but inside, they all want to curl up on the Big Bed. There they smile in their sleep and dream of singing "Gimme a pig's foot and a bottle of beer."

Cats are creatures that know how to lick life right in the face. I could learn a thing or two from them. If they could put it into words, they would say that most humans make a job of being happy. Or that we don't know happiness when we have it. It is easier for a cat. When you are a cat with a safe home, a full supper bowl, and all the freedom you choose, every day is like a whole new Saturday you have never seen before.

A Cat's Philosophy for a Happy Life

Take every day as it comes. Get some sunshine.
Every day, take a nap and moderate exercise. Play a little.
Every once in a while, chase something.
When you eat fish, lick your plate clean.
Don't ever go to bed wondering if you could have done
    that day better.
This is the secret of being a happy cat.

A Sextet about Gardening

False Spring

My friend Jackie says she knows it is spring when old boyfriends start showing up. "They're like trappers," she said, "coming down from the mountains when the snow melts."

Spring does that to us. Spring has us running around as if in a Shakespeare comedy singing "Hey nonny nonny."

The first springlike weekend, my gardening neighbors and I pop out of our homes like gophers. We bring rakes, shovels, and chain saws. We dig up bushes and move them to new locations. We drag lawn furniture out of the garage. We crop monkey grass until our arms ache.

I stopped by a plant store and was about to plunge headfirst into flowering plants when a seasoned old gent in overalls told me, "Sixty-degree weather in Oklahoma in March don't mean nothin'."

I screeched to a halt. He was exactly exact—it *don't* mean nothin.' Gardening too early in Oklahoma is much like those old beaux: one spring day soon, I'll look outside at the freak frost or late snowstorm and wonder, "What was I thinking?"

And yet, after hibernating all winter, we are starved for color, new life, and fresh air. Once I inherited a basement office from a woman so morose about her love life, she was as gray as a flounder. Her office had no windows. The cinder-block walls were decorated with two big paintings—one was a coiled snake, the other was a green corpse in a wooden coffin. A couple of days in that place and I would have been depressed, too. I took down the paintings and put up a border of bright paper flowers. Neither the office nor the job worked out, despite my paper flowers and cheery stab at cheap interior decorating.

I need color and light in my life, but a little common sense is good, too. I do not need to make a garden in March and sacrifice it to the elements. There is spring, and then there is false spring. Gardening is like the rest of life—there's a fine line between optimism and lunacy, much like old romances and bad jobs.

So in false spring, I compromise. I buy a couple of pots of blossoming geraniums, big enough to see but light enough to grab up and rush indoors when the cold threatens to freeze their buds off. I tie colorful ribbons to flutter on the bare tree branches. Sometimes I buy a dozen plastic pinwheels to stick in the garden, where they spin like animated jonquils.

Then I sit outside in the sunny yard all one afternoon, not gardening myself to a froth but sipping mimosas and making a garden plan on paper. Giddy with birdsong, pollen, and champagne, I do not give a thought to what lies ahead—Oklahoma summer with equal portions of heat and humidity, insects and mildew. But neither do I bring out the tender plants from my greenhouse before they are ready to face the world.

I hope Mother Nature is smiling on me and thinking, "She's a slow learner, but she's showing promise."

Gardening Fool

I know the adage "Two swallows do not a summer make," but I can't believe it for long. I hold myself back as long as I can in early spring; then I see one swallow and I run outside to the garden with shovel and trowel proclaiming myself Mother Nature's Favorite Daughter. I rush to nurseries and garden centers carrying my credit card above my head like the Olympic torch.

I tend to leap into things with more enthusiasm than sense. The first night of my landscape design class at the garden center, I sat with my head in my hands moaning quietly as I realized all the mistakes I have made in my garden and, even worse, how much time, money, and energy it was going to take to correct these mistakes.

I know one poor soul who had just planted a row of bamboo in his yard when he picked up the newspaper and read about the struggle Americans are having trying to reclaim their yards from the monster plant. A man in Pennsylvania tried to stop his bamboo invasion with a shovel, a pickax, a machete, a mini bulldozer, salt, fourteen gallons of poison, and an exorcism, and in desperation he even tried to shoot it with a revolver. He finally got rid of it, but doing so cost him about $1,500.

Bamboo, so fragile and graceful, is devouring suburban America.

It's much like the Chinese proverb about water: Water is soft and gentle, but water gently dripping can wear away a stone.

I may be a slow learner, but I did learn something in the gardening classes. I learned that when a plant's instructions say "full sun," it probably doesn't mean "full Oklahoma sun," which is a whole different enchilada from full sun in, say, Seattle.

I know that I sound like a song from *The Lion King*, but one thing I love about gardening is watching the circles of life. Every living thing has them, and the different speeds are interesting. Spring's azaleas, tulips, and forsythias roar through Oklahoma like they're trying to catch a train. Then here come the roses bursting center stage and the bosomy peonies preening for applause.

Soon it will be too hot and too dry to play in the garden. Then it's time to come inside with a book. For me, that's part of the cycle, too. Sometimes we dogtrot through life making families and careers, and sometimes we sit down.

This is much like Hinduism's four stages of life: first, the student, learning about life; second, the householder, busy with career, marriage, and family; third, that mature adult retiring from responsibilities; and fourth, the ascetic stage, seeking spiritual enlightenment and self-discovery. The last is called the Forest Dweller stage, and in extreme cases the seeker abandons all possessions, leaves home, and wanders the forest with a beggar's bowl. I plan to skip this stage.

Sometimes, I learned in the gardening class, the horticultural gene doesn't kick in until age fifty or so. It reminded me of Jonathan Rosen's book *The Life of the Skies*. It is not a book about bird-watching, not how to identify the red-winged blackbird, but a poetic, philosophic book. It says one reason we are drawn to admiring the birds overhead is that for most of us they are the only wildlife we see. In our urban lives we don't see deer or buffalo; our only connection with the natural world may be watching birds.

And, I would suggest, by gardening. It's a way to touch the earth. And when it snows on my daffodils or even hails on my tulips, I can identify with the farmers—and the pioneers—who wrestled with nature for their very lives.

The sad truth is, we don't always reap what we sow.

Summer Solstice

Oh my gosh, here we are in the heat of summer and I almost missed the summer solstice.

This is the day the sun balances *en pointe*. It is the longest day of the year. On this day in Oklahoma, we have fourteen hours and thirty-seven minutes of daylight.

Everybody else celebrated it. In Peru at Machu Picchu, which is the Temple of the Sun, a weeklong festival was held. In Sedona, Arizona, Native Americans performed a Sun Dance. In Barcelona at the Festival of Saint John the Baptist, dancing and music went on all night. At Stonehenge, in Norway, in Iceland, in Cairo—all around the world people celebrated the summer solstice.

And in Oklahoma, I let it slip by—unacknowledged, unappreciated. One of the best things about life is that we usually get another chance—another crack at it. So I am going to make amends by hosting a little alfresco summer luncheon.

Outdoor dining is the hot topic of all the gracious living magazines, the ones we used to call ladies' magazines. All of the photos look like a luncheon in Provence. There it is on the magazine cover—summer alfresco luncheon. And inside the magazine, a step-by-step guide including recipes. I will follow it to the letter.

Oklahoma summers used to be hot and dry. A woman told me about the legendary drought of ought-nine when it was so hot and so dry for so long that when the weather finally did break, even the cat stood out in the rain. That's changed now. With our manmade lakes and heavy spring rainfalls, we have humidity. Humidity that feels like a big, yellow dog breathing on us.

Not to worry. I am a slave to fashion, and if the magazine says summer alfresco luncheon, that's what it is to be.

However, since this is Oklahoma I will have to make a few adjustments.

For starters, I can't tell my guests it's to be alfresco. Nobody I know will come to eat outside in the midday Oklahoma sun; that is beyond mad dogs and Englishmen. I'll leave out that part. Unfortunately, my guests will arrive dressed for indoors air-conditioning—long sleeves, perhaps even a shawl against the chill. Little joke on them, isn't it?

I don't have a garden umbrella, so I will have to set the table as far as it will go under the shade of a tree. Half of the guests will be subject to bird droppings or falling ticks, poor them, and the other half will be in the sun's full glare, even poorer them.

The next hurdle is to decide which linen to use. I thought about my vivid Provence cloth with yellow and lavender, but the magazines this year are emphatic about blue and white. The magazines keep talking about the beach and the sea breeze. The closest thing I have in my yard is 50 percent humidity, which means whichever tablecloth I use will hang like damp laundry. But let's move on.

Hydrangeas from the garden can make a floral centerpiece, but even with the vase filled with ice cubes, soon the flowers will be hanging their heavy heads and moaning in wilting agony. I so dislike moaning at a luncheon, don't you?

Me at my garden gate *(author's collection)*

And now the menu. For starters, a nice chilled white wine. Perhaps a Spanish albariño, so lovely for spring and summer. Sadly, the heat index of 105 will take the chill right out of the wine, and the guests will be drinking warm white wine. And feeling slightly nauseated about it.

As dictated by the magazine, the menu will be crab salad and cold avocado soup made with cream. I can see the guests now, perspiring mightily and eyeing the luncheon dishes with real fear. I know what they're thinking—ptomaine. They're checking to see if their cell phones are handy, in case they need to call 911 and be rushed to the hospital with food poisoning.

Oh, why bother. With deadbeats like this for guests, maybe I'll wait until the autumn equinox for an alfresco meal.

Green Bouquets

I love to have fresh flowers in the house. I love to have them sent to me, but it's especially rewarding to make the bouquets myself. From my own garden. Flowers that have blossomed in my garden, not because of but in spite of my sincere efforts.

In Oklahoma, spring speeds through fast, and by the time we've passed the summer solstice, heavy heat has settled in and most blossoms have packed it up and headed north.

That's when I make green bouquets. I fill vases with green foliage, branches, trailing grapevines, and spikes of ornamental grass. All green, various shades of green—whatever I find in the garden. It's such a creative idea, I must have read it in some magazine.

Early one recent summer, just as I began to make the first green bouquets, I read about the death in Johannesburg of Albertina Sisulu. This tiny black woman was known as the Mother of South Africa. She was married to Walter Sisulu, head of the African National Congress, who was jailed on Robbins Island with Nelson Mandela for twenty- six years.

Mrs. Sisulu was a quiet but rock-solid force against apartheid in South Africa. She herself was repeatedly jailed and banned by the government. But she kept on, and as Archbishop Tutu said, "Try as they might, they could not break her spirit, they could not make her bitter, they could not defeat her love."

One of the events she is noted for is leading a historic march of twenty thousand women on August 9, 1956, to protest the pass laws that restricted the movement of blacks in South Africa. A slogan from that march is "You strike a woman, you strike a rock." That day, August 9, is now celebrated in South Africa as Women's Day.

I met Mrs. Sisulu when I went to South Africa to research a book I was writing. I found her to be as she is described—a tiny, quiet, humble woman but rock strong. We sat on her sofa and she spoke passionately about her current mission of building crèches, homes for the orphans and street children of South Africa.

The gift I gave her was a Native American dream catcher I had brought from Oklahoma. I told her that dream catchers are often hung over children's cribs to keep away bad dreams. She liked that.

About the same time I was making green bouquets and learning about the death of Mrs. Sisulu, I was reading a biography of Margaret Fuller. This incredible woman died in 1850. What an incredible, brave life she blazed for herself in the first part of the 1800s. She was a fierce intellectual, one of the very few women who were part of the nineteenth-century's Transcendentalist movement, which included Emerson and Thoreau.

She was an adventurer who traveled by carriage and stagecoach from her native Boston into the open West, which at the time was Illinois and Ohio. When she first saw the vast prairie with nothing but waving grass, she thought it was dull and desolate. Then she began to love it, and she wrote, "It is always thus with the new form of life; we must learn to look at it by its own standard."

She was a teacher at a revolutionary school and a writer who campaigned to become the first woman to enter Harvard's library. She was a champion of two forward-thinking, unpopular philosophies: abolition and women's rights. She supported herself by writing, as a journalist for Horace Greeley's *New York Tribune* and as an essayist for the radical book *Woman in the Nineteenth Century*, published in 1845. Fuller was brilliant, highly educated, and said to be the best-read woman in America. Her revolutionary theory was that women needed intellectual and religious freedom equal to men's. A true union, she said, was possible only when both man and woman were self-dependent individuals. The book was both praised and damned, but it is known as the first of its kind in America, and it launched the feminist movement. She is known today as a powerful influence in contemporary American thinking.

In 1846, the newspaper sent her to Europe to become the first woman foreign correspondent. In her mid-thirties, she was in Italy writing about the Italian struggle for unification. Alone except for friends she had made abroad, she fell in love with Giovanni Ossoli, a young Italian nobleman. He was a Catholic whose religion and family prohibited their marriage. The couple had a son, then left Italy for a new life in America.

Their ship had almost reached land when a hurricane drove it onto a sandbar. The ship was only fifty yards off the shore of Fire Island, New York, but the wind and waves were so strong, people standing on land in the storm could not go to their aid and the people on the ship could not reach the shore. The horrified crowd watched the shipwreck to its tragic end. They saw Giovanni with baby Angelo and Margaret in a white nightgown on deck struggling against the battering water. They saw those three and all other passengers swept overboard to drown.

Albertina Sisulu was ninety-two when she died. Margaret Fuller was forty.

Both women lived at times in history when so much was against them—the laws of their lands, society's convention, sometimes religion. Working against odds, they took what they had at hand, which was talent and courage and personal integrity and determination, and they made bouquets of their lives. They made green bouquets.

In fairy tales, girls spin straw into gold, but in life, some women make green bouquets.

Neighborhoods

Here's the skinny on neighborhoods from archaeologists and urban scholars:

> Fact Number 1: Neighborhoods in some form existed among primitive congregations of people and within ancient cities.
>
> Fact Number 2: Neighborhoods are generally thought of as a geographical space within a larger city or village.
>
> Fact Number 3: Neighborhoods can be defined as spatial units with lots of face-to-face social interaction.

You can say that again, the part about face-to-face interaction. Whatever it's called—parish, borough, residential community, or—in China—administrative division, neighborhoods can be heavy lifting.

Sometimes it's not even face to face. It can be anonymous unilateral action, everything from dumping garbage on a lawn to mean-spirited posts on social media. It can be pounding on the ceiling, shouting over the fence, phoning irate messages, or calling the landlord. It can involve regular communication on the mayor's Action Line. It can be having Animal Welfare on speed dial. It can involve police reports and attorneys.

It's not just neighborhoods; it's people. I can't think of any circle of people I've joined that hasn't come to some kind of hair pulling, but neighborhoods can be the worst. Officers, bosses, members, employees, colleagues—they all move on or straighten up. Neighbors usually stay put. And some of them stay difficult.

Former City of Tulsa mayor Rodger Randle told me he believes we have a civic duty to our neighbors to keep our front yards tidy. What about our backyards? Driveways? House color? Vehicle collection?

It is hard to keep everybody happy. It's hard to communicate and resolve differences. No wonder pockets of geography are always erupting in violence. Remember the Kingston Trio song,

> The French hate the Germans, the Germans hate the Poles;
> Italians hate Yugoslavs, South Africans hate the Dutch,
> And I don't like anybody very much.

Just as I was sinking into a permanent malaise, a ray of human sunshine appeared. It took a catastrophe in my garden to reveal it.

One fat, happy day was ruined when I looked out to see that all of my rosebushes had died or were dying. All of them—front yard, backyard, side yards of the house. "All of them" means some twenty rosebushes of different ages and varieties. Rosebushes that had been green and flowering one day were suddenly stricken down as if by Old Testament wrath.

It wasn't the recent rose disease that had decimated Tulsa's Rose Garden. This was different. This calamity looked as if someone with a flamethrower had gone through my garden blasting the rosebushes at waist height. Some bushes were completely dead; others were left with a two-foot-wide expanse of brown, dead leaves across the center of the plant.

That was the bad news. Here comes the good news.

I sent out an S.O.S. to gardeners, and they came on the run. They came by foot, by pickup truck, and by e-mail. They were nursery owners, master gardeners, amateur gardeners, rose experts, garden book authors, and concerned neighbors with gardens of their own.

The cause of this horticulture tragedy was determined to be excessive insecticide spraying in direct sun in the heat of the day by overzealous garden helpers. That's the best guess. Gardeners are opinionated people and the opinions vary, but what we have agreed on is a therapy of watering, pruning, watching, and waiting.

I have been shored up with such morale boosters as "Don't despair. All may not be lost." And "If the worst happens, we'll get you more roses." The roses and I are still despondent, but we're feeling somewhat better.

Gardeners may differ on politics, religion, music, noise, volume, wind chimes, bird feeders, cats, dogs, trees, insecticides, and God knows what else, but we agree on this: innocent gardens should not be destroyed, rosebushes should not die a mysterious death, and gardeners must join forces to save the day.

It's a very good start. From the neighborhood to world peace?

Grass: It's a Guy Thing

I'm a magpie when it comes to gardens. I want every shiny new garden I see. And I want it right now.

Oh, how my eyes sparkled when I read that the New York Botanical Garden had an exhibition combining Emily Dickinson's poetry and flowers. I wanted that garden for myself. "Emily Dickinson's Garden: The Poetry of Flowers" was a spring flower show with a self-guided poetry walk. The Poetry Society of America was the collaborator.

I called the Botanical Garden and ordered copies of the program for my book club. Here were pictures of Dickinson's favorite flowers from her nineteenth-century New England garden: peony, columbine, daisy, dandelion, and more. Here were her poems that were miniature word portraits of those flowers: columbine's bonnet, daisy's shyness, hyacinth's ruffled head.

This Dickinson poem is about a carmine-red tulip:

> She slept beneath a tree—
> Remembered but by me.
> I touched her Cradle mute—
> She recognized the foot—
> Put on her Carmine suit
> And see!

I read that during her life, she was better known as a gardener than a poet and that she frequently sent flowers or nosegays to friends. Often she tucked a tiny poem into the bouquet gift.

My appetite grew. Now I want a Tulsa garden exhibit of Emily Dickinson's flowers combined with a poetry reading. I want the whole package.

Although I'm as greedy as a magpie, my attention span is more like that of a mayfly. My memory flittered from Emily Dickinson to a lecture I heard about gardens of the Bible. What a fascinating exhibition that could be, with information ranging from historic irrigation skills required to literary interpretations of biblical vineyards, olive trees, oaks, cedars, thorns, herbs, figs, pomegranates, and fragrant paradises.

My own garden is an exuberant hodgepodge of roses, dahlias, hollyhocks, and whatever beguiling annual catches my eye. I describe it, rather grandly, as an Oklahoma version of a cottage garden. That means it is crowded, overplanted, and always a happy surprise.

One of my favorite escapes is to sit in the dappled sun of my back garden and read. This serenity has been shattered of late by two small children next door. I like the children, and to them, the three of us must seem like a scene from *To Kill a Mockingbird* with me as a friendly Boo Radley.

Guess how many times an hour small children can say, "Hi, Connie. Hi, Connie. Hi, Connie" in piping voices. A lot. A whole lot. This calls for a handyman and a taller fence. Is it worth the cost? Yes, although this time of the summer both the garden and I are burned out. All that remains is the grass with its malevolent mantra, "Mow me. Mow me."

As much as I enjoy my small patch of grass, we don't bond as I do with the garden of shrubs and flowers. Here's my take on lawns: grass—it's a guy thing. I don't know any women who enjoy edging and blowing and mowing their lawns as much as my male neighbors do. The men may not even look at flowers or shrubs, but their lawns are their pride, joy, and glory. For a while, to my gardening embarrassment, my neighbor was a single, straight, young man whose grass was far better than my own. I hired a lawn care company to get me up to speed. What is the reason for this attitude toward our lawns and gardens? My theory, totally without evidence, is that flower gardens represent domesticity to women. This is our nest and we beautify it.

I don't understand the male ego of grass. Maybe it is the masculine energy of mowing and edging large spaces. Maybe it is the suggestion of a golf course. Maybe it is the history of lawns that connect men to the lord of the manor.

Lawns are a sixteenth-century European invention. The original term, *launde,* meant a glade in the woods. Then, in the seventeenth century, lawns were cultivated around French and English castles. These were often planted with chamomile or thyme, and since they required cheap labor to maintain them, they were the province of the wealthy.

Fast-forward to the late 1800s and the invention of the rotary lawn mower and the garden hose. Every man could be a lord. Before that, Woodrow Wilson kept sheep on the White House lawn. And then came the nineteenth-century public parks and then post–World War II suburbs with miles of houses surrounded by lawns.

And here we are.

The neighborhood men are outside with their pride and their noisy lawn equipment defying the heat, and I am inside with air-conditioning and a book.

Vive la différence.

I Like a Vine

In my next life, I want to come back as a vine.

If you wonder why, clearly you do not spend August in Oklahoma. Hotter than words can describe in a G-rated book. Hot and dry and windy.

I scuttle around like a lizard, dragging the garden hose with me. In August, I personally finance the City of Tulsa's water department. And still the little leaves wilt, the bushes droop, and the hard ground rends itself in great, barren cracks like Alexandre Hogue's painting *Mother Earth Laid Bare.*

Then, in the heart of this blast furnace, like another Old Testament plague, comes the vines. Green vines everywhere: climbing, clawing, scrambling. Bind vine, smother vine, vines I've never seen before spewing up from the middle of the lawn. It is like a green, science fiction movie.

Everything else in the garden gasps for life, but the vines—oh, the mighty vines—how they triumph. And so, I want to be reincarnated as a vine. Just consider all of their virtues: strength, tenacity, determination, daring.

Vines don't take up much ground space and can cover something unsightly. Think of a big trumpet vine. It is beautiful and fragrant. Think of wisteria, jasmine, honeysuckle, clematis. (The problem with clematis is how to pronounce it: CLEMatis, clemAHtis. And the embarrassing suspicion that it sounds like some part of the human anatomy.)

Vines are educational, too. Some of my vines come back year after year to remind me that some mistakes just don't go away, such as the bushy old-fashioned purple morning glory I planted years ago.

Being a vine will let me explore my darker side. I'll be persistently annoying like a little eight-year-old boy I know named Michael. He was angry one day because he'd been told he couldn't go outside alone.

"It's not fair," he said. "I'm smart and strong. I wouldn't let anyone hurt me."

"You're too little," I explained.

He said, "Then I'd annoy them to death."

"That," I told him, "is a real possibility."

When I'm a vine it'll be all about me—my climb to the sun. I'll be a Joan Crawford vine, I won't care whom I step on to get ahead. I agree with that great actor/philosopher William Shatner, who said that the worst human emotion is regret. A vine has no regrets.

I'll also be cunning. I'll thread myself through the rosebushes and laugh when the cursing gardener tries to pull me out and ends up with thorns in her soon-to-be-infected fingertips.

And then, when I've overtaken the fence and the pole and the rest of the garden, I'll stand alone in glory. People will paint my portrait like Henry VIII in all his majesty, standing with legs wide apart and hands on hips.

But when I'm a vine I'll also inspire fables and songs and literature because, of course, my most famous vine relative is the grapevine.

Leif Ericson named the land he discovered, lush with grapevines—
Vineyard. People sing raucous and woeful songs about the fruit of
the vine. Steinbeck wrote about *The Grapes of Wrath.*

In the 1600s, the pastoral English poet Robert Herrick wrote a
poem titled "The Vine" that is so poetically erotic I dare not quote all
of it, but here's how it begins:

> I dreamed this mortal part of mine
> Was metamorphosed to a vine,
> Which, crawling one and every way,
> Enthralled my dainty Lucia.
> Methought her long small legs and thighs
> I with my tendrils did surprise:
> Her belly, buttocks, and her waist
> By my soft nervelets were embraced.

In his later years, Herrick wrote poems about spirituality, but in his
youth, oh, my, how he wrote about vines.

Let's move on to the many religious allusions to the vine. The
Bible is full of vines as parables, metaphors, and morality lessons:
Jesus as the vine, the Israelites from Egypt as the vine, the lazy
tenant of a vineyard, the vine that brings forth no good fruit. It was
coveting a particularly lush vineyard that tempted Queen Jezebel to
murder.

I particularly like this religious story about the vine. The rabbis
said that at the foot of the first vine planted by Noah, a fiend planted
three things: a lion, a lamb, and a hog. Therefore from the fruit of the
vine mankind can receive either ferocity, mildness, or wallowing in
the mire.

Oh, I so want to be a vine.

Pickles and Tomatoes

It's been an emotional summer. Remorse, worry, and a bit of guilt. First, I was remorseful and guilty about pickles. Then I began to worry about tomatoes. Let me start at the beginning.

I was reading a novel set in the early 1900s and came across a passage about a doctor having a breakfast of cold ham and pickles. Pickles! I thought. When I was a restaurant critic, I read books about food in history. Pickles had a starring role. Cleopatra ate them for beauty and spirituality. Julius Caesar ate them for health. Napoleon hauled them along to feed his armies on campaign. Aristotle wrote about them, as did authors of the Bible. Sailors ate them to prevent scurvy. Elegant menus of the 1800s often listed "assorted pickles." Shame on me for taking pickles for granted.

I vowed to take up pickling. First, I would have to overcome two fears bred into me from the 1950s: the dreaded pressure cooker ("They'll explode and kill you"), and any food left unrefrigerated for fifteen minutes will kill you with food poisoning.

I jumped into my new hobby by ordering a stack of books about pickling. *The Art of Fermentation* by Sandor Ellix Katz seems to be the primary authority. The author is so keen on the subject, he writes about his "love affair with sauerkraut." He writes with emotion about fermenting everything: yogurt, bread, cheese, fruits, vegetables, beer, wine, grain, beans, fish, eggs, and much more. Bacteria is our friend, he declares, not our enemy. "When it's late at night and quiet in the house," he writes, "I can hear my ferments gurgling contentedly." It's a joyful sound to him: "It means my microbes are happy."

Sadly, this fascinating book was too much for me. It was like taking a graduate class in bacteria, enzymes, and anaerobic metabolism.

I moved on to easier instructional books: *The Joy of Pickling* by Linda Ziedrich and *Pickled* by Kelly Carrolata. From them I learned the basics, that pickling means preserving food with salt or vinegar or both. I learned we have a national Pickle Day; that Hyderabad, India, is considered pickle heaven; and that some Chinese and Japanese travel with suitcases full of pickles. I read about pickle crocks and jars and seasonings. I learned that some people use pickle brine as a cosmetic and some as a hangover remedy. The more I read, the more making my own pickles seemed too labor-intensive. Lazy to the bone, I put away the instruction books and turned my attention to tomatoes.

Even I can grow a few tomatoes. I planted some of my favorite varieties in large pots, wondering again if the Cherokees really did bring the seeds of Cherokee Purple with them over the Trail of Tears. I set pots of grape and cherry tomatoes by the door so I can pop a tiny tomato into my mouth as I come and go.

I believe that everything goes better with books, so during a short rainy season, I read *The Big, Bad Book of Botany* by Michael Largo and learned fascinating facts about the tomato, *Lycopersicon esculentum.* The French call it *pomme d'amour,* love apple, and both the Serbs and the Croats refer to it as the paradise fruit. The name likely comes from the Aztecs' word *tomatl,* meaning "the swelling fruit." Summer's ubiquitous tomato was soaring to new stature in my opinion. I was like a crying drunk hanging onto the plant, saying, "I love you, buddy."

Sadly, I also read *Tomatoland* by Barry Estabrook. A blurb on the book's cover says, "It will change the way you think about America's most popular vegetable," and, boy, is that right. Except that according to my research the tomato is the *second* most popular vegetable, behind lettuce. Furthermore, botanically speaking, the tomato is a fruit, although in 1893 the Supreme Court ruled it was a vegetable for taxation purposes. (Michael Largo tells us that scientifically the tomato is neither fruit nor vegetable but a berry.)

In *Tomatoland* I learned the history of the tomato. It traveled from its ancestral home in the deserts of Peru and Ecuador to Spain, Italy, France, and eventually California. This book is a condemnation of the tomato industry in Florida, where the plant is grown in barren sandy soil and pumped full of chemical fertilizers and herbicides. These are picked hard and green, gassed with ethylene to a ruby red, then sold to us "as bereft of nutrition as they are of flavor."

Even if I could get past that unappetizing news, I couldn't overlook the book's report of the slavery of the Florida tomato workers. "Not virtual slavery, or near slavery, or slavery like conditions," according to the chief assistant U.S. attorney in Florida, "but real slavery."

No longer will I buy grocery store tomatoes. Until my own handful of tomatoes ripens, thank heavens for the local farmers' markets. I've also renewed my vows with Vlasic pickles.

The New Gang in the Hood

I live in a sleepy midtown neighborhood so quaint even Mr. Rogers would be bored. I'm surprised there's not a street in my neighborhood named Pleasant Street. And if there were, a plump and kindly Mrs. White would live here, cooling apple pies on her windowsill.

We're big on pets in my neighborhood. Around the corner, Mrs. Brown daily walks her black poodle named Jeffy, and trailing along behind them is her calico cat Chelsea. Some would find this scenario unusual. We don't, because a couple of blocks away, Mr. Graves walks his pug dog named Peco on a leash, and following them is his calico cat Blanche.

We know all the pets' names in my neighborhood.

Into this tranquil scene, a new gang has moved in. Six of them, all with one family. All at one house. Or, more precisely, all in one backyard. They're hens. It's big news in the 'hood. A very nice family with two little girls named Sarah and Lily has acquired six hens and named them: Lucy, Louise, Iolana, Fiona, Kelsey, and Cindy.

The father built a state-of-the-art cage, but during the day, the chickens are allowed out to wander around the backyard. The little boy next door tries to catch them. Lily and Sarah call the flock to come eat when it's suppertime.

Who knew you could keep chickens in the city? You can, but evidently not a rooster. We're so conditioned to think politically correctly, that seems a bit discriminatory, doesn't it?

I like the looks of chickens. I wondered if I resemble a chicken when my friend Maridel sent me a photograph of a fancy chicken, a Bearded Buff Laced Polish hen, with a note stating, "If you were a hen, this is the hen you would be. A glamour hen."

I've been to visit the local chickens several times. And like a good neighbor, I wanted to take them a welcome-to-the-neighborhood gift. What do you give the chicken that has everything? A covered dish is always safe, I thought. So I took them a mixed grill. A mixed ungrill, actually: grapes, sunflower seeds, and nuts with some parsley from my garden for garnish. The mother of the house said, "This is a gourmet treat for them. They're used to bugs and leftover oatmeal."

I think having a little garden and raising chickens is part of the human urge to touch the earth and get back to nature. At some point, most of us want to feel part of the greater universe around us. Most of us live in the city now. I don't often see the deer and antelope roam, but I see that the cardinals in my backyard are flocking. It's that season. They scatter the sunflower seeds with abandon, and I suspect that attracts mice under the bird feeder. The clue was seeing my cat Veronica trot toward the house with a tiny, gray mouse tail trailing out of her mouth.

We all feed one another, don't we? In many ways. One way is literal. The nice family with chickens brought me six fresh, free-range eggs. The eggs had yolks as orange as cling peach halves. They were so proud of the eggs, humans and chickens alike. It's not exactly a sustainable lifestyle they're aiming for, though. The father laughed and said they figured each egg being produced in the backyard costs about five dollars.

Then, sadly, the family's dog ate one of the chickens (Kelsey, I think). And then the rest of the chickens died during one of Oklahoma's spectacular heat waves.

Ah, Mother Nature—so red of tooth and claw.

A Duet about Birds

Wanted: Mockingbird

Although my neighborhood is a drowsy one, recent violence on my block has been front-page news. The crime wave was in the *Tulsa World* newspaper and covered on TV by the local Fox News affiliate. And, I'm not kidding about this—the post office distributed Wanted posters.

The perpetrator is still at large. I think I saw the guilty party myself, but I'm not sure. That's because the culprit is a mocking-bird—a.k.a. *Mimus polyglottos*. Description: about ten inches in length with a long tail and white patches on a gray coat. I don't want to stereotype, but all mockingbirds look alike to me.

According to the newspaper report, for some weeks an aggressive songbird has been harassing the mail carrier, flying from tree to tree, chimney to chimney, and swooping down to peck at her. The Postal Service issued the same letter it does for hostile dogs, saying if the animal isn't confined, mail service to the home might be interrupted. When the same thing happened in Houston twenty years ago, *Texas Monthly* magazine jeered the U.S. Postal Service for being a sissy-pants.

The response in our neighborhood has been what you might expect from neighbors. "Gee," we said, "he always seemed like such a nice bird, a quiet neighbor, and a devoted parent."

That seems to be the problem. Mockingbirds are such devoted parents, sometimes they defend their nests aggressively against predators—cats, snakes, opossums, raccoons, other birds, and even dutiful mail carriers.

But let us give the mockingbird credit for its other virtues. Sing-ing, for instance. The mockingbird is known as America's Songbird and the King of Song. The Latin name means "many-tongued mimic." Both male and female sing, but the male sings the most—and the loudest. He even sings at night. Mostly he sings a song of love to attract a mate and to define a territory. Usually he starts softly, often hidden in shrubbery, but as he gets carried away by passion, he sings louder and louder. He flies to a high perch for the finale.

Sometimes he flings himself into the air to hit a high note. What girl could resist that?

Mockingbirds sing a medley, imitating other birds with great precision. They also mimic other animals—frogs, chickens, crickets—and even machinery or squeaky gates. They repeat a song five or six times and usually have a repertoire of twenty or thirty songs. A mockingbird in Boston named Arnold holds the record; he could mimic fifty-one species.

Once the mockingbird's concert has won him a mate, he settles into monogamous domesticity and sings less. (If he were a male human mate, he would lose interest in going dancing, attending the theater, or doing home repairs. He would claim the TV remote control as his own.) When the mockingbird incubation and fledgling is completed, however, in about twenty-four days, he starts singing again. His outburst of song is a signal to the female for the nesting process to begin again. This goes on from March through August as the mockingbirds build five or six nests.

Even naturalists rhapsodize over the mockingbird's musical talent. They say he sings with more joy, power, abandon, and even more emotion than other birds. No wonder the northern mockingbird is the state bird of five states: Texas, Arkansas, Florida, Mississippi, and Tennessee. Artists write poems, songs, and novels extolling the mockingbird. Some say it is the very embodiment of the South. The Choctaw name for the mockingbird is *hushi balbaha,* which means "the bird that speaks in a foreign tongue." In Hopi mythology, the mockingbird gave humans the gift of language.

Yet because mockingbirds are so territorially defensive, some people think of them as bullies. One bird author says that up to 50 percent of the questions he receives are about how to deal with annoying mockingbirds.

I don't know if any of the inquiries are from the Tulsa post office, but I do know that a notorious mockingbird—singing for joy—is still at large in my neighborhood.

Four and Twenty Black Birds

Every once in a while it's good for us to take an unpopular stand. Go against the tide for something we believe in. And here is mine these days—starlings. Others may see them as a nuisance, but I love them.

I have developed an affection for almost all black birds. I like them in art and in nature. If three can be considered a collection, then I have a collection of Zuni blackbird fetishes carved of black marble with turquoise eyes. Each is no larger than a thimble. A fetish has a spirit and magic power. What is the difference between a fetish and a carving? According to Mark Bahti's book *Spirit in the Stone*, "If you believe it is a fetish, it is."

Black birds appear in poetry from nursery rhymes to this haiku:

> A lone crow
> sits on a dead branch
> this autumn eve.

The quoting raven is menacing in Edgar Allan Poe's poem, but in Native American stories it is a trickster who taught humans to enjoy life. An old folksong about blackbirds existed long before the Lennon/McCartney song that starts "Blackbird singing in the dead of night." The jazzy ballad "Bye Bye Blackbird" is largely why I was drawn to blackbirds in the first place. But what does that song mean?

According to my research, the song was written in 1926 and refers to a lady who was leaving the big city and going home to her mother. "Blackbird" may be a term for the men in the city or slang for the city itself. One thing is clear. The lady, sad and disillusioned, was out of there. A later verse in the original version is about bluebirds.

But starlings—now that's a bird of another order. These birds do not hop; they walk on legs that turn from brown to bright pink during mating season. (Think how interesting it would be if human legs did that. We would know so much more about one another.)

Starlings have a romantic nature. Males sometimes decorate a love nest with flowers, then woo females inside with a song, much like a troubadour. Adult starlings eat insects and grain, but juveniles have a particular fondness for cherries. I told a four-year-old boy this, and he said, "I wonder if their tongues are pink."

In winter, I see starlings sitting as silently as black ornaments in bare trees. In the spring, I watch them strut like drum majors across greening lawns. At twilight the aerial pyrotechnics of starling flocks are breathtaking.

The names of flocks of birds are charming: an ostentation of peacocks, a murder of crows, a paddling of ducks, and a stand of flamingos. Starlings? A group of starlings is called a murmuration.

One autumn evening in downtown Tulsa, just as the sun was setting in smears of gold and saffron, enormous swarms of starlings came in to roost. They came from the fields where they had been feeding, and one flock after another joined a huge murmuration circling overhead. The main group circled, looped, cut sharply left, then right, and spiraled in figure eights. Each arriving flock merged with the others. Eventually, the overhead sky was flecked with black. Thousands of starlings circled in one direction for about twenty minutes and suddenly descended as a whole into four trees, as smoothly as if drawing a shade. The birds chittered noisily for a few moments, saying their prayers and goodnights, then went to bed.

Below the starlings, as night darkened, musicians and singers in formal black attire filed into a Gothic church for a classical concert. Day ended with the black flock's spectacular flight, and night began with tuxedoed musicians.

What symmetry. What a joyful noise—musicians performing Mozart under a murmuration of starlings.

Charlie's Web

The afternoons feel like summer, but the calendar says early fall. Maples blush with color and the leaves rustle in the giant sycamore in my front yard. Autumn is slipping in.

In this bridge between two seasons, I almost walked into an enormous spiderweb that spanned the width of my driveway, strung between a white crape myrtle bush and a tall yaupon holly tree. The web itself was the circumference of a bed pillow.

What kind of spider can make a web this large? I wondered. How can a spider travel some sixteen feet across the driveway to establish the silken structure?

This was no itsy-bitsy spider climbing up the waterspout. What I found was a large, light brown spider, the size of a button. I learned that it is an orb-weaving spider.

The orb weaver is the spider that spins the classic web associated with Halloween. It is a nonaggressive and low-toxicity spider. The greatest danger to people, I read on the Internet, is walking into its web at night. The fright of feeling a large spider on your face can give people over forty a heart attack. Oh, come on. Who writes that stuff? Who believes it?

My orb weaver is not quite like Charlotte, the heroine of E. B. White's book *Charlotte's Web*. Charlotte was gray, and her family is most associated with barns. My spider—Charlie, I think is his name—is more ambitious. Traditionally he strings his webs between buildings and shrubs in summer gardens to catch flies and mosquitoes. I watched Charlie for several days, and I spied on him at night. I could see that he is shy. By day he hides in the holly tree. At night he comes out to check his catch and repair his web.

I read in the *Encyclopedia of Insects and Spiders* that the orb weaver is very nearsighted and manages his creative silk work by touch. To span such great distances, he lets out a long line of silk and waits for a breeze to catch it—and him—and carry him airborne to a tree or bush. This freewheeling travel is called ballooning. The dragline silk of the golden orb weaver is the strongest natural fiber known, more elastic than nylon and stronger than steel of the same diameter.

One day as I stood admiring the web, Louie the yellow cat batted playfully at a pot of tall ornamental grass and knocked loose one of the web's anchoring strands. That corner of the web rolled up as fast as a window shade. The next morning, the web had been mended perfectly.

After a particularly windy day, both the web and Charlie were gone. Had he chosen a less vulnerable place for his web? I read that webs located lower, closer to the ground, are more efficient for catching insects. Or had his short life come to an end? The spider has an ancient lineage—some 400 million years old—but many spiders live only one year. Yet what an adventurous and artistic year it is. During courtship, the male orb weaver attaches a thread to the female's web and spends hours plucking it like a harp, beguiling her to join him.

About this same time, I visited people in two separate nursing homes. I was full of energy. Some of the patients I saw were active and vital. A few others were slumped in wheelchairs. Some were there temporarily; for others it was a final destination.

We are all—Charlie the spider, Louie the cat, we humans—moving through our life cycles at different paces. We are much like Gerald Murphy's large painting of the gears of a watch—different sizes, different speeds.

Charlie the spider, the smallest of us all, has moved on from my sight. But perhaps that is his web I seek higher and in a taller tree.

Gilding the Lily

Lucky me. A little girl named Lily has moved into the neighborhood. She is nine years old and has lots of girlfriends who come to play. They roller-skate, bicycle, skip rope, wear matching headbands, and have sleepovers. They are fonts of energy and good deeds.

One sunny Saturday morning, Lily and her friend Macee ran up my driveway with an announcement.

"We want to make a difference," Lily said. "We want to raise money and give it to the SPCA. We were going to wash everyone's car in the neighborhood, but my dad said no."

"Your dad's smart," I said.

"Then we were going to ride our bikes through the neighborhood with a sign that says we'll wash everyone's dog, but my dad said no again."

"Another smart decision."

"So then we thought, 'We'll do chores for Connie!'" Bull's-eye.

They told me they were up for anything, any chore I didn't want to do. They told me they were experienced gardeners and good at weeding.

"How about sweeping out the garage?" I suggested.

"We can do that," Lily said. "I volunteer at the therapeutic riding center. I sweep lots of stuff there. Even yucky stuff."

The sweeping had barely begun when they decided the garage floor needed to be cleared. That meant me. I moved lawn mowers, dragged bags of soil, and scooted storage boxes to give them a clear shot.

Then they spotted several things like Christmas decorations that ought to be moved into the garage attic. They assured me they were strong and could do it.

"I don't know," I said. "This attic ladder is so narrow."

"We'll let Macee do it," Lily said. "She's little."

"I'm afraid you'll fall," I said.

"That's okay," Lily said. "Macee is a gymnast. If she falls she can nail a perfect landing. Like this—ta da!"

So it was I who climbed the narrow ladder to the attic, precariously hauling Christmas trees and boxes. They swept, but I got to be involved in this task, too.

"Hey, Connie. Do you have any trash bags?"

"Hey, Connie. Do you have a dustpan?"

Then we moved smartly to the weeding. My garden gloves came up to their elbows, like evening gloves. To protect their knees, I had one green, padded kneeler and one folded towel.

"I call the green kneeler," Macee said. ("Call" is equivalent to saying "dibs.")

"Do you have a banana?" Lily asked. "Because if you do, we can plant it near the rosebush and the roses will be beautiful. That's what my mom does."

We were all disappointed to learn that I had no banana.

"Do you have clippers?" Lily asked. "Because I'll need to clip off these dandelion heads or they'll spread. That's what my mom does." I silently questioned this approach to dandelions, quietly hid the clippers, and told them I had none. This saddened us.

Just before we plunged into weeding, Lily decided lunch was needed and went to place the order. Soon her mother arrived with two little plates. They went inside and sat on my cushioned window seat to eat.

"Not too long now," I joked. "You're on the clock." I chuckled. They didn't answer. They didn't smile. They looked at me expressionless with huge blue eyes as they ate their sandwiches and carrot sticks in silence. Evidently nine-year-olds don't joke about lunch. Neither do they chuckle.

Back in the garden, before weeding could begin, they applied more sunscreen and drank from their water bottles. Nine-year-olds are scrupulous about avoiding sunburn and dehydration.

By then, however, they decided it was too hot to weed in the direct sun. A far better task would be raking leaves out of shady flower beds. This job was full of amazing discoveries.

"Hey, Connie. Come look. We found a whole family of roly-poly bugs."

"Hey, Connie, look what we got you," Lily said, with an outstretched hand. "Three worms!" Who wouldn't be happy with that?

They couldn't reach all of the leaves, they told me with little regret, but they got almost all of them. Well, some of them. The others, I could deal with later. The immediate raking required more help from me.

"Hey, Connie, do you have a rake? Do you have any more plastic bags? Do you have a bigger dustpan?" We improvised with garbage pan lids.

Then someone arrived to take them swimming and they ran down the street.

Doing chores for a good cause can be exhausting.

I went inside to take a nap. I "called" the sofa.

Something Awful Has Happened

When I was thirteen, I hosted a New Year's Eve dance. In my small hometown, the only place available for big parties was the fellowship hall at Saint Catherine's Catholic church.

I couldn't have a big birthday party there, because my birthday usually fell during Lent, which I didn't understand at the time, since I'm not Roman Catholic. All I knew was that it was a blackout time for parties at the church. That didn't seem fair, since spring was the best time for pretty dresses. One spring I had a new dress with a gathered bodice, which made me look—almost—as if I had a bust.

All of the kids' dances, and even the dancing classes we attended, were held at Saint Catherine's. At my New Year's Eve party we danced to "Rock Around the Clock," "Dance with Me Henry," and "Cherry Pink and Apple Blossom White." At least, some of us danced. Most of the boys didn't want to dance. They knew how, since they had been forced to attend dance classes. They just didn't want to be that close to girls. They stood together on one side of the hall pushing and tripping one another and daring others to go ask a girl to dance. Every few songs, the chaperones would make the boys dance with us.

The party was over well before midnight. Although it was a Friday night and there was no school the next day, we were still kids and not allowed to stay up too late.

My friend Sparky Wilkinson—one of the few boys who would dance—asked me to take charge of his collection of 45 rpm records he had brought. He had come to the dance on his new motor scooter and was afraid he would drop them on the way home. Back at my own home, I spent considerable time organizing them for him.

The next morning, friends called to tell me, "Something awful has happened."

Sparky and some other boys had gone to one of their homes to see in the New Year. I think the parents were gone. At midnight, the boy whose home it was got his father's shotgun and fired a round into the sky to celebrate. As he walked back toward the house, the shotgun fired again. Sparky, age fourteen, was standing in the open doorway watching. The shot hit him in the chest, killing him immediately.

Days later, as a class, we walked in a line to his funeral at the First Baptist Church. It was an open-casket funeral. I was shocked at how white his face was; the color made his freckles more prominent. He would have been proud of his flat top, I thought, so waxed and perfectly straight.

A few weeks later, my father drove me to Sparky's home to return his record collection to his mother, a war widow and schoolteacher.

Half a Decade Later

One recent Saturday afternoon, a weeping woman woke me out of a nap with her persistent ringing of the doorbell. Something awful had happened. She said that her granddaughter Lily, who lives across the street from me, had been in terrible accident. Lily, the same perky little girl who did those Saturday garden chores with her friend Macee. Lily, who had helped me with many busy projects after that—painting the fence, cleaning litter boxes, and sweeping the garage apartment. Lily, by then fourteen, was one of six young teenage girls who had spent the night before at a birthday party slumber party. That morning all six climbed onto a utility terrain vehicle for a short ride. The UTV, designed for two people, tipped over, and the girls were hurt. Lily's injury was the most serious. At that moment, she was in a hospital's intensive care unit; her right arm had been amputated.

The news was so awful, I couldn't comprehend it. It was raining and I was sleepy; maybe that's why the message seemed incomprehensible. I made the crying grandmother tell me again. We both stood in the rain and clutched our hearts, and then one another. I wonder if collected broken hearts offer solace to the families with hearts smashed and shattered.

Just a week before, I saw Lily and some friends taking photos in her front yard. They were wearing party clothes, on their way to a school dance. "How she is growing," I thought. "Long blond hair, long legs that go on forever, and young-girl cute-beautiful."

Age fourteen. So invincible. So fragile. One minute a party, the next minute something awful has happened.

Every Little Bit Helps

My current philosophy is this: every little bit helps.

Take energy conservation, the whole Green Movement. I read that in England, Prince Charles has converted his Jaguar to operate on used cooking oil. See what I mean? Every little bit helps.

I can apply this philosophy to seasons, both the seasons of the calendar year and the seasons of life. As one season winds down, I feel wistful. Summer, like my future, used to stretch before me as wide as the Oklahoma horizon, so big I couldn't see around it. Then I looked up and summer had gathered her hat and purse and was heading out the door.

Had I squeezed every little bit of juice out of this season? Had I learned everything I could?

I had learned

- that the reason my orange cosmos sway in the breeze on tall stems is to attract pollinating insects;
- that the reason jalapeño peppers are hot is to discourage foraging mammals but to allow birds to eat them and spread the seeds; and
- that poet Billy Collins said Emily Dickinson's poems are so rhythmic, most of them can be sung to the tune of "Yellow Rose of Texas."

The more seasons I notch on my belt, the more fascinated I am about the natural world around me. Playwright Alan Bennett wrote as he was recovering from cancer that he wanted to spend every available minute out of doors. He read, wrote, dozed, and ate in a big chair on the lawn.

I am not recovering from anything. I am as fit, as the English say, as the butcher's dog, but as I sat outside, clinging to summer's twilights, I wondered with all the curiosity of Galileo pondering the stars, "Why do locusts rasp?"

It seemed like a question of great depth.

What I learned is that (a) they are not locusts, they are cicadas. Locusts are really what we call grasshoppers. And (b) cicadas don't rasp, they sing. Crickets and grasshoppers make a rasping sound by rubbing their legs together, but cicadas sing. The tymbals on the sides of their abdomen make one of the loudest noises of all insects.

Only the male cicadas make this sound, singing for love to attract the mute females. They make other sounds, too, some so high-pitched we humans cannot hear them. And they sing for other reasons, primarily to repel birds and other predators, including humans. The males' bodies are more hollow, which is what allows them to make that loud sound. I am reminded of the Chinese adage "It is the empty pan that makes the loudest sound." I refer to cicadas, not males in general.

I learned that humans from ancient Greece to China and the Congo have eaten cicadas, favoring the meatier and tastier female. Not I, but other humans.

Eating cicadas doesn't seem quite fair, since they do not sting us, bite us, or eat our crops. They can damage young trees or shrubs, but mostly they spend their lives making a loud, joyful noise and being part of the food chain for birds, raccoons, opossums, and other animals.

Here we like to keep our crickets outside, but in China, crickets are kept in special cages. Some Chinese species are fighting crickets, which are prized.

Just as I was becoming too gooey about the great outdoors, I had a final fling with gardening—and got a poison ivy rash.

Did you know that the itchy rash may not appear just where you came in contact with the plant? And that the rash cannot be spread from one part of your body to another by scratching the blisters or by touching a person who has a poison ivy rash? Washing the skin immediately after contact helps, but the toxin is quickly absorbed through the skin into the blood system. That is why rashes can break out days or even weeks later in places the plant didn't touch. And that is why some of us must treat poison ivy internally with some kind of cortisone.

Cicadas, poetry, poison ivy, and Prince Charles's energy-conserving Jaguar—maybe it's not a lot to learn one whole summer, but as I said, every little bit helps.

Airing Laundry

Here's a true story that I read in the *Wall Street Journal*.

One fine day in Bend, Oregon, a woman did a load of laundry and hung the sheets outside on a clothesline to dry. Oh my gawd—what a ruckus it caused.

It seems that she lives in a very chichi neighborhood. One that prohibits outdoor clotheslines. Her neighbors are up in arms—outraged, incensed, claiming that her behavior decreases property values. Gives the neighborhood a bad image. They're threatening legal action. Her defense is that fresh-air drying is part of the Green Movement and preserves energy.

What a cute little story, I thought. Then I read on and learned that some 60 million people live in 300,000 neighborhood associations that restrict outdoor laundry hanging. As my great-aunt Maude would say, "Good God Gertie, what's this world coming to?"

I'm of two minds about this. The only issue I have with clotheslines is that when I was in college, I hung a silky black-and-white dress—my favorite dress—on the clothesline to dry so I could wear it to a party that evening , and my father's bird dog ate it. Everything but the zipper.

At my own house, in midtown, I occasionally hang laundry on the back clothesline, and once I even spread freshly washed lace tablecloths on the green grass to dry because I read that made them whiter. And you know what? It did.

Nobody complained.

And if anyone complains in my neighborhood, it would likely be me. Even I, however, pull a few punches as the price of keeping the neighborhood peace. I heard of two neighbors who got into such a spat that it escalated to blows: they beat up one another's automobiles, hitting the cars with hammers and baseball bats.

A neighbor of mine had an unsuccessful garage sale and left the stuff that didn't sell on his front porch. For months. Through at least three heavy rains and an ice storm. It wasn't garage sale stuff anymore, it was junk. Everybody ignored it. We're peaceable folk. When neighbors leave Christmas lights up until Valentine's Day, we grumble, but among ourselves.

We're an old neighborhood, and we try to make the best of things. I planted a little evergreen in the front yard, which my dog immediately made a target. It was better than a water hydrant to him. The little tree died, but I made the best of it. I spray-painted it green, and the dog was happy for a couple more years.

Would I file a complaint if someone hung her knickers out to dry? Who cares? Corny yard art? Roll your eyes and move on down the sidewalk. Ignorant and misguided signs I don't agree with? Pray for their enlightenment.

What about a collection of old cars falling into ruin in the front yard? Probably. Upholstered furniture or car seats on the front porch? Yes.

Houses abandoned and overgrown with weeds and grass? Eventually, but not until I've mowed my own lawn or raked the knee-deep leaves. Domestic violence? You bet. Animals neglected or abused? Oh, I'm quick to leap into the fray on that.

But laundry drying? I don't think so.

Maybe it's age. A woman in her nineties wrote that we grow more tolerant with age. Impatient, perhaps, but tolerant. Sort of like the mosquito ring that teenagers put on their cell phones. Supposedly it cannot be heard by people over twenty, just as people after middle age can't hear the sound of bats.

No bat squeaks, no cell phone mosquito rings, no irritation at clotheslines. Life in maturity is good, isn't it?

Outing the Fruit Fly

This essay is recommended for adult audiences only.

Just for fun, let's play a little game of morality gymnastics. Here's how we start. Let's say I do not believe in homosexuality. Which means that I do not approve of it. That I am, in fact, opposed to it and even repulsed by the idea.

Let's say that I believe it is against the laws of nature and denounced in the Bible. I'll display one of those bumper stickers that say, "God declared it. The Bible says it. I believe it. That does it." Period. End of discussion. Close the mind and go home.

Let's say that I am adamantly opposed to the notion of same-sex relationships, same-sex marriages, gays in the military, gays in the church—no gay priests or bishops, thank you very much—and definitely no gays in education because what if they start recruiting?

Then let's say I tune in one evening to the Sundance Network and discover it is running films in honor of National Gay Pride Month. What gall, I might exclaim, awarding this abomination a dignity right beside National Prune Month or National Return Carts to the Grocery Store Month!

Then, let's say, I am still staggering from that assault when I open the *Wall Street Journal* and the *Tulsa World* and read about not one but two scientific studies that have documented same-sex relationships among others of God's creatures. Well, that's the liberal media for you. Now what are we supposed to tell the kids about the birds and the bees?

These scientists tell us about their discoveries of homosexuality in nature. They write about same-sex behavior among dolphins, penguins, killer whales, and manatees. They write about gay ducks, gay geese, and gay sheep (a real problem, I understand, for sheep breeders).

According to the scientific journal *Trends in Ecology and Evolution,* when two female albatrosses raise chicks, they are more successful at it than a single female.

That's a good thing, because nearly one-third of the female Laysan albatrosses in Hawaii form same-sex relationships.

Worldwide, some scientists say, 450 species have been identified as engaging in same-sex behavior. Giraffes are notorious for it: 80 percent of interactions between male giraffes are sexual.

Pink flamingos, at least the males, often spend part of their lives in same-sex relationships, from courtship to raising the young. But it is a small percentage compared to a species of Japanese monkeys; one-third of female Barbary macaque monkeys choose females as their longtime partners.

Worms, frogs, locusts—scientists are dragging all of them out of the closet. The scientists even outed the lowly fruit fly.

Ogden Nash wrote a little poem titled the fly, and here it is in its entirety:

> God made the fly.
> I wonder why.

As a tribute to Ogden Nash and with a nod to Mehitabel the cat from Don Marquis, I have written a little poem myself. I wrote it while I was giddy with this new perspective of the world of nature—enlightened about life and almost drunk with these revelations from the scientific community.

Here is my poem about the fruit fly:

> God made the fruit fly
> *Toujours gai* and fruity
> Rejoice and be glad, little fly
> And shake your little booty.

The Bearded Dragon and Me

Life is a series of discoveries, and I have—at last—discovered my soul lizard. She is a bearded dragon named Trixie. She is about ten inches long, the color of sand, and as spiky as a rock musician with a new jar of hair gel.

Let me start at the beginning. I have always suspected that I have a chronic case of inertia. The definition of inertia, as I learned it, is the tendency of an object in motion to remain in motion and of an object at rest to remain at rest. That's me.

When I am doing anything—house cleaning, working, reading—I am like a gerbil on a wheel. It is hard to stop. I keep going until I'm numb.

Same thing when I'm sleeping. I love to sleep. And once asleep, I find it hard to wake up. Other people tell me, "Oh, I may be sleepy at first, but once I'm up, I'm up."

Not me. Once I'm up, I'm in a stupor. I gave up attending dawn prayers at a Benedictine monastery when I fell so fast asleep one morning that I bumped my head loudly on the pew in front of me. I made such a clatter the nuns turned around to look at me. I hope they thought I had swooned in religious ecstasy.

Now I find that there *is* such a thing as sleep inertia. An article in the *Journal of the American Medical Association* describes the condition as that groggy, befuddled feeling we have when we wake. Some people feel this way for about three minutes, the article said. Other people suffer this trance for up to two hours. Pshaw! Two hours is child's play to me. I can sit motionless with a cup of coffee all morning. Then go back to sleep.

For a while I hoped it was just seasonal affective disorder, that sluggish feeling brought on by the short days of winter and a deprivation of sunlight. Unfortunately, I feel the same way all during the long days of summer.

I recognized the true cause when I saw Trixie. She was in her terrarium, freeze-frame still, with her head lifted toward an incandescent light bulb, and basking in the heat. That's me, I said to myself. That's how I start my day. It was at that moment I realized that I am part bearded dragon.

Trixie's ancestors are from the deserts of Australia and mine are from Oklahoma, but we have much in common. Temperature is important to both of us. We are both docile creatures by nature and low maintenance, although we both need lots of calcium and vitamins, especially vitamin D. We both like flowers, fruits, and vegetables, and neither of us is to be fed fireflies. (They are toxic to her, and I do not care for them as a food group.) She cannot eat iceberg lettuce; it dehydrates her. We both prefer mustard greens or Romaine lettuce. She eats more crickets than I do, and she likes to be sprayed with water each day. I am not fond of that myself.

When her light is turned off, Trixie falls asleep immediately, possibly because she and I follow the same bedtime routine. However jangled the day has been, at bedtime we think of three things we are grateful for. We remember what Charlotte Brontë said—"A ruffled mind makes a restless pillow"—so we do not brood about the day's failings.

But maybe not. Maybe Trixie never has a ruffled mind. Maybe she is smug as a bug in her glass house, relishing her nature as a bearded dragon. Maybe she drifts off humming a phrase from a Marlene Dietrich song: "I'm the laziest gal in town."

Baby Stars in My Eyes

This is a story about clarity and irony. The title could be "Why, There's Your Problem Right There."

The story begins with the stars. For years, I have made a wish on the first star I see. "Star light, star bright, first star I see tonight." It's a poetic way to button the day to the night. It's a private little ritual for tossing wishes into the sky. One persistent wish of mine is that more of my wishes would come true.

And then, just last week, I discovered that what I've been wishing on much of the time is not the first star but the bright International Space Station. That's the clarity part of the story. As my country uncles would have said, "Why, there's my problem right there." I have been wishing on a space station.

The irony is that I am in constant flight from modern gadgets. Apps, iPods, smartphones, even a cell phone—I hear the words and run the other way with my old-fashioned paper and pencil. The further I flee from gadgets that keep me constantly wired to other people, the closer I want to be to the natural earth. I'm reading *The Sea Around Us* by Rachel Carson and learning about rivers that flow deep in the oceans. I'm reading *The Natural Navigator* by Tristan Gooley and learning how to tell directions from a spider's web and the crescent moon. I am making an effort to unplug and look around me. Starting with the ancient navigational guides—the stars and the moon.

It's a humbling experience to realize that I can no longer pick out the constellations but the African dung beetle works at night using the Milky Way as its compass. Birds, seals, and butterflies also depend on the stars to find their way.

The moon, steadily waxing and waning across the sky, has a power of its own. It inspires romantic songs, tugs the tides, and plays hell with our moods. The full moon sends some people barking mad. Native American tribes identified the seasons by the full moons. The Cherokees called them the Cold Moon of January, the Bony Moon of February, the Green Corn Moon of June, the Harvest Moon of October.

I am as obsessed with time as are other people: wasting time, not enough time, time is going too fast, time heals, timing is everything, time is on my side. Just when I think I've roped and saddled time, the universe puts me in my place. I may parse my day with meetings and schedules and clocks that tick, tock, and chop the hour into seconds, but what is really happening is that my organs, tissues, and cells move to a great rhythm of day and night. I read that our biological rhythms are so intricate, each of us carries two trillion clocks inside us. Some are set by the way our brains and eyes react to the sun.

Our chemistry is tied to the spinning of the earth and the moon. Scientists tell us that our cells beat to an even bigger drum—the universe itself. The minerals in the soil samples the astronauts brought from the moon are similar to the earth's crust. That links us to the theorized Big Bang of four billion years ago: not only our earth's seasons but also our individual, internal clocks.

And this is the part I like best: our bodies are composed of elements from the supernova explosion and the birth of stars. The iron in our blood was created by an exploding star. We are connected genetically to the solar system; the stars are our ancestors. That's what Carl Sagan meant when he said we are stardust.

We are connected to everything. We are so mighty. And we are so small. That's why I think we must be mindful about our world, and we must be gentle and caring with ourselves and with one another.

Here's a quote about stars that I like: "Any star can be devoured by human adoration, sparkle by sparkle." Know who said that? Shirley Temple.

....

I tore myself away from the daily news recently—ripped myself away from the headlines—because I didn't care to know anything about the careers of Kim Kardashian or Charlie Sheen. I'm not much interested in TV stars or popular celebrities. I don't know the names of any of the *Survivor*s or *Idol*s.

What I did instead was watch a television documentary about the cosmos. It was so riveting, I want to share the story with everyone. However, having me explain astronomy and the planetary system is like having quantum physics explained by Daisy Duck. Lucky for me, people with sense and clarity like author Dava Sobel can explain it. One of the basic things I learned from her book *The Planets* is that an easy way to remember the names of the nine planets is this silly sentence: "My very educated mother just served us nine pies." Those initial letters are the names of the planets extending outward from the sun: Mercury, Venus, Earth, Mars, Jupiter, Saturn, Uranus, Neptune, and Pluto. Poor Pluto, however, has been downgraded recently into a dwarf planet, so the sentence no longer applies.

I moved from Sobel's book to Internet research and discovered sadly that I am easily sidetracked by the stories, fables, and music about the planets. Did you know that it is a myth that Mozart wrote the little song "Twinkle, Twinkle Little Star?" The song is a French melody from a popular English nursery rhyme. However, Mozart did write twelve variations on it.

So with all those confessions and disclaimers, here is my version of the cosmos, and part of it is true. Once upon a time and in the beginning—about five billion years ago—on the fourth day, God set the sun, moon, and stars in the firmament, and this is how it happened: first there were clouds of gas and dust, then something set off swirls and ripples of motion, then hydrogen atoms fused with one another and produced helium, and energy was released as heat and light. Voilà—a star. The end. That's enough science for me.

The story of a birth of a star is magical to me; it never occurred to me that our Sun is a middle-aged star. I know that old stars die, but I did not know that new stars are still being born. They are baby stars that have to learn their way across the heavens. With that image, I began to imagine an older and wiser star counseling the baby star. The old star might say this:

"Little star, every night, people will look up at you and say to you, 'Star light, star bright, first star I see tonight.' People will write books about you and compose songs and poems to you. They will question you in rhyme: 'Twinkle, twinkle little star, how I wonder what you are.'

"Every night, many wishes will be pinned on you like *milagros*. Some will be small and light, fanciful even. Flights of hope and full of laughter.

"But other wishes will be prayers—serious, solemn, and desperate. Hearts will be opened to you. You will hear dreams told to nobody else.

"In the night sky, high hopes of romance will find their way to you. Many tears will be shed on your small chest.

"You must hear them all and hold them in your arms. Just that. Remember that you do not have the power to answer the wishes or to make the prayers come true. However much you want to sprinkle happiness on all those upturned faces, you cannot make that magic.

"Your job, little star, is to shine. And to listen. That's enough. To sparkle with hope in a dark sky is plenty. It's a gift.

"Up above the world so high, you are a diamond in the sky."

Livin' on Tulsa Time

Who would have thought that the concept of time is so complicated? We take time for granted, like gravity or atmospheric pressure. We think it's as common as cornbread.

Not really. Just consider the definitions (plural) of time: from "a one-dimensional quantity to sequence events" to "one of the seven fundamental physical quantities in the International System of Units." Check out the orders of magnitude. Look up literary, musical, or historical allusions to time. Heavy stuff.

My favorite definition of time is by science fiction writer Ray Cummings: "Time is what keeps everything from happening at once."

Here's what I know about time: it changes. And as it changes, it drags along everything with it—fashion, customs, life itself.

A Little Etiquette, Please

I gave a party recently, and it went south so fast, I didn't even see the light change. The guests of honor were rude and I was a surly, snarling hostess.

What is needed, I decided, is a little review of good etiquette. Who better to consult than Emily Post, who was born in 1873, was raised in privilege in Baltimore and New York, went to finishing school, became a popular debutante, and then married a banker? They had two sons and lived an upper-society life until, evidently, the appearance of a showgirl. Divorce in 1905 was something of a scandal, but she did it.

To support herself, she began writing for newspapers and magazines. She wrote travel books. Then, in 1922, she wrote a best seller titled *Etiquette in Society, in Business, in Politics and at Home*. She wrote primarily for an audience in Boston, which she considered the pinnacle of society, and for Washington dignitaries and politicians. She published ten editions of the book over almost forty years, until she died at age eighty-six. The books are produced now by her great-great-granddaughter.

Emily Post became the quintessential American authority on proper social behavior and good manners, and she based her advice on common sense and courtesy. She described etiquette this way:

> Politeness is to do and say
> The kindest thing in the kindest way.

Yet she was no patsy. She said we must have our limits. Suffer bores gladly, she said, and you'll be surrounded by bores.

I got so caught up in Emily Post that I read four editions of her books, most of them from the 1950s. What fun, these detailed accounts of the social mores of the time. Who would have thought that the 1950s would come to seem as quaint as Edwardian England?

Here are some of the tips that cross eras, and some show just how much times have changed:

- It is not appropriate to take the president of the United States a gift without advance permission, not even a brace of pheasants after a successful hunting trip.

- It is not appropriate to have the television on when guests come to call, unless they are unexpected, in which case you may finish the program you are watching.
- On a hot night, a man may sit in his own house in his shirtsleeves when guests visit, unless they were invited in advance.
- A widow who remarries, then divorces her second husband, takes back her first husband's name.
- When dining out, a gentleman should never seat a woman on his left—it is a signal that she is no lady.
- When setting the table for a dinner party, you would no more put the folded napkin beside (instead of on) the empty plate than you would wear a ring over a glove.
- And speaking of gloves. When a gentleman meets a woman while walking down the street, he must transfer his walking stick and his cigarette to his left hand, put his hat in his left hand, remove his right glove, and then shake hands. A lady never removes her gloves to shake hands unless they are dirty gardening gloves.
- A gentleman never writes a letter that can be construed as damaging to any woman's good name. And he doesn't write in pencil if he can avoid it.
- In a well-run business, a gentleman stands when a lady or older man speaks to him, and he takes the cigar out of his mouth.
- Women in business should not waste time fussing with their hair, dabbing at their face, or engaged in conversation.

There is much more—such as how to eat corn on the cob at a dinner party without making snapping sounds or getting corn fragments on your chin, how to properly bow to a person, and what it means to cut somebody in polite society.

I am not making light of the books; they are helpful, especially on topics such as how to set a table and how to write invitations and thank you notes. The books kept up with the times, and by the 1990s, they suggested what a child should call a parent's living-together partner and how to explain being a single parent by choice.

Still, I think my favorite is this commonsense advice from an earlier edition: a bride, Emily Post wrote, should never smoke a cigarette while wearing her veil.

Work Clothes Are Hard Work

I've been following for some time now the business news about
clothes that are appropriate for the workplace.
To sum up the advice: nothing new here.
The attire recommended for office work is conservative. For
the employee who wants to be taken seriously, dress seriously. For
women, that means that if you want to get hired, get a raise, get
promoted, and get ahead, don't wear flashy clothes more appropriate
for the evening than for day.
Specifically:

- Don't wear dresses that are too tight.
- Don't expose too much cleavage or too much leg.
- Pantsuits are safer, but be careful of color. Pastel colors?
  Maybe. Red? No—too threatening. Shows you're trying
  too hard.
- Beware of showing your toes. Don't wear open-toed
  shoes. Don't even think about wearing flip-flops.
- Not too much jewelry. Certainly no hoop earrings.

Then I read that the City of Tulsa was thinking of adopting a dress
code for city employees: no spaghetti straps, no low riders, no span-
dex, no sleeveless dresses, no halter tops, no miniskirts, no clothing
with graphics, and no house slippers.

The last I heard, this policy has run aground because of employee
opposition.

Panty hose is an issue unto itself. A company in Kansas City
attracted national press attention when women protested the dress
code requiring panty hose. This brouhaha was followed by the male
employees' protest over wearing ties. All of this is interesting to me
because it reminds me of the maxim "It has always been thus."

On the one hand, dressing appropriately demonstrates that we
have a sense of time and place (and I suppose the money to pay for
costuming) when we wear specific clothes for play, for work, and
for social events. Most of us have different costumes for sports, for
church, and for special parties. We wear different colors and textures
for the different seasons.

But we're always pushing the envelope, aren't we? There are the people, young people mostly, who believe that flip-flops are all-purpose footwear for any occasion, including to the White House to meet the president. Dressing down didn't start with Casual Friday, although that was a major camel's nose under the tent when it comes to workplace costumes.

In the '70s, women's evening pants became fashionable. Remember them? Full, flowing, and dressy. They were followed in short order by tailored pantsuits. Not even pants and different tops, just pantsuits. We wanted to wear them to work. I was working at the University of Tulsa at the time, and as I remember it, our request had to make its way all the way to the president of the university. The answer came down: Yes, we could wear pantsuits to work. But only one day a week.

It would never have occurred to us to abandon our panty hose, though, no matter what we wore. Minidresses were the fashion then, but always with stockings of some kind. Today we call them tights. The rule of thumb for many of us was that if the hem of your mini-dress reached your fingertips, it was long enough.

A few years ago I met Tom Rhone, a legendarily tough principal of a tough Kansas City public school who enforced dress codes for his teachers. One of his rules was that the women teachers had to wear undergarments. Some protested. The protest went to court.

"Why do you want dress codes?" the judge asked him.

Rhone answered, "For the same reason I stand up when you enter the courtroom, Your Honor: to show respect for you and for this court. Appropriate dress shows respect for the students, the other teachers, and for the workplace of education."

"Case dismissed," the judge said.

Hot, Smokin' Hats

Here's some breaking fashion news: hats are back.

And I don't mean for women. For men.

Maybe it began with the Indiana Jones films starring Harrison Ford and his trademark fedora. Then Johnny Depp and Brad Pitt were photographed wearing fedoras. Leading them all may be Pharrell Williams with his famous, custom-made hats akin to that of a Royal Canadian Mountie.

That ought to cinch it, right? Celebrities wearing hats—hats are back!

But did we realize that fedoras were first women's fashion? Sarah Bernhardt introduced a hat of this style while playing Princess Fédora Romanoff in an 1882 play titled *Fédora,* which was also a novel and an opera. Men claimed the hat for themselves in the early twentieth century, and then Hollywood established it as an icon for newspapermen, Depression characters, film noir tough guys, detectives, and gangsters—Alan Ladd, Dana Andrews, Humphrey Bogart, Clark Gable, Dick Powell, Joel McCrea, Fred MacMurray, and later actors Gene Kelly, Frank Sinatra, Jack Nicholson—the list goes on. How about Dick Tracy? Marlene Dietrich added a sexy sizzle when she wore a fedora.

Hats have been so important in our culture, they have inspired an entire vocabulary:

To raise money, we'll pass the hat.

If you want to get into the fray, throw your hat in the ring.

You're so full of hot air, you're talking through your hat.

Something that happens quickly is at the drop of a hat.

Something else is so passé it's old hat.

I'll tell you a secret, but keep it under your hat.

And I'm so sure of this, if it's not true I'll eat my hat.

A newspaper fashion article quoted a spokesman for the venerable Manhattan haberdashery Worth and Worth as saying that its core customers had been conservative executives, bankers, and lawyers, but now new generations of men in their twenties and thirties have discovered the fedora. With felt hats in the winter and straw hats (with striped bands) in the summer, they are retro chic.

The newspaper's fashion article ended with this advice: when you go indoors, take the hat off.

Oh, dear, says I. What does this new generation know about proper hat etiquette? What do I?

So I turned to my vintage Emily Post books. And here's what I found out.

Do not wear a fedora with a tuxedo.

Lifting or tipping the hat is a gesture of politeness. Just lift it slightly off the forehead or tip it when you say, "Excuse me," "Thank you," or "How do you do?" or when greeted by a lady in passing.

Remove your hat and hold it in your hand when a lady enters a building or an elevator but replace it when you get into the corridor—unless the elevator is in a public building such as an office or a store, then keep your hat on.

If you stop in the street to chat with a woman, remove the hat and keep it off until she urges you to put it back on—unless you begin walking with her, then you put it on as you walk.

Remove your hat when passing the flag, when the national anthem is sung, in a church, or in the presence of a casket.

When bowing to someone on the street, a gentleman should not remove his hat with a flourish and should never sweep it down to his knee like a musketeer, and neither should he cover his face with it as if he's examining the lining.

But let's clear this up right away. A gentleman tips or lifts his hat to strangers; he only bows to friends and acquaintances. And, Emily Post says, a gentleman always—and I mean always—lifts his hat to his wife when he encounters her, joins her, or takes leave of her in public. And those are the rules of properly wearing a fedora.

I don't know which, if any, of them applies to wearing a ball cap, with bill either forward or backward.

....

The Oklahoma Highway Patrol, according to media reports, is trying to increase the number of troopers and their salaries.

Since I am both socially conscious and a deep thinker, my immediate reaction was "How did the Highway Patrol come up with those cool hats? I love those hats."

This is where the Internet is invaluable for those of us with wandering curiosity. A quick search showed me a vast variety of military and law enforcement headgear: fatigue caps, a U.S. Navy sailor hat, berets, a peaked cap with a stiff bill, triangular caps like those of an ice cream soda worker. Or think of the more flamboyant ones:

saucy French gendarme kepi hats like Jack Lemmon wore in *Irma la Douce*, the broad-brimmed cavalry hat pimped up like that of General William Tecumseh Sherman, the cute little French navy cap with a red pom-pom on top. And there are helmets and pith helmets and slouchy jungle hats like a fly-fisherman's headgear.

To my mind, none outshines the Oklahoma Highway Patrol's campaign hat with its stiff brim and four smart creases. There's a hat that says "authority." But the patrol uniform didn't start out like that. The highway patrol was established in 1937 by Governor E. W. Marland in response to a problem. As the highway system had grown, so had the number of motor vehicles. Life on the open road was wild and woolly. Oklahoma citizens, being the way we are, resisted the idea of traffic regulations, but the story goes that the patrolmen won us over with their courtesy and respect. Plus, they had laws they could enforce.

In 1937, a trooper drove a Ford sedan equipped with a two-gallon gasoline can, a red spotlight, a siren, and a ticket book. He had no radio, of course, in those days, and the only phones were those at farmhouses.

The early uniform included jodhpurs—riding breeches tucked into knee-high, shiny black boots. The jacket was belted with a Sam Browne belt that carried a holster holding a .38 revolver. The uniform was topped with a hat that looked like a bus driver's or that of a guy pumping gas. As the uniform evolved into a more modern—dare I say, friendly—look, the riding breeches and tall boots disappeared. But authority was maintained, maybe even increased, when the squashed cap was replaced by the campaign hat.

This hat originated among the armies posted in the West in the 1800s; the soldiers preferred a hat with a broader brim to keep the sun off their faces. It became part of the official uniform of British and Canadian troops serving in Africa and during the Spanish-American War. By 1911, the crown was pinched into a four-crease Montana peak. By the 1930s, the flat brim was permanently stiff. And so it has remained.

Now it is the hat preferred by the Royal Canadian Mounted Police, military drill sergeants, U.S. park rangers—the Smokey Bear hat—Boy Scout leaders, and the highway patrols of many American states, including Oklahoma.

And so, back to the original question. Do I approve of more personnel and higher salaries for the Oklahoma Highway Patrol? Heck yes. Sharp dressers like that deserve it. Plus, they keep me safe on the open road.

The Many Wonders of the Modern World

I'm never surprised by my own ignorance—I guess I'm used to it—but what surprises me is the ignorance of other people. I assume everybody knows at least what I know, which is usually enough to stumble through the day.

To be polite, I should refer to ignorance in others as innocence. Let me give you a couple of examples with American history.

A junior high school teacher who teaches about the Civil War told me that every year she is surprised by the number of her black students who have never heard of slavery in this country. She says the only reason she can come up with is that their families think the subject is too harsh for them, that it would upset them to know about slavery.

And then there are the efforts to get out the vote among young women and minorities. To encourage female voting, suffragette history pops up like a cork from time to time. The HBO movie *Iron Jawed Angels* is an example. This is the story of an incident that occurred in November 1917, known as the Night of Terror. Suffragettes were picketing the White House and President Woodrow Wilson for the right to vote. Some forty officers of the law arrested thirty-three suffragettes for "obstructing sidewalk traffic." The men beat, choked, and kicked the women, then imprisoned them in a Virginia workhouse. For weeks, their sewage system was an open pail and their only food was slop infested with worms.

When a woman named Alice Paul went on a hunger strike, she was tied to a chair, a tube was forced down her throat, and liquid was poured through it until she vomited. President Wilson and others tried to persuade a psychiatrist to declare her insane so she could be permanently institutionalized. The doctor said that she was strong and brave but not crazy. He told the men, "Courage in women is often mistaken for insanity."

....

At a meeting of my book club recently, a roomful of professional women, including two professors at two different institutions of higher learning, said, "Do you know what the young women of today say they want? To get married and have someone take care of them."

A stunned silence drifted through the room like noxious fog.

"That's their life's ambition?" I asked.

Nothing against marriage. I'm all for marriage. I've had some myself. It's that other part—"and have someone take care of me." That's the disturbing part.

"What about women's lib?" I asked. "All that stuff we went through in the seventies? What about the suffragettes before that?"

"Oh, they don't know anything about that," the college professors said.

Don't know anything about it? Don't know what it was like when you didn't have to be paid equally with your male counterparts? Don't know what it was like when a woman couldn't get a credit card in her own name or a bank loan for a house or car?

In the heat of women's lib I applied for a job at a big Tulsa insurance company that had advertised that they particularly wanted a woman for the job. But when the job was described to me, it sounded like three jobs rolled into one. For the price of one.

"Why exactly do you want a woman?" I asked.

And the male interviewer told me, "Because we find that women are more reliable. And frankly, we don't have to pay them as much."

You could say that back in the '70s. That's what the workforce was like forty years ago. And that's why we went through all that hassle.

But if we think we had it tough, I just learned about hiring practices before that, back in the '40s. I read an excerpt from the July 1943 issue of *Transportation Magazine,* a publication written for male supervisors of women in the workforce during World War II.

Here is some of the advice. I quote from the magazine.

- Pick young married women. They usually have more of a sense of responsibility than their unmarried sisters. They're less likely to be flirtatious and they need the work or they wouldn't be doing it.
- Retain a physician to give each woman a physical examination, one covering the female condition. This not only protects the company against lawsuits, it reveals whether the potential employee has any female weaknesses which would make her mentally or physically unfit for the job.
- Allow for feminine psychology and give every girl an adequate number of rest periods during the day. A girl has more confidence and is more efficient if she can keep her hair tidied, apply fresh lipstick, and wash her hands several times a day.

- When possible, hire husky girls, those who are just a little on the heavy side, because they are more even tempered and efficient than their underweight sisters.

There is more advice: don't ridicule a woman, because it breaks her spirit; provide a variety of uniforms so each girl can have a proper fit; and avoid strong language. You get the drift.

Back to my book club and the accounts we were getting of contemporary young women and their life goals. Surely this is a bad sampling, we decided. Surely this is not a cohort that reflects accurately all young women's career ambitions. So we asked the professors, "What about young men in your classes? What are their ambitions?"

"Oh, that's different," their professors told us. "They don't have any ambition at all."

. . . .

Despite the growing Hispanic population, a ripe audience for politicians, my sister in Tucson reports that many of her Hispanic friends and relatives never vote. "Most of the time," a young Mexican American woman told her, "I don't even know who's president."

Lest we think this ignorance/innocence is limited to minorities, a friend told me of leaving the movie *Pearl Harbor* and hearing a young white couple discussing it. "So," the young man asked, "was that based on a true story?"

Yet people seem to be remarkably intolerant of my ignorance and incompetence, especially when it comes to gadgets. I unwittingly test this theory a lot. When it comes to things like cell phones and remote controls, the sales and service people and I are eons apart. They look at me as if I'm talking to them about Morse code. Their attitudes range from controlled impatience to scorn. Whatever happened to the kindness of strangers?

USA Today has a term to describe people like me who resist technology—e-mail, the Web, texting, cell phones, digital cameras, Blackberries, iPods, Facebook, texting, electronic books, and all the rest of it. The term is "tech-no's." A tech-no is someone who says no to all the gadgets that keep us constantly wired. This stubborn lot is a dwindling minority, the newspaper says, akin to an endangered species.

I may not be in the deep end of this tech-no pool, but I am definitely in the shallow water. I have some gadgets, it's just that I don't always know how to use them. They give me the digital willies. And here's the blasphemy: I don't want to know. The Information Age is passing me by at Wile E. Coyote speed.

I have a cell phone, but I only turn it on when I want to call out. I have a DVD player, but it's always chancy that I can get it to work; I promise you, the remote control never operates the same way twice. My computer delights in tripping me up. Electronic devices seem to smirk, knowing they are smarter than I am. No wonder I felt so triumphant the first time I mastered self-checkout at the grocery store. I took a victory lap around the produce department.

Since I am already so far behind, it is discouraging to know that the gadgets I rarely use are becoming outdated at the speed of light. Even before I master them, they are figuratively rusting. The new cell phones I see advertised, for example, have capabilities I can't grasp, described in a technical language I don't understand. My own technical possessions are starting to remind me of collections I have seen of quaint antique kitchen tools—apple corers and milk churns, for example. My connected friends lecture me with scorn: "You have to text and use Facebook! You have to keep up with the times."

And yet, although 81 percent of adults use the Internet and 78 percent use cell phones, the newspaper article says, it may become fashionable to go the other direction. To disconnect. If so, I'll be right there waiting, like vintage clothes coming back in style.

Or maybe not. There's the chance the tech-yes trend could keep going and leave me even further behind. If so, there's another word for people like me. Every year the American Dialect Society chooses a new word to be the word of the year—a neologism, an invented word. That new word for 2006 was "plutoed." It means to be devalued or demoted, like the planet Pluto sent down to the minor leagues.

That could be me and my handful of rascally gadgets. Today I'm a semi-tech-no; tomorrow I could be totally plutoed.

The Angry Bandwagon

Everybody seems to be mad about something these days, so I thought I'd jump on the bandwagon. While there's still room. First I had to choose a subject. What was worthy of my being really, deep down outraged? The answer: the U.S. Postal Service. Oh, not for the reasons you might think. Not because there is always a line of customers and not enough windows open. Not because there is no parking. Not because the dear, sweet soul in front of me cannot decide which stamp to buy or has a complicated issue with a forwarding address or a rented postal box or a package to be sent to some far-flung destination. Pishposh—those are too trivial for a fit of Rumpelstiltskin proportions.

So, then, exactly what is it about the U.S. Postal Service that has teed me off? Simple. I learned that the U.S. Postal Service—that fine, American institution that delivers the mail through rain, sleet, gloom of night, and most snow—has spent millions of dollars sponsoring a U.S. professional bicycling team.

In the years 1996–2004, the U.S. Postal Service spent something like $32 million on the USPS Pro Cycling team. Maybe as much as $60 million; the federal investigation is still under way.

What was somebody thinking? Did anyone think that could bene-fit America? Make people abroad think more highly of us? Encourage U.S. business and persuade Europeans to "Buy American?"

In short, yes. The intent was to increase revenue created by Postal Service products on a global basis, to boost morale among the some 500,000 employees of the Postal Service, and to identify the United States with an international athletic championship team.

I imagine this scenario: A nice Frenchman, a cycling enthusiast who had just seen Lance Armstrong and team in the Tour de France, is overcome with American sympathies—just go with this, it's fiction—and walks into the nearest Paris *La poste* to mail a letter to Marseilles.

"*Je voudrais un timbre* [stamp]," he says. "American."

"*Quoi?*" asks the French postmistress. "*Qu'est-ce que vous veux?*"

The customer says in French, "I want to mail this letter from Paris to Marseilles with a U.S. postage stamp. And do you have the black baseball league stamp? Or the Katherine Hepburn?"

And the postmistress answers in French, *"Vous êtes fou?"* Which translates roughly to "Are you nuts?" The postmistress would go on to explain, "This is France. We sell only French stamps."

"Mais, non!" the irate French customer shouts. You know what short tempers the French have. *"Non, non, non. J'insiste!* I insist. It must to be the American *timbre-poste.* God bless America!"

The postmistress, being French also and believing far more in *égalité* than in customer service, shouts back, "French stamps only sold here!" Then things get loud but shouted in beautiful French. No American postage stamp is sold. An American business transaction is lost.

Sponsoring a pro cycling team? Talk about a bad idea.

The U.S. Post Office Department was established in 1775 by Benjamin Franklin and the Second Continental Congress. Federal law declared it a "basic and fundamental" government function, intended to "bind the nation together." It is owned by the U.S. government, but in 1971 Congress set up the U.S. Postal Service as an independent agency. It operates like a business, but a bad business.

The U.S. Postal Service, which receives no tax dollars, loses about $1 billion a month. In one year recently, it closed almost five hundred post offices. It is considering closing as many as another two thousand post offices in the near future and is reviewing another sixteen thousand (half of the post offices in the nation), which are operating at a deficit. Most of these are in small towns and rural areas. Periodically, it toys with the notion of ending Saturday mail delivery. Ker-plunk. There goes an American institution.

I blame this on the nincompoop who decided to fund a pro cycling team. And the same, or another, nincompoop who spent $98 million of Postal Service money sponsoring the 1992 Olympic Games. And whatever nincompoops approved these expenditures. It's more than a French comedy, more than a monumental business blunder. It's wrong in any language.

Now I learn that branches of the U.S. military have spent millions on NASCAR racing. Stand by for another tirade from me.

See the Bear

This essay should be titled "I Could Have Told You That."

Prepare yourself: it is deliciously sexist.

You may say, "Oh, how awful," and I would reply, "Oh, but what fun." After a lifetime of being called Darlin' and Sweetie and now Little Lady, what fun to take a swipe at the male sex and say, "Back at you."

This is my own observation—with a few men I know—and not at all scientific or objective. Isn't that the best kind of outrageous stance to take?

I was in a budget meeting with several men, and I was talking about a spreadsheet of budgets for three years. All of these men are accomplished and successful businessmen. One of the men suddenly said, "Wait, wait. Which year are you talking about?" And I said, "I'm talking about all three years. Last year's budget, this year's budget, and next year's projected budget."

"No, no," he said. "We have to talk about one year at a time."

I sat back in my chair and thought—here comes the sexist comment—"I get it. He's a 'See the bear, shoot the bear' guy. He can't remember last year's bear, he can't imagine next year's bear, all he can do is shoot this year's bear.'"

I, on the other hand, am a female, which means a natural gatherer and a multitasker. Females can hold the baby, stir the soup, talk to the plumber on the phone, and nudge the cat out of the door with one foot at the same time. As a female, I can see all of the bears—and what kind of shoes they're wearing. I feel vindicated in that thought. There seems to be an ongoing discussion, year after year, about the differences between males and females. It smolders constantly and occasionally erupts into flames and fiery debates. As in, "Are you implying that women are less capable?" An academic scientific journal reported a new study by researchers that reveals that the brains of young men and women are wired differently. The gender differences are how the brain hemispheres are connected. To summarize the findings with a broad brush: women are better at multitasking and analytical thought, and men are better at focusing on one thing at a time.

Here's my smarty-pants observation: I could have told you that. I read about this study in the *Wall Street Journal*. The journalist pointed out that the conclusions of the study were—speculative. The article was written by a man. I could have told you that.

Those Darling Little Cookie Monsters

Is it safe to come out?

Are they gone, those darling little cookie monsters?

We used to have a narrow, sweet-free window between Valentine's Day chocolate and Easter basket edibles. That time has been filled by Girl Scout cookie sales. First the little salesgirls sold boxes of cookies door to door. Now they have enlisted adult sales crews, and temptation is coming at us by the case. Colleagues at work take orders, and parishioners at church set up displays during the coffee hour. Parents drag red wagons full of cookies through the neighborhood or drive slowly with the car's backseat overflowing with cookies while the girls go house to house making the sales pitch. This year I saw pop-up cookie shops all over town—tables set at busy street corners, on sidewalks in commercial districts, and in front of big box stores. Some enterprising Girl Scouts are selling cookies online.

Girl Scout cookies come at me from all directions. Happily I follow the path of least resistance and buy cookies right and left. It's for a good cause, I rationalize. Plus, it salves my conscience about my personal history in Girl Scouts.

I did not excel at much of anything when I was a girl, except reading and memorizing. I certainly wasn't a success at being a little Girl Scout. I had my Girl Scout handbook and my Girl Scout neck scarf. I had brown oxfords, a little white shirt (usually with the tail out), a green skirt, and—best of all—my Girl Scout sash. I longed to have the sash covered and weighted down with badges, but it wasn't. I had only two or three, and those were the beginner badges they gave me out of pity.

I had either a short attention span or a low level of dedication, because I wasn't in Girl Scouting long enough or with adequate perseverance to earn badges. It was definitely not my goal to go on a camping trip. My most memorable camping experience was with my family, and it ended about sundown when I managed to step into a pot of coffee on the campfire. I howled, my father was furious, and I was sent back to my grandmother's house. Fine with me. She had Neapolitan ice cream, cookies, and no bugs.

I'm not an outdoor girl. I don't like to venture beyond my garden gate. I am, however, 100 percent in favor of cookies. In fact, I'm 100 percent for Girl Scouts as an organization to empower girls and to teach them to become self-confident and civic-minded. I like that it was founded by a woman overcoming a painful marriage.

I have visited the Savannah, Georgia, birthplace of Juliette Gordon Low, who began the Girl Scouts just over one hundred years ago. She was born in 1860 as Juliette Magill Kinzie Gordon but was always known as Daisy. Her father was a Confederate officer, and she grew up as a genteel southern lady whose goal in life, customary in those days, was to make a good marriage. She didn't.

She chose the wrong man, a scoundrel named Willy Low. At their wedding in 1886 was a small mishap that might be considered an omen. When the couple was showered with rice, a grain of it lodged in her ear. Bungled medical treatment and an existing ear infection resulted in near deafness for the rest of her life.

The marriage was a disaster. Her husband was a drunk and a womanizer. At one point he installed his mistress in the family home, and he tried to leave most of his fortune to her in his will.

In 1911 Mrs. Low met Robert Baden-Powell, a hero of the Boer War who had written a military training manual titled *Scouting for Boys* that was enormously popular in England. She was captivated with the concept and immediately began a similar program in the United States, but for girls.

In 1917, history was made in Muskogee, Oklahoma, when the Mistletoe Troop baked and sold cookies as a service project. This was the first Girl Scout cookie sale. Today, the Girl Scouts' cookie program is a $760 million business, and a Girl Scout statue stands in Muskogee to honor those first little entrepreneurs.

Not that it is always been sunny weather for the Girl Scouts. Initially, the idea of an organization for girls met with some resistance. Some people were concerned that so much female independence might lead to the radical idea of women's suffrage. Lest we think we've come a long way, baby, recently an Indiana legislator made news as the party pooper trying to squelch the Girl Scouts' hundredth anniversary. The Girl Scouts are the tactical arm of Planned Parenthood, he said, and promote a homosexual lifestyle.

We live in an era of scrutiny. Occasionally, someone raises the tedious issue of trans fats and palm oil in the Girl Scout cookies or the question of child laborers picking cocoa beans. Until all of that is sorted out, hooray for Thin Mints, Samoas, Trefoils, and the Girl Scouts.

Immigration—¿Qué Pasa?

Let's talk about immigration. Why not? Everyone else is.

I can tell you a story about immigration that will break your heart. I know because it broke mine. It is a true story, and it happened in Kansas City. The people who told me about Tony called it a horror story.

His official name was Leon, but he went by Tony. He thought he was born somewhere in Central America and raised in Mexico, but he was abandoned as a child, so he wasn't sure where he was born. As a boy, somehow he ended up in Texas. He hopped a train and found his way to the west side of Kansas City, Missouri. Someone there told him that if he went to school and told the officials that he was sixteen, they would admit him and he would be fed every day. That is how he became a student at Westport High School; it was a place to eat.

And then—a miracle. Along came a program for the students funded by Kansas City philanthropist Ewing Kauffman, a graduate of Westport himself and a self-made millionaire. He promised to pay for the entire high school's college education if they would graduate from high school. For Tony and his classmates, this would be a free ride. All he needed was to have his parents sign the documents. Or a guardian.

This was a real problem for Tony, because he had no family. He had no guardian. So to help him out, someone signed it for him. She became his pseudo-guardian-mother to help him get the grant to go to college.

He went to a community college for two years and graduated with a 3.0 grade average. He decided to go on to a university and become a physical therapist. With the advice of his academic counselors, he applied for Washburn, a small school where everyone was sure he would do well. All hell broke loose.

Tony began getting letters from the Social Security office telling him that his Social Security number was invalid. He didn't know where he got the number; someone gave it to him when he was a teenager. Now he was scared.

He talked to a local attorney, who didn't believe the story. He talked to Legal Aid and got nowhere. He talked to the legal office of the foundation giving him the scholarships. It appeared that nobody could help. Things got worse. The final recommendation was for him to go back to his country of birth and reapply to the Immigration Service to enter the United States. He had been in the United States most of his life, but he had no birth certificate and didn't know who his parents were. He didn't know the country of his birth. Was it Guatemala? Mexico? The likelihood of his ever being documented to live in the United States seemed hopeless.

It became too much pressure for him. He killed himself.

Tony jumped off the Paseo Bridge in Kansas City, they told me. They saw it on the TV news that night. It was winter, during the holidays, and very cold. The news team was pulling up just as he jumped. The TV station drew a red circle on the screen; the audience could see his head in the water. They could see him bobbing for a while, and suddenly he went under. When the ice comes down the Missouri River, I'm told, it is really cold. Tony never came up. They never recovered his body. Not in the winter in the Missouri.

Who knows why he committed suicide? Who knows when anyone feels enough depression to kill himself? I believe that one factor could be total despair.

As the current immigration issue bubbles and troubles, one group has moved on: the business community selling products. Pick up almost any product in the stores, and it is bilingual. We may be debating the issue of what to do with Hispanics and Latinos in this country, but the marketers are ahead of us. That's why whenever I buy a package of soft white light bulbs, it also says *suave blanco*. The bulb may be soft white, but too many of us Caucasians are not. We're hard white, monolingual, and determined to stay that way.

....

As if we haven't done enough to proclaim this state unfriendly, periodically there is an idea afoot about a bill to declare English as Oklahoma's official language. Not to put too fine a point on it, what kind of crackpot idea is that?

What must the Native Americans think about this, the same Native Americans who were given title to this part of the country by the federal government for as long as grass grows and water runs? What languages were they speaking when the area was overrun with white settlers? And what languages did they hear when Oklahoma settlers turned out to be from Italy, Germany, Poland, Ireland, and Russia?

English as the official language? Is that supposed to give us a feeling of superiority? How superior can we be if most of us can speak only one language and, too often, not all that well? Let those of us answer who can correctly use plural pronouns in the possessive case. If the answer is "Huh?" I rest my case.

Maybe I feel the way I do about languages because I worked for fifteen years for Tulsa Ballet Theatre, where I came across lots of people who spoke different languages. Roman Jasinski, the founding artistic director, was Polish and also spoke Russian. Moscelyne Larkin, his wife and the founding co–artistic director, was Russian and American Indian. She spoke fluent English, Russian, Spanish, and pig Latin. We had dancers, choreographers, and conductors from all over the world. They all spoke some French, because that's the language of the ballet steps. Before a performance, dancers of any nationality don't tell one another "Break a leg" for good luck, they say *merde.* It's French slang for poop. For a while we had a board president from Beirut, and he could speak Arabic.

Appreciating languages is something I acquired, but not because I came from a multilingual home—although my mother's maiden name was Don Carlos. Her father and uncle chatted in Spanish, and my mother cleaned house singing "Cielito Lindo."

I studied French in college and a little Russian after college but not enough to brag about in any language. My parents were born and raised in Oklahoma, but they loved to travel to other parts of the country and to talk to people. They enjoyed accents and regionalism. They liked the way people in Minnesota said "youse" instead of "you all." They enjoyed the drawls they heard in New Orleans and the Cajun cadences along the bayous as women taught my mother recipes that began, as she heard it, "First you make a rue [roux]."

When I began college, I commuted. One day I came home from college and told my mother, with great trepidation, that I'd met a girl who wanted me to share an apartment. Leave home? The first child to leave the nest? Oh, what would my parents do? Flatly forbid it? Would my mother weep and cling to me?

No, none of that. What she said was, "I'll help you pack." Because she also said, many times, "I believe in seeing the other side of the mountain." And it went without saying that over there, they probably spoke another language.

Rumi, the thirteenth-century Persian poet and mystic, said, "Speak a new language and the world may be a new world."

Also he said, "The heart knows a hundred thousand ways to speak."

But what did he know? He wasn't from Oklahoma. He probably didn't even say these things in English.

It all starts with education, doesn't it? And, too often, lack of same. How embarrassing that I, a card-carrying citizen of the Cherokee Nation, did not know until I was well grown that many Indians won't carry a twenty-dollar bill because it pictures the hated Andrew Jackson.

One of my favorite high school teachers, Mrs. Richardson, lectured enthusiastically about Jackson. He was her idol—general, war hero (battle of New Orleans), and president of the United States. Also, I know now, thanks to the power of continued education, slave holder, Indian fighter, and the power behind the forced relocation of the Five Tribes, officially titled the Indian Removal Act of 1830 and popularly known as the Trail of Tears.

Yes, Mrs. Richardson told me years later, she knew about Jackson's faults and failures. "We didn't teach like that then," she explained.

That style was not quite the same as revisionist history. Which is what the Texas State Board of Education is trying to do by rewriting history in social studies textbooks with a more conservative spin on politics and religion: minimizing Thomas Jefferson because he advocated separation of church and state, describing the slave trade as the Atlantic Triangular Trade, and brushing aside slavery as a "side issue" of the Civil War.

How can this be? History's history, isn't it? In a word, no.

Just ask both parties of a divorce.

We should prepare ourselves for a major demographic shift coming down the pike. Very, very soon in this country, nonwhites will outnumber whites of European ancestry. Already in Oklahoma, the second largest religion, after Christianity, is Muslim.

This means we white, Christian majority will one day become the minority. We'll be "you people," as in "How do you people celebrate Christmas?" and "What do you people eat for breakfast?"

My sister lives in Arizona, and we seem to be trying to top one another to see whose state has or is trying to have the nuttiest, most intolerant attitudes toward immigration and racism.

If I were writing Oklahoma school history books, I would borrow heavily from a series first published in 1980 by the University of Oklahoma Press, titled Newcomers to a New Land. This ethnic history of Oklahoma is a series of ten little books, so colorful and lively they rival any Hollywood epic. Each book focuses on one nationality of ethnic settlers to Oklahoma's frontier: Czechs, Poles, Russian-Germans, Jews, Mexicans, Italians, British, Irish, blacks, and the native settlers, American Indians.

The creator of this ethnic history series was Anne Morgan, not the philanthropist of the World War II cookbook but the Oklahoma historian who believes in the bones and sinews of history—history in full, real drama. Dull history books, Morgan said, focus on dates, battles, and laws. "That's not what history is about. History is the daily lives of ordinary people."

The Newcomers series tells the personal stories of men and women of courage, determination, and self-reliance. They were people with a powerful work ethic who struggled in the raw land against incredible hardships.

The Russian-German immigrants were a people dedicated to three F's: farming, faith, and family. They smuggled hardy Russian wheat into the country sewn into the hems of the women's long dresses; this turned the prairie into the breadbasket of the world.

The earliest Polish immigrants were a handful of coal miners in the McAlester area in 1876. Later Poles to the state were the refugee priests who survived the World War II holocaust. One of these was Father Kasimir Krutkowski, a political prisoner of the Third Reich and medical guinea pig at Dachau. Ironically, he was rescued by the Thunderbirds from Oklahoma's Forty-Fifth Infantry Division.

The Mexicans are described as Oklahoma's "invisible minority," vital to the state's economic development. Between 1910 and the Depression, Mexican immigrants provided the majority of the workforce for railroad crews and a significant part of coal-mining labor.

Sometimes they "passed" for Indians and found work in government WPA projects. In school, one Mexican girl remembered, "They treated us like Negroes"—segregated and forced to walk in the street by Anglo children.

This spirited history series shows us the legacy that immigrants to Oklahoma left to our keeping. It tells us what we owe foreigners.

For years, the out-of-print books could be found only on the Internet and in libraries. "I had about two hundred calls a year asking for copies," Morgan said. And then, one of those little miracles that lifts the heart; the University of Oklahoma Press reprinted the series in 2011. We need it now more than ever. We need tolerance. A seed for that may lie in knowledge about our own state, its history, and its peoples. I hope Oklahomans find the series and read it. This is my wish for education in Oklahoma.

Burnout

According to a burnout expert, if you want to know why a cucumber became a pickle, look at the vinegar.

That's one conclusion of Christina Maslach, quoted in a *New York* magazine article about burnout. Originally burnout was thought to afflict those in social service agencies and caring professions—teachers, nurses, social workers. Now we know it can affect any profession. Apparently three-fourths of workers experience burnout at some time.

I attended a burnout seminar once where everybody was sitting around like zombies. "I work at the zoo," the man sitting next to me said. "I'm in charge of large animals. I've had the same job for twenty years. I'm tired. Let someone else chase the gazelle when it gets loose."

Sometimes burnout is not just about overwork but more about the gap between expectation and rewards. That's why idealistic younger workers can be candidates as well as realistic older workers. And that's why some people change professions midlife, to get into something that gives them more control and more satisfaction.

Causes of burnout include working too much, an unjust environment, little social support, no control over work, insufficient reward, or values we do not respect. Even a cursory Internet search turns up information about other kinds of burnout—volunteer burnout, for example, and disaster burnout from following too much disaster news.

Another professional problem is described by Sara Davidson in her book *Leap! What Will We Do with the Rest of Our Lives?* She writes that one day when she was in her late fifties, her children were out of the home, her lover left her, and her work dried up. She felt stripped of her identity and rejected in every way.

What do we do when we reach into our quiver to find that our best arrows (youth, idealism, promise) are all gone and what we're left with are our weak and crooked arrows (age, fear, depression)? It's a stage Davidson calls "the narrows," a rough passage from one phase of life to another. It's a time when you wake up at two in the morning afraid and worried and ask yourself, "What am I supposed to do for the next twenty or thirty years?"

A solution to both conditions—burnout and life passage—seems to be change. I agree. However, I know that it is better if we make changes by our own choice. This is because I've had some unwelcome help with change in my life. In relationships and in jobs, people have said to me, "Here's your hat, what's your hurry?"

The burnout experts say find something that fulfills you. The life-passage author says discover something that fuels you creatively, something that makes you feel alive. I know people who have done this. I know an attorney who stopped practicing law and started teaching middle school literature. He's happy as a bug. I know a TV personality who stopped working in television and started teaching middle school English. Hated it. Well, teaching is not for everybody.

Davidson said for her, the trick was to stop creating for a purpose—that is, for pay—and create for joy alone. I don't think the soul knows the difference. All the soul feels is that creating is being done.

And this is the hard part: she taught herself to be half in love with uncertainty. That is quite an accomplishment, because living with ambiguity is hard. So is living with burnout and life-passage depression. The trick is to tackle these things with grace and hope and joy. And to know that others are doing the same thing.

Davidson writes that this stage of life is what the Buddhists call the second arrow. "The first arrow is the bad thing that happens. The second is what you do to yourself because of the bad thing that happened."

Let's All Just Calm Down

When all else fails to bring peace and tranquility, I go for the two standbys—in common-folk English, a lovely lie-down and a nice cuppa. A nap followed by tea.

The human species has a gift for folderol. Just look what we have done to religious ceremonies: candles, bells, flowers, hand gestures, marching, costumes, special utensils, everything up to and including snakes and whirling in circles until we're dizzy. I love the bells and whistles of my own Episcopal church, but I realized that being on the altar guild was not for me when I came upon the directress down on her hands and knees combing the fringe of an Oriental carpet in the side chapel.

So, with this propensity for detail, it's no wonder that we have developed an entire literature out of a concept as simple as a nap. Books, articles, research data—it's all there, elevating the common siesta to a science. The literature tells us the importance of napping, cites the benefits of naps, names famous nappers, spells out the best times to nap, and shares tips for the best nap techniques. A holiday is even devoted to napping—National Napping Day, which is the first Monday after the beginning of Daylight Saving Time.

Some of the world's celebrated nappers include Presidents Kennedy, Clinton, and Reagan, as well as Churchill, Napoleon, Edison, Einstein, Johannes Brahms, and American newsman Jim Lehrer, who calls napping "a magic bullet for life."

Why are naps in the news? Because researchers tells us that 50 percent of us are sleep deprived. Millions of Americans. Some say it is an epidemic.

Older people need naps because of reduced blood circulation in the brain. So do people who have poor health, poor eating habits, or lack of exercise or fresh air and those who work under artificial light. But lest we think naps are for the infirm, Lance Armstrong's coach says naps were an important part of his athletic training. In Iraq, the Marines insisted on power naps before a patrol.

The benefits of napping are extolled in new literature. Books include titles such as *The Art of Napping, Power Sleep: The Revolutionary Program That Prepares Your Mind for Peak Performance, Permission to Nap: Taking Time to Restore Your Spirit, Take a Nap!*

Change Your Life, and perhaps my favorite, *The Art of Napping at Work.* This last book tells us that workplace napping is a natural, no-cost way to increase worker productivity. One book with a nap chart and a workbook says we can design naps to inspire creativity or to improve memory.

This literature is not written by slugabeds like me looking for kindred spirits. The authors are scientists and university researchers. They tell us that power naps boost learning, memory, concentration, alertness, creativity, and reaction time. One scientist concluded that napping benefits heart function, hormonal maintenance, and cell repair. Long-term benefits include reducing the chance of heart attacks and strokes and limiting stress. Another study showed that an afternoon nap improves productivity and problem solving for 93 percent of workers. That's why some progressive companies are building nap rooms and nap lounges. Napping is natural, the experts say. Every animal on the planet naps, and evolution has not raised humans beyond this basic need.

Once we're sold on the concept, the questions are how long should we nap and when? The other animals might answer, when we feel sleepy in the middle of the day. My cats would say anytime 24/7. We humans, however, have scientific data to help us know how to nap.

The simple answer is that morning people might need a nap at noon, and night people about three or four in the afternoon. If we follow the human circadian rhythm, we feel the need for a nap eight hours after we get up in the morning or twelve hours after the mid-point of the previous night's sleep. That is, between two and four in the afternoon.

How long to nap? This can range from the nanonap of a few seconds to the micronap of about five minutes to the lazy nap of up to ninety minutes. But the consensus seems to be that the best is a power nap of about twenty minutes, enough to get the benefits of the first two phases of sleep.

I'm sold. Time to grab forty winks. Get some shut-eye. Take a little snooze. Catch a catnap.

······················

And then, tea, anyone?

I was at an upscale restaurant in Tulsa for lunch one hot day, and my server said, in an English accent, "I didn't know Americans drank so much iced tea."

I never thought of that summer drink as a cultural phenomenon. Now that I think about it, I've been to lots of banquets where glasses of iced tea are preset on the tables along with water. How did iced tea get to be a ubiquitous beverage?

Not that I am maligning tea. I love afternoon tea with all the little sandwiches, scones, and cakes. On a trip to Ireland, I learned to appreciate a bracing cup of tea instead of coffee in the morning. In the *Nutcracker* ballet I like the "Tea" variation in Act 2, also known as the Chinese dance. I feel healthy when I drink green tea, virtuous when I drink white tea, and exotic when I have tea out of tiny Chinese cups. When I read that health-conscience and gorgeous actor Antonio Banderas said that white tea is the first thing he puts into his body in the morning, I immediately loved white tea, renowned for its delicate flavor and antioxidant quality.

On the other hand, I once drank far too many Long Island Iced Teas and only later learned that it is made not with tea at all but with vodka, tequila, rum, gin, triple sec, sweet and sour mix, and a splash of Coca-Cola for color. No wonder I had to be driven home.

But like the knife in "Old McDonald Had a Farm," iced tea stands alone. Its history began at the extravagant world fairs. In 1893 at the Chicago World's Fair, a concessionaire sold iced tea and lemonade, but it was during the St. Louis World's Fair in the steaming summer of 1904 that iced tea's popularity took off like a Fourth of July rocket.

Americans had been making a version of iced tea since the early 1800s. Often it was a green tea spiked with liquor and called tea punch. As icehouses and iceboxes became more prevalent, so did iced drinks. By 1920, special tall glasses and long spoons were being manufactured especially for iced tea.

Tea originated in China more than five thousand years ago. Traders carried it around the world, its mystique growing country by country. In Japan, the tea ceremony became an art form and inspired a special architecture, the teahouse, with specially trained hostesses, the geisha. The Dutch introduced tea to Europe, where it became fashionable but was so expensive that only the wealthy enjoyed it. The Dutch also brought tea to America in 1650 for the Dutch colonists at New Amsterdam, later renamed New York.

When tea reached England, it became a mania. Specialty tea foods were made—Scottish scones and English crumpets. In Russia, by the late 1700s tea was so popular that a special large teapot—the Russian samovar—was devised so it could sizzle along all day.

In the late 1800s, grand hotels in America and England began to offer tearooms for Victorian ladies and gentlemen. And by 1910 when dance crazes followed one after the other, afternoon tea dances became the fad. When green tea became scarce during World War II,

Americans began drinking black tea from English colonial India. In the course of tea history around the world, the United States offers two inventions: the tea bag and iced tea.

It all originated from the *Camellia sinensis* plant, which originally grew wild in the monsoons area of Southeast Asia, what one author called Mother Nature's "primeval tea garden." Now most of the tea consumed in the United States comes from Argentina, China, and Java.

Tea is a booming business. In the United States, sales have tripled in the past two decades, and now tea is a $6 billion industry. According to the Tea Association of the U.S.A., Americans consume more than two and a half billion gallons of tea a year. About 85 percent of that is iced tea. On any given day, about half of the American population drinks tea.

For a less scientific account, I asked the maitre d' at another classy Tulsa restaurant if everybody who came in for lunch in the summer ordered iced tea.

He thought it over and then said, "Pretty much."

Statue of Liberty

One of the things I like best about summer holidays is that about the time of Flag Day and the Fourth of July, a wealth of new U.S. history books and articles are printed. They are stories about our founding fathers, our historic documents, battles, places, and events in American history.

I confess, though, that when the Declaration of Independence was read in its entirety on public radio one July Fourth, I found some of the language so antiquated I could barely understand it. That was hearing it orally. When I read it, slowly and carefully, the logic is as solid as laying bricks and the conclusion as strong as a pile of bricks falling on our British brethren.

So I was delighted to read some new works about the Statue of Liberty. There's a woman I've always taken for granted—stodgy and solid in her shapeless drapes but strong and courageous, too, with her crown and torch welcoming the tired, huddled masses of immigrants. Well, not as welcoming to immigrants now, but historically. Or so I thought.

The lady is not without blemish. Her history is full of disrepute and tarnish. Here are some of the facts I didn't know about our august Statue of Liberty. Mark Twain hated her. Said she was too hearty and well fed. To him, she looked like "the insolence of prosperity." But let's start at the beginning.

The old dame is now in her second century, and her full name is *Liberty Enlightening the World.* She stands as a monument to liberty, but it is a myth that she was a gift to the United States by the people of France in solidarity of independence. Although France's own symbol of liberty is a bare-breasted young woman carrying a flag into battle, the American statue is a more matronly woman wearing a toga. She represents the Roman goddess of freedom, named Libertas.

French sculptor/entrepreneur Frédéric Auguste Bartholdi first tried to sell the idea of a colossal statue of a woman holding a torch to Egypt, where he envisioned it standing at the mouth of the new Suez Canal. When that project fell through, he turned his sights to the United States and generated revenues from fund-raising events in France and America. Newspaper publisher Joseph Pulitzer helped gin up support on this side of the ocean.

American Jewish poet Emma Lazarus gave the statue a welcoming elegance. In 1883, she wrote a poem titled "The New Colossus" for an auction to raise money for a new pedestal for the statue. This sonnet ended with the soaring line, "I lift my lamp beside the golden door." The U.S. government donated the island on which the Statue of Liberty stands. The fifteen-story statue was dedicated October 29, 1886. The mayor of New York proclaimed the day a public holiday, and President Grover Cleveland officially accepted the statue.

You'd think Americans would have greeted the statue with a polite "Welcome," but that wasn't the case. Mark Twain wasn't alone in his carping and complaining. Protestant clergymen declared the Statue of Liberty both pagan and idolatrous. One Roman Catholic theologian said it shouldn't be a Roman goddess at all but a statue of Jesus Christ.

The statue was never intended to be a beacon for immigration, and that is certainly not the way the Americans saw her at the time. In the early 1900s, the arriving shiploads of poor immigrants—Slavs, Jews, Irish, Italians, Greeks—were immensely unpopular. One American cartoonist drew the Statue of Liberty holding her nose at what was called the "European garbage ships."

In 1903 the American writer O. Henry quoted the statue—most politically incorrect—as saying, "I was made by a Dago and presented to the American people on behalf of the French Government for the purpose of welcoming Irish immigrants into the Dutch city of New York."

It was another thirty years before the nation embraced this notion of welcoming the world's forlorn, and that was only after the tsunami of unwelcome immigrants had slowed. In 1936, upon the fiftieth anniversary of the statue, President Franklin Delano Roosevelt identified her as an icon for America as a melting pot where newcomers helped build one nation. FDR quoted President Cleveland from 1886: "We will not forget that Liberty has here made her home."

And yet—the United States was slow to relax its immigration quota as World War II began and then made feeble efforts to rescue the European Jewish victims of Nazi Germany. That's one of the interesting facts in Edward Berenson's book *The Statue of Liberty*. *Liberty's Torch* by Elizabeth Mitchell tells the story of Liberty's bumpy road to creation.

The old girl has had a tough life and a checkered past, but to paraphrase a lyric from a Stephen Sondheim musical, "She's still here."

More Sins and Social Mores

An old country-and-western song says, "I fell in with evil companions, now I'm having the time of my life."

I remembered that lyric when I read that the Catholic Church has added some sins to the age-old Seven Deadly Sins. The new ones include drug use, pollution, genetic manipulations, and social and economic injustices.

Oh, no, not more sins! I haven't even mastered the old ones.

Actually, that is not quite true. I have mastered some of them. Perhaps mastered is too strong a word. Let's say, instead, that I am naturally inclined toward some of them. "Incline" is such a good biblical verb, as from Proverbs: "Incline thine ear unto wisdom, and apply thy heart to understanding."

I was brooding over this—"brood" is another fine biblical verb, as a hen broods over her chicks—when I began to study the Seven Deadly Sins. Guess what? They're not listed in the Bible. The list of seven was compiled and refined by a monk in the fourth century, by Pope Gregory the Great in the fifth century, and finally by Dante in his epic poem *The Divine Comedy* in the fourteenth century.

The early Church divided sins into two categories: minor and mortal. Minor, or venial, sins are forgivable through sacraments and penance. Mortal sins, the big ones, are thought to destroy the life of grace, to separate us from God, and perhaps to condemn us to eternal damnation.

The Big Seven are lust, gluttony, greed, pride, wrath, sloth, and envy. Life is short, so I'm selective about my sins. I try hard to avoid five of them. It's those other two—sloth and envy—those are my slippery slopes. I am particularly susceptible to sloth, although I think of it as laziness or, when I'm feeling high minded, fatigue.

Sloth was decried by the moral fathers as another word for apathy or, worse, melancholy. They seemed to consider sloth not a vice or a sin but rather a weary sorrowfulness edging toward dangerousness. "Idle hands are the Devil's workshop" means that a lack of joy and a lack of work (either for God or for the good of society) open the door to sin. Sloth is what our parents were on the lookout for when they told us not to sleep the day away but to get up and get busy. Carl Sandburg was describing the opposite of sloth when he wrote that God gets up in the morning, puts on his overalls, and works regular hours.

For me, sloth is the big sister of avoidance and procrastination. These naughty little girls look so innocent with pigtails and freckles. Oh, but they are sly. Especially when it comes to a writing project. As much as I love writing, I delay and dawdle. Instead of getting down to work, I hang out with avoidance and procrastination as long as possible. Instead of putting hands to the keyboard or the butt in the chair, I suddenly feel the need to clean the refrigerator, tidy the desk drawers, or straighten the linen closet.

I used to beat myself up about this habit, but one of my favorite university professors, Winston Weathers, explained his theory of writing: any sort of creating is a way of putting order to chaos. So it seems natural that we would start on the outside ring of that chaos and work our way into the center, which is the real creating. For me and writing, I have discovered that it is a way of ginning up the energy for that work. There's a limit to it, of course. I can't kid myself that taking a nap in the sunny garden room is anything but laziness, but the rest of it—the cleaning and straightening and refilling the coffee cup—that's like getting ready to hop into a game of jump rope.

One sin of the Big Seven I have found to be helpful, and that is envy. And here's how I discovered that. I have always been a writer. Sometimes writing full time, sometimes writing as part of a job, usually freelancing and writing at night while holding a full-time job. Then I had a job as an arts administrator that began to eat me up and left me no time or energy for writing. About that time, a friend wrote a book of short stories, *The Silver DeSoto,* that was not only published but also reviewed favorably on the front page of the *New York Times Book Review.* I was literally sick to my stomach with envy.

It wasn't that I resented her having this success. I was happy for her. It wasn't that I wanted that publishing success instead of her. It's just that I wanted it, *too.* The more I brooded on this, the more I pondered it in my heart (to keep the thread of biblical allusions), the more I realized that I was not living what some describe as an authentic life. Which means, I wasn't doing what I wanted to do. Envy was a signal to me that something was wrong.

And so I changed my life a bit. I changed jobs and began writing more. I had magazine articles and columns and books published. I went on honest-to-god book tours. (Disclosure: my idea of an honest-to-god book tour is if I drive on a highway to get someplace. Across town doesn't count.)

Once I felt comfortable with my position among the Seven Deadly Sins, I turned to the Seven Heavenly Virtues to see how I stack up. Those are chastity, temperance, charity, diligence, patience, kindness, and humility. My score is 4–3, and details are personal.

So much for sins and more sins. Social mores (pronounced more-AYES) are more flexible. They change over the years, like a shoreline reshaped by the ocean.

When I was a young woman in a small Oklahoma town, girls who were pregnant when they got married went to some lengths to hide the fact. They wore white wedding dresses tailored even tighter to avoid looking pregnant. In college, it did not strike us as unusual that literature professor J. Henry Hedley—whom we all adored—dropped little nuggets of morality into his lectures. One class session he said, "In my day, if a girl got pregnant before she was married, she left town. And she ought to have."

Today, 180 degrees later, I saw a catalog advertising wedding dresses for pregnant brides. The caption was "Show off your baby bump!" Just another social more that has changed.

And also changing, slowly, is the prejudice of race. At least sometimes. At least for some races and for some people.

Oklahoma's famed historian Angie Debo told me that someone—and maybe it was she—abandoned the project of writing the biography of the great Creek Indian Alexander Posey when it was discovered that he was part black. That would have been a scandal to his name in the 1940s.

And in the 1950s another race scandal was whispered about blond singer Dinah Shore. It was rumored that she, too, was part black but passing as white. At that time, it was believed, to have even one drop of black blood meant that you were categorized as black—a second-class citizen. For a while it threatened her career. As it turns out, she was the daughter of Russian Jewish immigrants.

I was coauthor with Ambassador Edward Perkins of his autobiography, *Warrior for Peace.* He was born and raised in segregated Louisiana, Arkansas, and Oregon. His story alone illustrates the progress of the black race in the United States.

Perkins's great-grandparents were among the black slaves on the cotton and sugarcane plantations in Louisiana in the 1800s. The Civil War brought a few rights, but equality was a long time coming. In 1898, Louisiana called a special state convention to stop the tide of black votes. A revised state constitution decreed that only adult males could vote, and then only those who could read, write, tell time, and remember dates and places, or those who owned property valued at three hundred dollars or more. This precluded many black men, including Perkins's grandfather.

Race was such an obsession in the South as late as the 1930s that an entire vocabulary was developed to identify the degree of interracial heritage. This was the terminology of the time: a Griffe was a person with 75 percent Negro and Mulatto blood; a Marabon was a person with 62.5 percent Mulatto and Griffe blood; an Os Rouge was 50 percent Negro and Indian; an Octaroon had 12.5 percent white and Mulatto—and so on. Perkins's grandfather was classified on U.S. Census documents as Mulatto—50 percent Negro and white.

In 1947, when Perkins was nineteen, he joined the army. He rode alone in a segregated railroad car while his white fellow soldiers rode together in the white car. Almost twenty years later, in 1986, he became the first black American ambassador to South Africa. He went on to become the first black director general of the U.S. Foreign Service.

It interests me that Barack Obama is described as the United States' first black president. During his first campaign, only one newspaper I read referred to him as of mixed race. He is routinely described as black. Why is that? His father is from Kenya, but his mother is a white woman from Kansas.

I asked two friends, both black, male professionals. The black priest said, "It's because he looks black." The black professor told me, "It's because he can get more political mileage out of being black."

Is that it, because he defines himself as black? Or do we, the press and public, define him? Are we still in an era when one drop of black blood identifies a person? Will the day come when we don't describe Americans by race at all?

Or, come to that, by age? Women tell me that about age sixty, we become invisible, without authority, power, or presence. I see it myself. Seems like only yesterday young men approached me murmuring, "Foxy chick." Now if they speak to me at all it's in the grocery store to ask me about produce: "Is this a cucumber or a zucchini?" I look like a mature woman who knows her vegetables.

The definition of social mores is this: the accepted social customs or moral attitudes. Sometimes it's a good thing when they change. Sometimes, and probably much of the time, change is difficult. Our hearts, emotions, and bodies can't seem to keep up with the real time whirling around us. It's like a ride on a roller coaster; my body is down here but my stomach is back there.

Every society thinks that change is happening too quickly—too much technology, no respect for traditions, diminishing values. It is hard, painful even, to live with ambiguity. It is scary to feel the earth fall out from under us, to not know what is going to happen to us next, and to feel as if we have no control over what is happening. Talk about high anxiety. Don't think that I'm smart enough to have figured this out on my own. I'm not. God bless therapy and books. The ultimate change is death, and there's not much preparation for that. When Eleanor Roosevelt was asked if she feared death, she answered, "Whatever it is, I'm sure I'll be up to the task." That's courage I aspire to.

I enjoy religion, and although my personal theology keeps changing—evolving, I think—I genuinely enjoy reading about biblical archaeology, history, interpretations, and even crackpot theories. It is as comforting as reading a murder mystery set in an old-fashioned English village; I am familiar with the stock characters.

And so I understand and sympathize with people who need to feel stark black-and-white religious tenets. It is comforting. How discomforting it must be when books come out such as *God and Sex: What the Bible Really Says* and *Unprotected Texts: The Bible's Surprising Contradictions about Sex and Desire.* If these books are read by conservatives with strong views about core family values, homosexuality, and sex outside of marriage—yo mama! Are they ever in for a shock. They will read, for example, that biblical authors sometimes used the euphemisms "hands" and "feet" when referring to genitals. In the Old Testament, Ruth anoints herself, lies beside the sleeping Boaz, and "uncovers his feet." Not only that, she spends the night "at his feet." Oh, my, what does that do to the New Testament's story of Mary Magdalene's washing Jesus's feet and drying them with her hair? The erotic "Song of Solomon" is simply too steamy for thought.

Better for some of us to live on the straight and narrow roads of Twelve Commandments and only Seven Deadly Sins.

I know where I stand among the seven sins. I may be slothful and envious, but I'm no snob. I gather my philosophies where I may. And so I hold up, as a fine philosophy, Michael Jackson's song "The Man in the Mirror." I'll start with myself.

I'm rotten at quiet, seated meditation. It's either a struggle of impatience or I fall asleep. I do like walking meditation. I like to repeat an ancient Buddhist prayer when I walk—very short and simple, just four lines. Sometimes I focus on just one aspect of it, say the bit about being healthy. I walk and explore all the ways I could be healthier—physically, emotionally, financially, spiritually, mentally, back to financially.

I share the following fourth-century Buddhist prayer with you:

> May I be filled with loving kindness.
> May I be healthy.
> May I be peaceful and at ease.
> May I be happy.

On the Subject of High Heels

French may be the language of diplomacy, Spanish the language of love, and English an international language, but I have discovered a universal language among women. Shoes.

I have struck up involved conversations with strangers in shoe departments by saying, "I don't know about these. What do you think?"

Complimenting a woman on her shoes is another surefire conversation starter.

One woman during intermission at the opera leaned on her date's arm and removed her shoe so I could see it better.

"Put your shoe on," he said, mightily embarrassed.

"Oh, she'll want a close look," the woman explained to him and told me the brand and purchase location.

Uncomfortable shoes, foot problems, sensitive feet, and long walks through airports—oh, we are kindred sisters.

A podiatrist once prescribed a cure for my own foot pain. "Wear men's shoes," he said. "They're flatter and wider."

I looked at the diplomas on his office wall. "All that education," I said, "gone to waste." I'd rather wear clown shoes.

My metatarsal problems, he said, are caused primarily by high heels, the modern-day equivalent of foot binding. So how did I get into this mess?

In a word—fashion. About six centuries of it.

It is a myth that the high heel was invented by Leonardo da Vinci. High heels can be traced to early Egyptian times, when butchers wore them to keep their feet out of blood and guts. They came into fashion in the sixteenth century when fashionable women in Renaissance Europe wore platform shoes called chopines. They're mentioned in *Hamlet.*

Sometimes chopines were two feet tall, and women in Italy, Spain, and France used a cane to keep their balance or had an escort hold their arm. Hence, another tradition—"Take my arm."

When tiny Catherine de Medici wore her chopines for her wedding in the French court, high-heeled shoes immediately became the craze, even among men. Louis XIV liked them so much, he decreed that only the privileged class could wear them—on penalty of death.

A younger version of me, "Connie Jo," in my Rainbow
Girls formal *(author's collection)*

The term "down at the heels" referred to the lower classes, whereas
"well heeled" meant the wealthy and aristocratic.

Madame de Pompadour popularized high, narrow heels, and court
ladies taped their feet to make them seem smaller. Sometimes this
hurt so much they fainted. During the French Revolution, however,
high heels went out of fashion quicker than you can say "flip-flop."
Suddenly nobody wanted to be identified as aristocracy. In the late
1800s, high heels crept back into fashion among women, although
men occasionally wear heels. Think cowboy boots with heels and the
disco 1970s with John Travolta, Elton John, and others.

In naughty Victorian times, the glimpse of a lady's ankle boot
was titillating, but it was the 1950s that brought one of the sexiest
high heels—the stiletto, so long and thin it was named after a type of

dagger. This shoe was invented by Roger Vivier for Dior and came with pointed toes. Jane Mansfield had two hundred pairs of spike heels. Oh, the variations on the theme: French heels, kitten heels, Carmen Miranda platform shoes, wedges.

Why do we go through this misery? Appearance. The calves look better, the legs look longer, the posture shifts so the back is arched, the chest sticks out, and the tush protrudes 25 percent more when we wear heels.

This effect fails, however, if you can't wear heels properly and walk around in a crouched position with knees bent like Groucho Marx. Wearing heels takes practice. Evidently it also takes study, because there's even a book titled *How to Walk in High Heels*. The downside of wearing high heels is that it shortens the stride, makes it difficult to run, and can damage the feet over time. Wearing heels and arching the back can even contribute to back pain.

What, I wonder, is the historical psychology of hobbling women? Of women hobbling ourselves? Why don't we want equality in foot-wear? Is it a sense of sexual allure, like a flower exposing its pollen? I don't want to even think about the subject of sexual foot fetish. Women's shoes are a deep, dark mystery. I don't know the answers to the appeal; I only know that I love to wear heels.

Throughout history, women's shoes have wrought danger and adventure. Remember Cinderella's glass shoe and Dorothy's ruby slippers.

When it comes to shoes, we are all—here comes a flat-footed pun—sole sisters.

The Little Black Dress and Me

Once upon a time, I thought the epitome of elegance and glamour was a little black dress.

Know what? I still do.

I learned about adult fashion as a skinny little girl in pink-framed glasses in a small Oklahoma town. This was the 1950s and '60s, and I learned it at the movies. I saw the glamorous Lana Turner, Ava Gardner, and Elizabeth Taylor as a woman of the evening in *Butterfield 8*. The naughty Rita Hayworth stripped off long, black gloves while singing "Put the Blame on Mame." I watched the joyful abandon of Anita Ekberg in *La Dolce Vita*. I saw Audrey Hepburn give the long, black dress elegance in *Breakfast at Tiffany's*.

When I was being imprinted by fashion etiquette, we had a defined sense of time and place. We honored a sharp sense of occasion by dressing for parties and special events. This sense of propriety—matching costume to event—carried into my adulthood.

I fantasized that I would escape that small Oklahoma town and would sit in a New York bar wearing a little black dress, smoking a cigarette in a long holder, and drinking something in a stemmed glass. I actually did that, minus the cigarette holder, and as much fun as it was, I would not identify it as a highlight of my life.

From the late 1970s to the early '90s, I was general manager of a ballet company, a job that involved dressy occasions, opening nights, and New York premieres. To me, that meant a little black dress.

In Las Vegas so late one night it was morning, I was among a small party in a private, posh restaurant atop a casino. I was wearing a little black dress and pearls. At another table sat Dean Martin and Frank Sinatra. So quickly I could have imagined it, I saw Sinatra lean forward and take a closer look at me. I was very slim and had short, short blond hair. He must have wondered if I were Mia Farrow. I was not Mia Farrow, of course, and he lost interest in a nanosecond.

Gradually I accumulated a closet full of little black dresses. My friend Maridel Allinder is as thin as a pencil and loves vintage clothes, so I offered them to her. She said, "You don't have a closet full—you have a collection."

And so I did. Different silhouettes, hemlines, necklines, fabrics. We talked to Teresa Valero, our mutual friend in the University of

The little black dress and me *(author's collection)*

Tulsa art department, and her creative mind spun the idea further; she curated an art exhibit around some of my little black dresses. We chose fourteen dresses for the exhibit, and we named the dresses as suggested by their design: "All That Glitters" for its showy gold embroidery, "Frock Noir" because it reminded us of film noir movies, "Tango Nights" for the ruffled skirt, and so on.

Valero then enlisted fourteen women artists to each create a work of art inspired by the dress assigned to her. Their works, and the dresses, constituted an art exhibit titled *Little Black Dress: New Takes on a Timeless Old Classic.*

One of the first artists contacted was another mutual friend, pianist Anna Norberg. She composed "A Suit of Dances" (a play on the word "suite") for the exhibit's opening. It includes "Not Just Another Rag" and "The Take-It-Off Tango."

The artists worked in a variety of media—painting, photography, poetry, film, sculpture, mixed media, and more. Beside each piece of art stood a mannequin wearing the dress it inspired. Who wears a little black dress? Bad girls, call girls, sirens, movie stars, nuns, widows, witches, Goths, and women having a special occasion. To learn the power of the little black dress, read *Strapless: John Singer Sargent and the Fall of Madame X*, by Deborah Davis. It's the dual biography of the painter and the model, covering the scandal that rocked the 1884 Paris Salon when the famous portrait was first displayed.

Was the Tulsa exhibit equally shocking? No, but it was historic. More people attended that opening than any previous art show on record at the university. Most of them were women. The publicity encouraged attendees to wear a little black dress to the opening, and most did. The gallery was crammed with women of all ages and sizes, all wearing little black dresses.

What we discovered in putting together that exhibit is that there is no such thing as a simple little black dress. Add imagination and the variety is endless. Like women ourselves.

Coda

Many ballets end with a coda. "Coda," meaning "a look back," derives from the Italian word for tail.

The coda is the ballet's finale, or big finish. The dancers appear on stage in waves—demisoloists, soloists, corps de ballet, principal dancers. They set the stage afire. *Danseurs nobles* leap in *grands jetés* so high they get nosebleeds; ballerinas do about two hundred *fouettés*. Everybody lifts everybody else high into the air. Curtain.

Sounds exhausting, doesn't it? The rest of us finish more quietly. We turn out the lights and go home. At the soup kitchen, we wash the dishes and mop the floor.

I grew up in a small town in northeastern Oklahoma where everybody knew who you were and what you were up to and called your mother and told her. I hated that part. One day I realized to my surprise that Oklahoma and I had settled down together comfortably. Lucky me. A Spanish philosopher said, "Tell me your landscape and I'll tell you who you are."

In this book, I have looked back at some of the people and things I've known in Oklahoma in my work and life. I have many more stories to tell—painter Charles Banks Wilson, Native American artists, cowboy champion Tom Ferguson, wheat farmers, and Indian chiefs, famous Oklahoma love stories and crimes, and more funny but true ex-husband adventures.

But in Oklahoma, we are humble people. We don't want to outstay our welcome or toot our own horn too loudly. We identify with writer S. N. Behrman, who said, "I've had just about all I can take of myself."

In Appreciation

Kathleen Kelly
Sally Boyington
Steven Baker

and also
Kendall Barrow
Anne Brockman
Carol J. Burr
Jay Cronley
Scott Gregory
J. Henry Hedley
Joy Jenkins
Ed Johnson
Missy Kruse
Morgan Phillips

and especially
the late Joseph A. Kestner

All of them smart and helpful
editors, teachers, proofreaders, and cheerleaders.